A to Z
of Whisky

FOREWORD BY CHARLES MACLEAN

GAVIN D. SMITH

Neil Wilson Publishing • Glasgow • Scotland

First published in 1993 by
Carcanet Press Limited, Manchester

This edition published in 1997
by Neil Wilson Publishing Ltd
303a The Pentagon Centre
36 Washington Street
GLASGOW
G3 8AZ

Tel: 0141-221 1117
Fax: 0141-221 5363
E-mail: nwp@cqm.co.uk
http://www.nwp.co.uk/

A catalogue record for this book is available from the
British Library.
ISBN 1-897784-66-X

3 5 7 9 10 8 6 4 2

Printed by Interprint, Malta.

Foreword

I have 98 volumes in my library about Scotch whisky. Only seven of these are on my desk for constant reference: *The Whisky Distilleries of the United Kingdom* by Alfred Barnard, *The Making of Scotch Whisky* by Michael Moss and John Hume, Philip Morrice's *Schweppes Guide to Scotch*, my own Mitchell Beazley *Pocket Whisky Book*, H Charles Craig's *Scotch Whisky Industry Record*, *The History of The Distillers Company Ltd* by RB Weir ... and this book by Gavin Smith.

As a source of reference it is reliable and quickly accessed. As an aide memoire it is invaluable. But it is more than this. Mr Smith's style is at once scholarly and entertaining. He has an eye for the telling etymological reference, the revealing quotation which casts new light upon old and familiar topics. Yet he does not allow his scholarship to become dry and didactic. Wherever possible he enlivens his text with humorous and curious anecdote. His tongue is often in his cheek.

The words used by the whisky trade derive from its long and colourful past, and owe their existence to courageous and forthright people. Whisky itself is convivial and lends itself to heroic tales and adventures, romance and accidents. It is also mysterious: it defies scientific analysis, and although simply made from the simplest ingredients, nobody can truly explain why one malt differs from the next, why blended whisky has universal appeal.

Gavin Smith catches something of this magic, the spirit of the spirit, in this engaging, entertaining and useful book. I cannot recommend it too highly.

Charles MacLean
Edinburgh, February 1997

Acknowledgements

Many individuals and organisations have taken an interest in the preparation of this book, and have provided information, opinions, advice and encouragement. I raise a grateful glass to them all, and offer apologies to anyone I fail to mention by name. Thanks are particularly due to Dr Christopher McCully and Dr Gerald Hammond, for thier faith, enthusiasm and practical assistance, and to John Dumbreck for his invaluable help in respect of matters Gaelic.

I am also indebted to Ian Allan, retired manager of Bruichladdich Distillery, Islay; Roger Brashears Jr. of Jack Daniel Distillers, Tennessee; Trevor Cowan; Leila Edwards; Owen Dudley-Edwards; Dafydd Gittins; Janice Mack and United Distillers; Helen Maclean; the late Sorley MacLean; George Melville of the Scotch Whisky Heritage Centre; Prof. D. Llwyd Morgan, University of Wales, Aberystwyth; M. Nicholson of The Mitchell Library, Glasgow; John Clement Ryan and Irish Distillers Ltd; Vicky Salmon of the Irish Distillers Information Bureau; The Scotch Malt Whisky Society; Janet Smith of Liverpool Record Office; Dr David Thorne, University of Wales, Lampeter; Tony Tucker and Campbell Evans of The Scotch Whisky Association; Jack Williams and Lancashire Whisky Producers Ltd; and Ian Urquhart, director of Gordon & MacPhail Ltd.

My friends and colleagues at The Wordsworth Trust, Grasmere - where library facilities were kindly made available to me - have been a welcome sourse of support and happy diversion, and members of staff at Scottish distilleries from the now silent Bladnoch in Galloway to Highland Park on Orkney have been unfailingly courteous, informative and helpful. Especial gratitude is due to my parents for introducing me to the greatest of all drinks, and to Margaret Kirkby and Janet Haynes for more reasons than I have room to relate.

The following publishers and agents have been kind enough to allow the reproduction of copyright material: Robin Clark for *Drink To Me Only* ed. Alan Bold; David Higham Associates Ltd for *Highland View* by James Bramwell; A. P. Watt Ltd for *The Century Companion to Whiskies* by Derek Cooper; André Deutsch Ltd for

Scotch Whisky by David Daiches; Guinness Publishing for extracts from *The Guinness Drinking Companion* by Leslie Dunkling, copyright © Guinness Publishing Ltd, 1992; Judy Piatkus Publishers Ltd for *The Little Whisky Book* by Susan Fleming; excerpts from *Floyd on Hangovers* by Keith Floyd reproduced by permission of Michael Joseph Ltd; Speymalt Whisky Distributors Ltd for Gordon & McPhail's *Corporate Brochure*; Warner Books for *The Spirit of Whisky* by Richard Grindal; Souvenir Press Ltd for *Whisky and Scotland* by Neil M. Gunn; Mainstream Publishing Company Ltd for *Scots on Scotch*, ed. by Phillip Hills, and *Spirit of Adventure* by Tom Morton; Irish Distillers Ltd for *Irish Whiskey: The Water of Life*; Jack Daniel Distillery for *Product Description* literature; Dorling Kindersley Ltd for *The World Guide to Whisky* by Michael Jackson, and *Michael Jackson's Malt Whisky Companion*; Mitchell Beazley Publishers Ltd for *Michael Jackson's Pocket Bar Book* by Michael Jackson; The Edinburgh Publishing Company Ltd for *The Whisky Connoisseur's Book of Days* by John Lamond; The Malt Whisky Association for *The Malt File* by John Lamond and Robin Tuček, and *The Malt Letter* (for membership details and lists of mail-order whiskies, send an SAE to the Membership Secretary, The Malt Whisky Association, Largs KA30 8BR); The Bodley Head for *Scotch* by Sir Robert Bruce Lockhart; John Murray Ltd for *The Whiskies of Scotland* by R.J.S. McDowall; The Appletree Press Ltd for *In Praise of Poteen* by John McGuffin; Lochar Publishing Ltd for *Tales of Whisky and Smuggling* by Stuart McHardy, and *The Scots Cellar* by Marian McNeill; The Society of Authors as the literary representative of the Estate of Sir Compton Mackenzie for extracts from *Whisky Galore*; Macmillan London Limited for *Scotch Whisky* by Donald Mackinlay (and others); Rogers, Coleridge and White Ltd for *In the Highlands and Islands* by John McPhee; Neil Wilson Publishing Ltd for *Wallace Milroy's Malt Whisky Almanac* by Wallace Milroy, and *Scotch and Water* by Neil Wilson; Ravette Books for *The Bluffer's Guide to Whisky* by David Milsted; James and James Publishing for *The Making of Scotch Whisky* by Michael Moss and John Hume; W. & R. Chambers Ltd for *Chambers Scottish Drink Book* by Michael Moss (and others); and *Scotch Whisky* by J. Marshall Robb; West Highlands and Islands of Argyll Tourist Board for *Campbeltown's Distilleries – A Guide for Visitors* by Norman S. Newton; The Scotch Whisky Association for *Scotch Whisky Questions and Answers*; The Hamlyn Publishing Group Ltd for *The Scotch Whisky Book* by Mark Skipworth; Iain Sutherland for *Vote No Licence*.

Every effort has been made to contact copyright holders, but in the event of any inadvertent errors or omissions, please contact

Carcanet Press Ltd.

In the text, references to frequently-cited sources are given in shortened form, but full details may be found in the References at the end of the book. Where no reference is given, details have been taken from the *OED*, and thanks are due to the Oxford University Press for allowing the inclusion of such material.

Introduction

Whisky – as I shall spell it throughout this book, except where locational or stylistic conventions dictate otherwise – has made a long journey from its obscure origins as unsophisticated *firewater* distilled in remote Irish and Scottish glens to its present position as one of the world's great drinks. Along the way it has inevitably acquired its own extensive vocabulary, which has grown and altered with the centuries, borrowing from other languages and from parallel technical processes. It is also one of the world's most interesting drinks in terms of historical development and character. It may be argued that one vodka is very much like any other, but not even the most *silent palate* could fail to discern that an *Islay malt* is a totally different drink from a *Highland* Speyside malt, and that both differ profoundly from a bottle of supermarket own-brand *blended* whisky. The mystique of whisky and its creation is perfectly captured by Neil Gunn, one of the most literate and original writers on the subject when he comments, 'To listen to the silence of 5000 *casks* of whisky in the twilight of a warehouse while the *barley* seed is being scattered on surrounding fields, might make even a Poet Laureate dumb' (*Whisky and Scotland*, 152).

Economically, whisky is a significant factor on the balance sheets of many producing countries, but none more so than Scotland, where in 1991 the industry employed some 15,000 people and earned £1.8 billion from overseas sales, actually making more money for Britain than North Sea oil. Since the first imposition of tax on the manufacture of whisky, illegal distillation has militated against the acquisition of revenue in terms of *excise* duty, and the illicit product has contributed to the lexicon of whisky words such as *innocent*, *peatreek*, *poitín* and *moonshine*. The making of illicit *spirit* represents an important aspect of whisky 'heritage' and more general social history.

The specialist vocabulary of whisky has inevitably been influenced by Irish and Scots Gaelic – terms such as *uisge beatha* and *poitín* for example – and as the process of distillation is believed to have originated in the East, so the influence of Arabic in words like *alcohol* and *alembic* is evident. Whilst some terms such as *draff*, *foreshot* and *rummager* are peculiar to whisky distillation, perhaps the most important influence on the specialist language of whisky production is that of the brewing industry. It should be borne in mind that brewing is a far older craft than distilling, and as the two processes run parallel up to the point where the *still* comes into use to create whisky, it was inevitable that the whisky lexicon would borrow heavily from that of brewing. Terms such as *mash, tun* and *wort* are common to the creation of both beer and whisky.

There is currently an unprecedented interest in whisky around the world, perhaps engendered by the greatly increased availability of Scottish *single* malts during the past few years, and the consequent realisation that whisky is a product with a rich history and great character and diversity. Notably old and rare malts have fetched 'telephone numbers' at auction in recent years: in November 1991 a bottle of sixty-year-old Macallan sold for a Scottish record of £6,375 to Osaka bar-owner Yusaku Matsuda, giving it an English one-sixth *gill* bar value of £212.50 per measure. This appeared a veritable bargain, however, in December 1992, when a fifty-year-old Glenfiddich went for no less than £49,604 at a charity auction in Milan. After many decades of almost scandalous neglect, distillers have finally woken up to the commercial value of the raw material they had previously been pouring into blends. The promotion of single malt whiskies by the 'major players' in the whisky markets such as United Distillers has been accompanied by the development of distillery visitor centres, complete with guided tours and the obligatory end-of-visit *dram*. William Grant and Sons of Glenfiddich distillery in Dufftown was one of the first companies to actively promote malt whisky in a market almost totally dominated by blends, opening Scotland's first distillery visitor centre in a disused malt barn in 1969. Glenfiddich has now received well in excess of 1½ million visitors, and is one of eight distilleries on the highly popular seventy-mile Speyside Whisky Trail. Such is the interest in whisky that Jack Daniel's Tennessee distillery regularly plays host to 300,000 per year, and in Ireland the latest whisky-related tourist development is the ambitious Jameson Heritage Centre, which opened in May 1992 in the old Midleton distillery in County Cork.

The progress of whisky from a parochial drink of the rural Irish and Scottish poor until the mid-nineteenth century to its current position of world economic importance owes a great deal to the development of *blending*. It also owes much to entrepreneurial and marketing skills, and the seductive vocabulary of the advertising industry. It hardly requires an expert to point out that whisky is more likely to appeal to the average member of the public if it is portrayed as a lovingly produced 'craft' item from a little whitewashed distillery in a romantic Highland glen, rather than the product of computer-aided technology and blending vats in a concrete 'factory' in Glasgow's industrial hinterland. Hence the success of advertising campaigns such as that designed to promote the Highland malt Glenmorangie, which features woodcuts and the 'Sixteen Men of Tain' who produce the whisky.

The vocabulary of Scotch whisky advertising tends to focus on terms which stress the exclusivity of the product in respect of age, as though *maturation* ad infinitum necessarily makes for fine whisky, along with its elements of tradition and 'Scottishness'. It may be, of course, that a sharper, 'trendier' image is required when targeting younger drinkers who tend to prefer 'white' spirits to 'brown', but Jack Daniel's, for one, has done well out of stressing its folksy 'down-home' image through more than thirty years of black and white photo advertisements featuring the distillery workers of Lynchburg, Kentucky's version of the Sixteen Men of Tain. Terms such as 'old' and *de luxe* are deployed in cavalier fashion in whisky advertising and labelling to connote exclusivity, yet they have no legal definition and can be comparatively worthless. Interestingly, the promotion of blended whiskies has traditionally been remarkably reticent in making any mention of the *flavour* of the product in question.

The language of advertising is, of course, designed to sell a product, and style and image are extremely important in whisky promotion. Only, perhaps, in Australia would the slogan 'Glen *Rat-arsed* gets you *pissed* quicker' sell significant quantities of spirit. Yet all the advertising verbiage masks the true role of whisky as an intoxicant, something it is easy to forget when reading Michael Jackson's *Malt Whisky Companion*'s *tasting* notes rather than thinking of a half bottle of Asda own-label blended. Like it or not, drinking whisky can – and frequently does – get one *drunk*, and therefore perhaps maudlin, nauseous, violent, or all three in no specific order. There is an old Scots proverb which declares that there is no such thing as bad whisky, they all make you drunk. Perhaps more sinister is the Gaelic toast 'You are the prowler of the night to the beds of virgins, Oh God what powers you have to gain kindnesses from girls'.

Even drinking single malts can get you drunk, a fact almost no commentators on whisky seem prepared to acknowledge, with the refreshing exception of Tom Morton. 'There is no such thing as a small whisky,' wrote Oliver St John Gogarty, and Neil Gunn says of Old Pulteney, the malt whisky of his native Caithness, 'I have childhood memories of seeing it in a bottle perfectly white and certainly new. In those days it was potent stuff, consumed, I should say, on the quays of Wick more for its effect than is flavour!' (*Whisky and Scotland*, 183).

Thus this Book of Words strays into the vocabulary of drinking and drunkenness as well as that exclusively pertaining to whisky. There are, perhaps, almost as many synonyms for drinking and being drunk as there are for sexual activity, with Benjamin Franklin offering a list of 228 terms for drunkenness in 1722, and Paul Dickson of the United States having recently compiled a similar index of 2,241 words connoting inebriation. It is interesting to consider the traditional difference between the vocabulary of drinking in Britain and America. The established Scottish terms for measures of whisky include *dram, nip* and *tot*; all cosy and unthreatening words. What could be more fraternal than the offer of 'a wee *goldie*'? Yet in the United States we find *belt, blast, slug* and other forceful, 'masculist' words in synonymous usage. Susan Fleming notes that the American whisky lexicon is 'rather aggressive and *fast*', the words used being 'all evocative of the cowpoke knocking back a glassful in one!' (*Little Whisky Book*, 39). The meta-language of drinking and intoxication has provided an apt source of terminology for drug-taking, just as brewing had supplied whisky-making with a ready-made vocabulary, albeit on a more technically-orientated basis. This development of the popular language of drinking initially occurred in America, where words such as *snifter* and *snort* were first applied to drugs from the mid 1920s and 1930s respectively.

Whisky has its origins as a medicine, with the Guild of Surgeon Barbers in Edinburgh being granted a monopoly on its distillation in 1505, and it was only legally available as such in America during *prohibition*, though if abuse was not widespread, then America in the 1930s was clearly a very sick country. In Compton Mackenzie's comic novel *Whisky Galore*, the local GP Dr Mclaren has no doubts that only whisky can sufficiently raise the spirits of his patient Hector MacRurie if a terminal decline is to be arrested, and the death of Captain MacPhee is directly attributed to his shock at its unavailability. It is in *Whisky Galore* that we find one of the most eloquent espousals of whisky's cause anywhere in fiction, when Norman Macleod exclaims: 'What is it gives me the necessary sagacity to outwit the Inspector? Whisky. What is it that helps me to know just where to put down the net in Loch Sleeport for Waggett's sea-trout? Whisky. What makes me a good shot at a grouse or snipe? Whisky. What is it makes Maclaren such a hell of a good doctor? Whisky. Love makes the world go round? Not at all. Whisky makes it go round twice as fast.'

Aftershots See *feints*.

age By law, *Scotch* whisky must be matured in wood for a minimum of three years prior to being sold for consumption, though most distillers and blenders consider five years to be a more acceptable period for *maturation*.

David Lloyd George, as Chancellor of the Exchequer, introduced the Immature Spirits (Restriction) Act in 1915, in an effort to reduce whisky consumption during wartime, and particularly to restrict the sale of relatively new and fiery spirit. The Act stipulated that new whisky was to be kept in *bond* for a minimum of two years – increased to three years in 1916 – and that was actually a modest compromise compared to the ideal of almost total *prohibition* that Lloyd George had in mind, but which met with great opposition both in parliament and in the country at large. His personal views on the subject were well illustrated in a typically headline-grabbing speech made at Bangor in North Wales in February 1915, when he stated, 'We are fighting Germany, Austria – and Drink. And as far as I can see the greatest of these deadly foes is Drink!'

The imposition of a compulsory three years' bonding period was of little consequence for the Scottish and Irish *pot* distillers and reputable *blending* companies, who already tended to observe such a period of bonding on a voluntary basis. However, as Malachy Magee relates in *1000 Years of Irish Whiskey*, 'The new measure...came as a bitter blow to the Coffey still operators, many of whom sold off the spirit almost straight from the still and had no warehousing facilities. It meant, in effect, a three-year setback in marketing operations, a crushing penalty that put many distillers out of business' (p.47). Subsequently the government took control of the *Coffey* or *patent still* distilleries and used them for the production of spirit for explosives. By that time there was a new Minister for Munitions, none other than David Lloyd George.

The Republic of Ireland continues to insist on a minimum maturation period of three years for its whiskeys, as do the Canadian and Japanese governments, whilst in the United States of America the legal requirement of bonding is four years.

According to The Scotch Whisky Association, 'The law requires that when the age is declared on a label, it must refer to the youngest whisky in the blend. For example, if a blend is described as being eight years old, the youngest whisky in that blend must have been matured for at least eight years' (*Questions and Answers*, 24).

ageing See *maturation*.

alcohol From the Arabic *al-koh'l*. Dunkling notes that '*Kohl* is a black powder used as eye make up in eastern countries. The word was later applied to other fine chemical powders, then to essences'. He goes on to write that 'The present meaning of *alcohol* derives from the phrase "alcohol of wine", referring to the spirit obtained by *distillation* or rectification' (*Guinness Companion*, 16).

Neil Wilson writes that 'Alcohol accumulates whenever yeast ferments and since yeast cannot utilise alcohol, it becomes one of the major by-products of *fermentation* which may be summarised as: $C_6H_{12}O_6 \longrightarrow 2C_2H_5OH + 2CO_2$
Glucose   Ethanol   Carbon Dioxide' (*Scotch and Water*, 6).

The standard European measure for strength of liquor, that is, the amount of *alcohol* it contains, is now the percentage of alcohol by volume, which has largely replaced the expression of strength in terms of *proof*.

Ambrose Bierce (*The Devil's Dictionary*) provides the definition: 'Alcohol, n. (Arabic *al kohl*, a paint for the eyes.) The essential principle of all such liquids as give a man a black eye'. Libavius (*Alchymia*, 1594) has 'vini alcohol vel vinnum alcalisatum', a misprint or perhaps misconception for *alcolizatum*, and the word first appeared in English in the sixteenth century. Sillett writes, 'The Arabians excelled as distillers . . . and it is indeed fitting that the word alcohol should be derived from an Arab word meaning pure spirit' (p.1).

From alcohol comes the adjective *alcoholic*, containing or relating to alcohol, and as a noun alcoholic has the sense of one addicted to alcoholic liquors. Dunkling (op. cit.) points out that 'In its addict sense the word has given rise to neologisms such as 'workaholic'. The slang abbreviation *alky* derives from alcoholic as a drunkard, being first attested in 1929 according to *The Oxford Dictionary of Modern Slang*, which also records the use of *alky*, *alchy* or *alkie* as meaning '(illicit) alcoholic liquor', principally in the United States, where the term originated in 1844. Dylan Thomas is reputed to have defined an alcoholic as 'Someone you don't like who drinks as much as you do', while Grindal quotes a solicitor acquaintance as making the observation that, 'In Scotland, the definition of an alcoholic has always been anyone who drinks more than his doctor' (p.227). In his introduction to *Drink*

To Me Only, Alan Bold quotes Constantine Fitzgibbon: 'I had had a semantic hold-up over the noun "an alcoholic". Was I one or was I not? Nobody seemed able to tell me, nor was the word listed, as a noun, in my *Oxford English Dictionary*. I therefore clung to the fact that I was not an alcoholic, for how could I be something which was semantically non-existent?' (p.153).

Scots writer John Broom has memorably described his own life as an alcoholic in an essay 'Alcoholic Odyssey', and whilst vividly portraying the horrors of delirium tremens, he also makes the point that, 'The notion that the alcoholic's life is one of unalloyed misery is quite false. Indeed, I can in all honesty say that I have never been happier, before, or since, than during those first few months of 1964. I was in an almost continual state of mental and spiritual exaltation, which must be akin to the experiences of the mystics' (Broom, 75).

In a letter of 1955 Raymond Chandler writes of many American writers of his generation, 'our emotional systems are tuned to the stimulation and the sedative effect of alcohol', and the American psychologist, William James, says in his *Varieties of Religious Experience*: 'The power of alcohol over mankind is unquestionably due to its ability to stimulate the mystical faculties of human nature, usually crushed to earth by the cold facts and dry criticisms of the sober hour'.

alembic   Defined by the OED as 'An apparatus formerly used in distilling consisting of a *cucurbit*, a gourd-shaped vessel containing the substance to be distilled, surmounted by the *head* or *cap*, or alembic proper, the beak of which conveyed the vaporous products to a *receiver*, in which they were condensed. It is now superceded by the *retort* and *worm-still*'.

The first recorded use of an *alembic* was apparently by Sicilians in *c*. AD 1100, according to McNulty; the idea came from the Arabs, and it was used in the medical school at Salerno.

The alembic soon came to be used for the production of spirit to drink, which McNulty describes as being '...flavoured with raisins to make a kind of primitive liqueur. This secret arrived in France a couple of centuries later' (p.9). The first English attestation of alembic occurs in *c*. 1374, 'This Troylus in teres gan distille, As licour out of *alambic*, fulle fast'. The English word is adopted from the French *alambic*, itself an adaptation of the Arabic *al-anbīq* (*al* – the, plus *anbīq* – a *still*), and the OED records that the term was aphetized from as early as the fifteenth century to *lembick*, *limbick*, and that the full form rarely appears again until the seventeenth century. '*Al-anbik* is particularly interesting because it adapts Greek *ambix* "vase for distillation" and thus demonstrates the Greek-Arab connection', Dunkling notes (p.169).

Missionary monks are thought to have brought the secret of whiskey-making to Ireland from the Middle East around the sixth century AD: 'They had discovered the ALEMBIC being used for distilling perfumes; Aristotle mentions the alembic circa 4th century' (Irish Distillers, n.p.).

The Dictionary of Drink records the spelling variant *alambique* as having current usage in France, Portugal and Spain, and notes that alambic occurs in the French name for a modified *continuous* still used in Armagnac – *alambic Armagnaçais* – and in *alambic Charentais*, a type of pot still used to produce Cognac.

Figuratively speaking, alembic can have the sense of a means of transmutation, and is first recorded in this respect in 1613, 'Making a brokers Shop his Alembicke, [he] can turn your silkes into gold'. The subjective *alembicated*, meaning 'over-refined, as if by distillation' also occurs in relation to literary style.

Allan o'Maut   See *John Barleycorn*.

American Barrel   See *barrel*.

angels' share   A distiller's term for what accountants in the trade more prosaically refer to as 'maturation losses', and the *excise* authorities allow for a maximum loss of 2 per cent per year. The term is not exclusive to the whisky business, also being current in French brandy-distilling circles. 'During maturation there is a significant reduction in the quantity and strength of the whisky from the 120° (or 68.5 per cent alcohol by volume) at which the law requires newly distilled spirit to be filled in casks. This is due to evaporation and the loss of alcoholic vapour through the porous wooden casks, this lost whisky being known as 'the *angels' share*' (Morrice, 35).

Writing in 1985, Bell observes that 'In fact, something like 20 million gallons of whisky (just imagine that as 160 million bottles!) evaporate into the atmosphere every year. Which may explain why visitors find the air of Scotland so delightfully invigorating' (p.20).

anker   Dutch and German, also found in medieval Latin as *anceria, ancheria*. A measure of wine or spirits approximately equal to ten gallons, or a *cask* or keg holding that quantity. *Anker* is first attested in 1673, 'Recd one halfe Ankor of Drinke'.

Dr John Mackenzie – whose previously unpublished manuscript volumes of *Highland Memoirs* were incorporated by his nephew, Osgood Mackenzie of Inverewe in Argyllshire into his celebrated book, *A Hundred Years in the Highlands* (1921) – wrote: 'My father never tasted any but smuggled whisky, and when every mortal that called for him – they were legion daily – had a dram poured instantly into them, the ankers of whisky emptied yearly must have been numerous indeed.'

aqua vitae   From the Latin for water of life, originally an alchemist's term applied to ardent spirits or unrectified alcohol. *Aqua vitae* is first attested in 1471, 'With Aquavite ofttimes, both wash and drie'.

The first recorded usage of aqua vitae in a specifically whisky-related context is in the Scottish Exchequer Rolls for 1494, where there is the following entry: 'eight bolls of malt to Friar John Cox wherewith to make aquavitae'.

Moss and Hume note that during the first third of the eighteenth century, 'the term aqua vitae, or in the Gaelic "uisge beatha", began generally to be corrupted, first to usky, then to whisky' (*The Making of Scotch Whisky*, 34). They also make the point that by the middle of the eighteenth century, 'the term aqua vitae seems to have come to mean malt spirit which was drunk as such, whereas usquebaugh was reserved for compounded cordials'.

'The first people known definitely to have distilled fermented liquor', writes Moss, 'are the Arabs and it is believed that the craft was brought to northern Europe by men returning from the Crusades who had witnessed the miraculous restorative powers of spirits on the human body. Hence, distilled spirits soon became known as aquavitae – the water of life' (*Chambers*, 88). Jackson suggests that 'It is a measure of man's community that so many European tribes agreed at an early stage that spirits were – as acquavite translates – "the water of life". *Acquavite* is an Italian general term for spirits. The more common *Akvavit* and *Aquavit* spellings belong to Scandinavia. The French follow suit by calling their brandies collectively *Eaux-de-vie*, and the idea recurs in the Gaelic uisgebeatha, etymologically the parent of whisk(e)y' (*Pocket Bar Book*, 26). It is also interesting to note that the Russian word *voda* means water, with *-ka* being a diminutive, hence *vodka*.

Atholl Brose   The word brose is a Scottish form of *brewis* or *broth*, deriving from the Middle English *browes*. In Old French *broez*.

Brose is oatmeal with boiling water or milk poured over it, and *Atholl* or *Athole Brose* is a mixture of oatmeal, whisky and honey. The drink appears in Sir Walter Scott's *Heart of Midlothian* (1818) – 'His morning draught of Athole Brose' – though it is supposed to have its origins in the fifteenth century, when the Perthshire Duke of Atholl captured his great enemy the Earl of Ross, reputedly by filling the well at which Ross regularly drank with the mixture and then taking him prisoner as he slept off the effects. The term *whisky brose* is first recorded in 1822, 'Whisky-brose shall be my breakfast'. McNeill makes the point that 'Strictly, Atholl Brose is not brose, but crowdie, for that is the generic name for any mixture of meal and cold liquid. But Atholl Brose it has been called for centuries, and Atholl Brose it is likely to remain' (*Scots Cellar*, 213).

The following recipe comes from The Scotch Whisky Association: 'Mix an equal quantity of honey (preferably heather honey) and fine oatmeal in a little cold water. Add the Scotch and stir until frothy. Bottle and keep for two days before serving. Two pints of whisky will be needed for a half-pound of honey and a half-pound of oatmeal' (*Questions and Answers*, 51).

Back Traditionally a large, shallow vessel, chiefly for liquids. The word is now restricted to brewing and distilling usage, and shallowness is no longer a defining characteristic. *Back* is thought to be adopted from the Dutch *bak*, a trough or tub, from the French *bac* – a ferry boat or punt, and also trough, basin, wash-tub. In Medieval Latin *bacus, baccus* – ferry boat. Back has had the sense of a brewers' or distillers' vessel since the seventeenth century, the first attestation being in a 1682 edition of *The London Gazette*: 'To be Sold, six Backs, several Stills and Worms'.

Back is usually now used as part of two compound words: an *underback* is located in the distillery **mash house** and a *washback* in the **tun room**. The washback is often simply referred to as a back, and in recent years stainless steel has superceded the traditional construction materials of larch or spruce in many distilleries.

backings See *feints*.

ball of malt An Irish expression for a glass of whiskey, though it is also sometimes used with reference to beer. In a whiskey context the phrase is used in contemporary Irish, such as in a 1991 magazine advertisement for The Lord Begenal Inn in County Carlow, 'relax by a blazing open hearth fire with a glass of vintage port or a ball of malt', and the bar-style *tasting* room of the 'Irish Whiskey Corner' in Dublin is named The Ball of Malt.

Occasional application in the context of Scottish malt whisky would seem to be derived from Irish usage, as in Fergus Pickering's poem 'Civilised Drinking, Civilised Chat'. 'Here, the right side of Watford, balls of Malt/Are more than just the prelude to assault'.

Ball here is perhaps an anglicisation of the Irish Gaelic word *beal*, which means 'mouth', though in Scots Gaelic *Ball* can mean 'bowl'.

Flann O'Brien uses *malt* in this sense as synonymous with whiskey, 'Lowers self into seat with great care, grips table to arrest devastating shaking in hands. Calls for glass of malt. Spills water all over table' ('Bores', quoted in Bold, ed., 113).

barley From the Old English *baerlic*. A hardy, awned cereal of genus *Hordeum*. The grain is first attested in 1124, 'þaet baerlic þaet is þae sed laepas to six scillingas'.

Barley is the principal raw material in the whisky-making process in Scotland, Ireland and Japan, and as such its quality and consistency is obviously of paramount importance. It is considered to be the choicest grain for whisky production as it has a high starch content which is utilised during *malting*, and the seeds are protected by double skins which reduces the chance of air getting to the starch and producing mould. It is perhaps surprising that the optimum barley for malting purposes is grown on comparatively infertile land, as too much nitrogen increases protein content at the expense of starch.

Scotch *malt* whisky is distilled from malted barley, and Scotch *grain* whisky from a mix of malted and unmalted barley, along with other cereals. Irish whiskey is usually made from both malted and unmalted barley, though Bushmills Distillery in Co. Antrim has marketed a *single* malt since 1984, and the Cooley Distillery in County Louth has also been producing malt whiskey since 1989.

Much of the barley used in Scotch whisky-making now comes from Europe, the United States and Australia rather than from the 'home' market. The nationalist Neil Gunn asserted in 1935, 'No foreign barley, however, beats good home barley either in quality or quantity of spirit produce, and personally I am persuaded that the home communicates a soft maturing excellence which the foreign barley never has to the same degree' (*Whisky and Scotland*, 129), though McDowall is inclined to believe that too much emphasis has been placed on the importance of the source of barley for whisky-making. According to Derek Cooper, when it comes to selecting barley, 'What the distiller is looking for is a grain that can be easily dried – so that it won't become mouldy when stored – rich in starch, not too high in nitrogen or protein and easy to germinate' (*Century Companion*, 19). The first stage in the series of processes that convert barley to whisky is known as *malting*.

barley – cream of the   Fanciful nickname for whisky, and taken as the brand name for a blended whisky now produced by Allied Distillers. The OED states that cream was 'Used in the names of some cordials and liqueurs with reference to their viscid character, or acknowledged excellence'. The word seems to have been applied to gin in England as well as to whisky in Scotland, often as 'cream of the valley' or 'wilderness', with Cream of the Valley first being attested in 1858, 'Is it cream of the walley or fits as has overcome the lady?'

This transferred use of cream clearly stems from the sense of what the OED terms '... the most excellent element or part, the best of its kind, the choice part, the quintessence', first attested in 1581, 'The gentleman which be the creame of the common'.

barley – juice of the   Synonymous with *cream of the barley*, the expression is used in Ireland and Scotland: 'with the aid of one of two more jorums of the juice of the barley, I would be feeling that poor old Bible-and-Sword Oliver Cromwell had made a mistake...' Criostoir O'Flynn, *A Stone on the Cairn* (in O'Brien et al., eds, *On the Counterscarp*, 1991, p.42).

With the sense of the liquid part from vegetables and fruit which contains characteristic flavour, *juice* is first attested in *c.* 1290, but the more figurative usage applicable in the case of juice of the barley is first recorded in *c.* 1380, denoting the essence of something, 'þo prestis þat geten out of juys of Goddis word'.

barley bree   Can refer to either strong ale or whisky, *bree* being a Scots variation of *broth*. Partridge *(Historical Slang)* dates the term with the sense of ale from before 1785, and with reference to whisky it was certainly in use by 1746, when a Jacobite officer in 'Bonnie Prince Charlie's army, one Robertson of Faskally in Perthshire wrote in his diary of "...that mellow barley bree from the caverns of Ben Vrackie".'

The sometime *exciseman* and committed whisky consumer Robert Burns uses the colloquialism as a synonym for whisky in his adulatory poem 'Scotch Drink', composed in 1785.

> When neebors anger at a plea,
> An' just as wud as wud can be,
> How easy can the barley-bree
> Cement the quarrel!
> It's aye the cheapest Lawyers' fee
> To taste the barrel.

Barleycorn – John   Personification in respect specifically of the grain from which whisky is made. The earliest record of the expression dates from 1620, 'A pleasant new ballad...of the bloody murther of Sir *John Barleycorn*'. Robert Burns refashioned the ballad of the barley's death at harvest time in *John Barleycorn* (1782), 'John Barleycorn was a hero bold,/Of noble enterprise,/For if you do but taste his blood,/T'will make your courage rise.'

The theme of *Dutch courage* also occurs in Burns's epic poem 'Tam O'Shanter', (1790) where Barleycorn again makes an appearance.

> Inspiring, bold John Barleycorn!
> What dangers thou canst make us scorn!
> W' tipenny, we fear nae evil;
> Wi' usquabae, we'll face the devil!

An earlier incarnation of John Barleycorn was *Allan o'Maut* (Allan of Malt), who appears in the poem of that title which describes the whisky-making process in some detail. It was orally recorded in the nineteenth century but is believed to date from the sixteenth century. Another poem – in the Bannatyne Manuscript collection of Scottish poetry which dates from 1568 – also sings the praises of one *Allane a'Maut*.

The writer Jack London called what Alan Bold describes as his 'alcoholic autobiography', *John Barleycorn*, and he uses the name as a synonym for drink generally, rather than whisky. 'At every turn in the world in which I lived, John Barleycorn beckoned. There was no escaping him. All paths led to him' (p.10).

barrel In Medieval Latin *barile, barillus, baurillis*. A cylindrical wooden vessel, generally bulging in the middle and of greater length than breadth, formed of curved staves bound together by hoops, and having flat ends or heads; a *cask*. In whisky-making, the cask has a dual role as both a container and a significant contributor to the process of *maturation*.

Whilst *barrel* is often used as a synonym for cask with no specific capacity being implied, in the whisky industry a barrel is a cask with a capacity of approximately 40 gallons (180 litres), between a *quarter* and a *hogshead* in terms of size. It is almost always referred to as an *American barrel*, as it is made from American white oak.

batter On the *batter*, cognate with on the *booze* or *piss*, indulging in a drinking bout. Partridge *(Historical Slang)* has 'to be on a riotous *spree*', dating its use from the late 1830s. 'On the batter' also has the sense of walking the streets as a prostitute, according to Partridge, with a sense of debauchery clearly common to both usages.

In general use, the verb to batter means to beat continuously and violently, so as to bruise and shatter, and the transference of application to the worlds of prostitution and heavy drinking bouts is easy to appreciate, and is comparable with other drinking terms such as *smashed*.

The expression 'on the batter' tends now to be restricted principally to Scottish and Irish usage, 'But if ye hev' tuck a sup, or been on the batther for two or three days...' *(Poor Rabbin's Ollminick*, 1861).

belt Principally an American expression for a *nip* of whisky, a single measure, though the word also tends to be used to mean a mouthful or gulp taken from a fuller glass. Andrew Malone uses the term in a contemporary Scottish context when he writes 'making sure he is not needlessly wasting effort by taking a couple of belts at his glass now that he has roused himself to speak' (*Scotland on Sunday*, May 1992). The drink-related usage of belt has its origins in the transitive slang verb 'belt', first attested in 1838 with the sense of to hit or attack, and intransitively in the United States from 1890, to hurry or rush. As with *slug*, the sense of a heavy blow or stroke also occurs.

beer From the Old English *bēor* and the Old High German *bior*. The word is rare in Old English, except in poetry. It became common as a name for hopped malt liquor only in the sixteenth century, perhaps deriving from *bere*, the Old English word for *barley*.

In the sense of an alcoholic *liquor* obtained from the *fermentation* of *malt* and flavoured with hops or other aromatic bitters, its first usage occurs *c.* 1000, 'He ne drincð win ne bēor'.

As McDowall points out, prior to *distillation*, 'the process of whisky making is very like brewing beer. Indeed, the man in charge is known as the brewer of the *distillery*' (*Whiskies of Scotland*, 104). Just as brandy is distilled wine, so whisky is effectively distilled beer, and Hills maintains that 'The brewer is as important a person in the distillery as the stillman' (*Scots on Scotch*, 12).

The end product of fermentation – the stage of whisky-making before distillation – is fermented *wort*, known as *wash* in Scotland and Ireland, but in the United States as beer, which it very nearly is. According to the makers of Jack Daniel's *Bourbon*, 'The end result of the fermentation process is "stiller's beer", which is sent on to the still for distillation'.

bender Originally a Scots dialect term for a hard drinker, first attested in 1728, 'Now bend your lugs, ye benders fine, Who ken the benefit of wine'. The OED also notes bend – to drink hard. Partridge *(Historical Slang)* records the first use of *bender* in the only sense to have survived, as a drinking bout – 'on a bender' – in the United States in 1827, noting that it had become anglicised by the 1890s. Also sometimes 'on a bend'. The origins of bender as slang for a heavy drinker perhaps relate to the fact that in the seventeenth and eighteenth centuries bender was used as a medical term for the flexor muscle, and was commonly taken to mean an arm or elbow.

bere Also known as *bear* or *bigg*, *bere* was the Old English word for *barley*. According to *The Dictionary of Drink* it was 'The Medieval name for barley from which *beer* derived'. The OED notes that the name 'bere' was 'in later times retained only in the north, and especially in Scotland; hence specifically applied to the coarse variety ... with six (or four) rows of grain in its ear ...'. This type of barley was particularly suited to relatively cold and wet climates, but as Moss and Hume point out when writing of 1799 *excise* legislation, 'A lower rate of tax on malt made from bere or bigg, allowing for the difference in yield of *spirit* between malted bere and barley, was introduced' (*The Making of Scotch Whisky*, 58).

The first attestation of *bere* occurs in *c*. 950 in the *Lindisfarne Gospels*, 'Fife hlafas bero and tuoeʒe Fisces'. Cooper writes that 'Small quantities of bere are still grown on the island of Orkney for making beremeal bannocks. Modern strains of barley are preferred for whisky-making, however; they are full of starch and low in protein' (*Malt Whiskies*, 7).

binge   A serious drinking bout. The word possibly derives from a Lincolnshire dialect term meaning 'to soak', though Partridge (*Historical Slang*) is more inclined to think it has its origins in the word 'bingo', (late seventeenth and eighteenth centuries), a slang term for spirits, especially brandy. *Binge* was in dialect use by the 1850s, and was common among Oxford University undergraduates by 1889. Describing communal heavy drinking sessions in the Hebrides, Neil Wilson remarks, 'These binges were the only means available to the chiefs of relieving the unremitting gloom of the 17th Century' (p.13).

bitters   According to Dr Jamieson's *Dictionary of the Scottish Language*, *bitters* were 'a dram much used in the Highlands as a stomachic, made from an infusion of aromatic herbs and whisky', and the *Encyclopaedia Britannica* (1892) considers them 'a class of liqueurs by themselves'. Jamieson believes that Dr Johnson had bitters in mind when he penned his *Dictionary* entry on *usquebaugh* (See **Uisge beatha**).

The first recorded use of the term dates from 1713: 'Two hogsheads of bitters'. Whisky bitters remained common in the Highlands and Islands of Scotland until well into the second half of the nineteenth century, as Sir Archibald Geikie (*Scottish Reminiscences*, 1904) makes clear when recounting being offered 'some acetates' as a pre-breakfast dram while staying with Jessie Nicolson of Lonfern in Skye during a geological field trip. The acetates, concluded Sir Archibald, were probably 'a decoction of bitter roots in whisky, often to be found on Highland sideboards in the morning'. He opted for whisky and milk as an alternative, but records that 'I did not discover that the draught in any way improved my breakfast'.

McNeill offers a recipe for Highland Bitters which includes gentian root, coriander seed, orange peel, cloves, cinnamon stick, camomile flowers and whisky (p.227).

blending   From the Old English verb *bland-an* and the Old Norse *blanda*, to mix. In the context of whisky, *blending* is the process of mixing *malt* and *grain spirit*. When two or more malts, or more rarely, two or more grains are blended, the result is known as a vatted malt or vatted grain whisky (see *vatting*).

According to one blender quoted by Cooper the end product of blending should be a whisky 'so perfect that it strikes the consumer as being one liquid, not many – i.e. having absolute unity, tasting as a whole' (*Century Companion*, 46). Samuel Bronfman, the founder of Seagram, the world's largest distilling company, maintained that '. . . distilling is a science and blending is an art'. The blender's 'art' is essentially an olfactory one. Rarely if ever will a blender taste whisky while on duty. He can tell by smell the age of a malt he is analysing as well as its area of origin, and he can often pinpoint the exact distillery that produced it. Mackinlay describes the task facing a blender in selecting whiskies as being not unlike that facing a host choosing guests for a dinner party. 'There are some which clash with each other, producing a discordant result, while others enhance one another, bringing out their best qualities to advantage' (*Macmillan Scotch Whisky*, 75).

It has been suggested that 'master blenders, like great poets, are born' (Morrice, 40), but one great poet who would probably not have appreciated the analogy was C.M. Grieve, better known as Hugh MacDiarmid. Grieve was a respected connoisseur of single malts, and it was clearly blended whisky that he had in mind when he wrote in *A Drunk Man Looks at the Thistle* (1926), 'Forbye, the stuffie's no' the real Mackay'. Daiches calls *A Drunk Man Looks at the Thistle* 'the great counter-statement to the music-hall tradition about the Scot and whisky' (*Scots on Scotch*, 118).

Daiches is one of the most literate and accomplished of writers on whisky, and he considers Neil Gunn's work on the subject to have been a major influence in his own subsequent interest. Gunn was no great advocate of blended Scotch either, seeing it almost as the adulteration of a noble and characterful spirit to please the timid palates of foreigners – particularly Englishmen. Single malts had become something of a rarity by the time he wrote his highly original and polemical *Whisky and Scotland* in the mid 1930s, and he lamented the fact that in 1935 only fifteen distilleries were active in Scotland, with six of those producing grain whisky. 'The future of Highland malt whisky, other than as a flavouring ingredient of patent spirit, is very obscure,' he wrote (p.169). Happily, that situation has altered considerably in recent years, as malts have found a significant market in Britain and abroad, albeit a modest one in terms of total whisky sales.

A typical blended Scotch whisky may consist of anything from fifteen to forty single malts along with grain whiskies, which are appreciably quicker and cheaper to produce in *patent* stills than malts in *pot* stills. The aim of the blender is not simply to dilute a range of malts with less characterful and less expensive grain whisky, as Mackinlay makes clear. Thus the lightness of a blend – and the American market traditionally likes its Scotch whiskies light for mixing – is produced not by increasing the quantity of grain whisky but by using a greater number of lighter malts, perhaps more *Lowlands*, in proportion to the heavier and fuller flavoured *Highland* and *Islay* malts.

De-luxe blended whiskies generally contain a higher ratio of malt to grain than standard blends, sometimes more than 50 per cent malt, and while there is no legal reason why a blended whisky has to contain more than a minute quantity of malt, even the cheapest supermarket 'own brand' blends will usually contain at least 5 per cent malt. The average malt content for an established brand of blended whisky is 10-40 per cent, though during the early 1980s, when over-production caused something of a *whisky loch*, some blends were produced with significantly increased percentages of malt – sometimes up to 65 per cent – in an attempt to drain the loch of matured malts.

The physical process of blending the chosen whiskies in their correct proportions takes place in a blending vat of up to 25,000 gallons capacity, in which compressed air mixes the contents. The resultant blend is then casked for between six months and a year to allow a full *marriage* of the component whiskies. Some firms keep the grains and malts separate until bottling, while others blend them before the period of marriage. In either case, prior to bottling the whisky is usually diluted to market strength, caramel is added to ensure continuity of colouring, and finally the spirit is filtered to prevent cloudiness from developing when water is added by the consumer.

Most Irish whiskies are now blends of pot still whiskey and grain whiskey, but unlike blended Scotches they are composed of a very small range of pot still whiskeys. Irish distillers prefer to use the term *vatting* rather than blending, with Irish Distillers making the point that 'in Scotland...a blender buys whisky, either new or mature, from many different distillers or brokers and mixes or "blends" them all together according to his own formula. In Ireland, we believe the art lies in the distilling rather than in blending, so all our component whiskies are distilled by us under our control – not bought in'.

Unofficial blending by merchants and publicans had been practised in Scotland for some time prior to the launch in 1853 of the first commercial blended whisky, Usher's OVG (Old Vatted *Glen-livet*), which was developed in Edinburgh by Andrew Usher, and, as Gunn reminds us, 'The great blending industry in Scotland arose with the *patent* still' (p.164). Moss and Hume point out that not only had various whiskies previously been mixed, but also 'Sometimes, the whisky had been blended with other spirits like brandy or flavoured with herbs and other additives in the same manner as gin' (*The Making of Scotch Whisky*, 98). Not surprisingly, the distillers of malt whisky were less than happy with such practices designed to produce inexpensive but low-quality drink, considering that 'it damaged their market and the image of whisky'. Mackinlay makes the important point that 'it is on blended whisky that the international popularity and reputation of Scotch has been built. If the practice of blending Scotch whisky had never begun, the whisky trade in Scotland might not have developed beyond a cottage industry' (p.72).

In the mid-nineteenth century, malt whisky was a relatively unknown drink outside Scotland, generally being considered too heavily flavoured for popular taste. Blending malt and grain whiskies to produce a drink with an altogether lighter character therefore presented great opportunities to expand sales beyond the traditional Scotch whisky markets. There was also the important consideration, as Cooper notes, 'that the whisky merchants realised that there could be a substantial economic advantage in mixing cheaper grain whisky with the more expensive and mercurial products of the pot still' (*Century Companion*, 42). One reason for the great commercial success of blended whisky during the second half of the nineteenth century was the havoc wreaked on the French brandy industry by the insect *Phylloxera Vastatrix*, which destroys vines by attacking their leaves and roots. It was first identified in France in 1865, and during the 1880s it caused the production of Cognac to cease almost totally, with brandy drinkers in England soon requiring a substitute. As Daiches puts it, 'It was the combination of the results of phylloxera in France, the development of blends of malt and grain whiskies in Scotland, and energetic commercial activity and brilliant salesmanship, that put blended Scotch whisky on the sideboard of the English gentleman at the end of the nineteenth century' (*Scotch Whisky*, 63).

The group of distillers whose fortunes were made during the blended whisky boom included Buchanan, Dewar, Walker and Peter Mackie of White Horse fame, whilst the already well-established whisky house of Haig grew in stature and in wealth. 'The "big five" of blended whisky', as Daiches terms them, ultimately all came under the control of The Distillers Company Limited, which now belongs to Guinness Plc, and trades as United Distillers. The company produces the leading brand of Scotch whisky in five of the top ten markets in the world, and it is interesting to note that approximately 20 per cent of the bottled Scotch whisky exported is Johnnie Walker. United Distillers currently produce eighty different blends for sale throughout the world, and operate twenty-seven malt distilleries and three grain distilleries in Scotland.

Before blended Scotch arrived on the scene, Irish was the whiskey most usually drunk in England, where its relatively light character found favour. The traditional Irish distillers were naturally less than delighted to see their market in England seriously threatened, but more worrying still was the fact that some grain whisky merchants shipped quantities of their product from Scotland to Ireland, where it was blended with small quantities of quality native whiskey before being re-imported and marketed as 'Irish Whiskey'. By the 1880s the product of patent stills in Belfast and Londonderry was also finding its way across the Irish Sea to Scotland to be blended with pot still malt. The Scottish Malt Distillers Association protested about this aspect of the blending trade as vehemently as their Irish counterparts, and there was considerable general and medical concern about the quality of much of the blended whisky on the market.

The year 1905 saw a very significant test case when the Borough Council in the unlikely setting of Islington, North London charged a publican and an off-licence operator under the Merchandise Marks Act with retailing as whisky 'articles not of the nature, substance and quality demanded' in what became known as the 'What is Whisky?' case. Finally the matter became the subject of a Royal Commission of Inquiry in 1908-9, which effectively found in favour of the grain distillers and whisky blenders. It rejected the proposal for a compulsory bonding period for all whiskies, and concluded: 'We are unable to recommend that the use of the word "whisky" should be restricted to spirit manufactured by the pot-still process'.

Domestic sales of blended whisky in 1990 accounted for 39.51 million litres of pure alcohol (one litre of pure alcohol = 0.386 imperial *proof* gallons) compared with just 1.76 million lpa of malt whisky, while on a worldwide basis bottled blended whisky accounted for 209.72 million lpa, and bottled malt sales for 10.58 million lpa. However, bulk malt exports, chiefly to Japan, accounted for a further 21.58 million lpa. The market leaders in Britain and abroad include Bells, Teachers, Haig, The Famous Grouse, Johnnie Walker, White Horse, Dewars, Whyte and Mackay and Vat 69.

blotto   Twentieth-century slang for very drunk. The OED suggests *blot* ('disfigurement; blemish; defect; disgraceful act or quality in good character') as a possible source. Partridge *(Historical Slang)* offers *c.* 1905 for its first usage, which he attributes to P.G. Wodehouse. 'He was oiled, boiled, fried, plastered, whiffled, sozzled and blotto'. He considers that the word may have been suggested to Wodehouse by the porousness of blotting paper, and possibly also influenced by the Romany 'motto', intoxicated.

Blue Blazer   One of the more spectacular – not to say hazardous – whisky *cocktails*, the *Blue Blazer* was invented by the principal bartender at New York's Metropolitan Hotel. Showmanship and an element of dexterity are as essential to the creation of this drink as whisky itself, and the principal ingredients are usually 2 fl. oz. of whisky and 2 fl. oz. of boiling water, both of which start off in separate one-*gill* jiggers. The name of the drink derives from the manner in which the ingredients are mixed, as the whisky is ignited and the contents of the two jiggers are then poured from one to the other four or five times until thoroughly mixed. As Jerry Thomas *(The Bon Vivant's Guide)* puts it, 'If well done this will have the appearance of a continued stream of liquid fire'. Once mixed, the drink is sweetened with white sugar and served with lemon peel in an *Old-fashioned* glass (a tumbler usually used for serving cocktails *on the rocks*). 'The *Blue Blazer* does not have a very euphonious or classic name', adds Thomas, 'but it tastes better to the *palate* than it sounds to the ear. A beholder gazing for the first time upon an experienced artist compounding this beverage, would naturally come to the conclusion that it was a nectar for Pluto rather than Bacchus'.

Blue Blazer coffee is a more recent British variation on the theme, consisting of a cup of strong black coffee into which is poured 1/5 gill of ignited Irish whiskey.

body   A common term in the vocabulary of the whisky expert or would-be expert, as in that of the wine buff. Jackson writes that 'body and texture . . . are distinct features in the overall character of each malt' *(Malt Whisky Companion*, 22). Along with colour, *nose, palate* and *finish, body* is one of the elements Jackson treats when examining the anatomy of individual whiskies, and comments vary from 'very light' and 'soft' through 'medium' to 'full', incorporating other adjectives such as 'quite luscious', 'rounded' and 'smooth'. Springbank warrants 'Big, tongue-coating', under its body heading, while a Signatory bottling of Glen Mhor earns the nicely apt description of 'Very soft and voluptuous'.

When applied to drink in the sense of substance or substantial quality, as opposed to insubstantiality, thinness and weakness, body is first attested, relating to wine, in c. 1645, 'In Greece there are no wines that have bodies enough to bear the sea for long voyages'.

boilermaker   American term for a measure of *neat* whiskey with a beer *chaser*, though Chapman *(The New Dictionary of American Slang)* notes 'Drink of whiskey with, or in, a glass of beer'. He thinks that the term derives from *boilermaker's Delight*, 'Any very strong or rough drink, inferior whiskey... because it would clean the scales from the inside of a boiler'.

'Boiled' is recorded as a slang synonym for 'drunk' from 1886, so the sense of 'a drink which makes you boiled' is another possible derivation, particularly as the combination of beer and whiskey can be a comparatively swift intoxicant.

Hugh MacDiarmid writes 'What beer was consumed was used simply as a "chaser" to the whisky in precisely the same way as a "boilermaker" in New York' ('The Dour Drinkers of Glasgow'). In England a *boilermaker* can denote a mixed pint of mild and brown ale.

boll   Probably Old Norse *bolli*, a bowl. In Scotland and Northern England a measure of capacity, particularly of grain, and in Scotland it usually contained six Imperial bushels.

The first attestation occurs in c. 1375, 'Off Ryngis... He send thre bollis to Cartage'. (For first recorded use relating to whisky see *aqua vitae*).

bond   In Middle English *bond*. Relating to whisky, the relevant sense is of 'The storage of excisable liquor on which duty and taxes have not been paid' (Edwards, 106). The bond is essentially an agreement to pay relevant duties at some future time. When the duty is paid the goods are said to be taken out of or released from bond.

In this context the word bond first appears in 1851: 'More foreign corn was let out of bond'. The liquor-related usage of bond developed from the sense of what the OED calls 'An agreement or engagement binding on him who makes it', with the first attestation occurring in 1330, 'If þe Kyng . . . had þat bond, & drawen it'.

Bonding takes place after the process of *distillation* has been completed. 'The casks are transferred to the warehouse for maturing and here again they are placed under lock and key by the distiller and the excise officer and cannot be removed without the knowledge of both. Such whisky is said to be in bond and duty is not paid till the whisky leaves for the bottler. In some cases for convenience, however, the latter may have a bonded warehouse to which the casks may be conveyed while still in bond' (Mc-Dowall, 129).

bootlegging A term dating from the period of *Prohibition* in the United States of America, and originating from the practice of carrying a flask of illegal whisky in the top of the boot. Initially a *bootlegger* was a smuggler of illicit alcoholic drink into the United States, though the term also developed a more general currency for anyone involved in the distribution of illicit liquor.

The writer and diplomat Sir Bruce Lockhart spent time in the United States during and after the period of Prohibition, and writes, 'Illicit distilling began almost at once, and, aided by a buoyant Stock Exchange and an unprecedented "boom", the boot-leggers entered into their paradise' (*Scotch*, 141).

The term bootleg has now gained acceptance as a colloquialism for illegally procured material, e.g. bootleg albums in the music business. 'Taiwan police have raided a bootleg compact-disc factory and seized over 1,000 counterfeit CDs by major artists...' (*Daily Telegraph*, June 1992).

booze A variant of the Middle English *bouse*, to drink, first attested *c.* 1300, 'Hail ye holi monkes...depe cun ye bouse.'

The early Middle Dutch verb *buizen* and the German *bausen* both have the sense of drinking to excess, which is still implied by modern British and American usage of *booze* as both noun and verb. The Dutch *buizen* probably relates directly to *buise*, a large drinking vessel.

Some etymologists suggest the Egyptian *bouzah*, 'a kind of beer said to be named after a city, Bousiris' as a possible origin, Dunkling notes; 'Bouzy is a village in the Champagne area of northern France. Chapman, in his *Dictionary of American Slang*, thinks that the use of the word was influenced "by the name of a 19th-century Philadelphia distiller, E.G. Booze"' (p.17).

Note also: *on the booze* (from 1850), *boozed* (from 1850) for drunk, *booze-up* (late 19th century) for a drinking bout, *boozy* (16th century), and *boozer* (pre-1611 in the sense of *drunkard*, and late Victorian as colloquial synonym for a public house).

bottle A vessel with a narrow neck for holding liquids, now usually made of glass, but originally of leather. *Bottle* is a Middle English noun, from the Old French *bouteille*, from Medieval Latin *butticula*, diminutive of Late Latin *buttis*, vessel. See also *butt*. The first recorded English use occurs in *c.* 1375, 'þes newe hoolis, þat been maad in oold botelis'. As well as having a nounal sense, 'bottle' can be also a transitive verb.

Grindal (p.140) suggests that Dewar's may have been the whisky firm to blend Scotch and sell it in bottle during the second

half of the nineteenth century, and it was in 1860 that whisky
was first allowed by law to be exported to England in bottles
rather than in *casks*, though it was not until 1917 that bottled
whisky really took over from sales direct from the cask in Britain.

The problem of the amount of space a cask took up on a bar
counter was solved in the early nineteenth century 'by the creation
of a whisky jar; a large glass container holding anything from one
to three gallons. These were filled from the cask by the publican
and had a tap in the bottom from which the spirit could be drained'
(Lamond, *Book of Days*, 32).

The standard bottle size used in Britain, Ireland and many
export markets contained 26¾ fluid ounces or 76 centilitres, until
an EC directive decreed that from January 1992 capacity had to
be reduced to 70 cls in order to standardise spirit bottles throughout the Community. In late 1992 the Safeway supermarket chain
introduced a range of four own-label *single-malt* whiskies to represent the Scottish producing regions which were marketed in
50cl bottles.

Litre bottles have gained in popularity in recent years and are
particularly favoured by duty-free outlets, whilst the licensed
trade also uses imperial quarts (1.136 litres), magnums (1.5 litres),
tregnums (2.25 litres) and giant size (3.75 litres). The miniature
whisky bottle has acquired notable currency among collectors,
and a book, *Scotch in Miniature* by Alan Keegan, is devoted to
the subject.

As well as being a practical container for whisky, the bottle has
inevitably become a fertile ground for designers and those charged
with marketing the product. Under their influence there has been
a move towards the much wider use of clear bottle glass in order
to highlight the attractive golden colour contained within. For
some distillers, an idiosyncratically shaped bottle is perceived as
having eye-catching value.

Most authorities contend that once whisky is in the bottle, the
process of *maturation* ceases: 'Neither it [malt] nor any other bottled Scotch will be affected by the length of time you keep it. It
should not suffer in any way by clouding nor should it change in
colour or taste, so long as it is kept in the original sealed bottle'
(Morrice, 17). An alternative view is provided by McDowall
(p.108), who maintains, 'After twenty years it [a Highland malt]
is liable to acquire a woodiness probably due to slight rotting of
the cask. It continues, however, to improve in the bottle. It is
said to "brandify" by those who know, but for some reason, which
I do not understand, the idea that a change takes place in the
bottle is not generally approved of'.

Neil Gunn describes drinking some 104-year-old Scrabster whisky from his native county of Caithness:

> Whisky is generally believed to mature in wood but not in bottle. Assuming this liquor was bottled immediately after it was made – and the 1830 on the glass would imply as much – then here was an occasion for the perfect experiment!
> Let it be said at once that the liquor in that bottle was matured to an incredible smoothness. I have never tasted anything quite like it in that respect, yet it had an attractively objectionable flavour, somewhere between rum and tar to our palates. (Gunn, 159-60)

With the growth of interest in single malt whiskies many more Scotch whisky distillery companies now bottle and market their own malts than they did a couple of decades ago. Their bottlings tend to be relatively standardised to eight, ten or twelve years old, and 40% vol (70° *proof*), but rarer bottlings are available from several specialist companies in Scotland, who also bottle whiskies which are not available from their distillers and the products of distilleries which are now *silent*.

William Cadenhead of Edinburgh and Gordon & MacPhail of Elgin bottle malts at a wide range of ages, with Cadenhead favouring 46% vol. rather than Gordon & MacPhail's 40% vol. Many single malt distillers are reluctant to allow casks of their products on to the open market where they cannot monitor the effects of maturation and thereby maintain stringent control of quality and continuity. In 1982 The Macallan – generally regarded as one of the 'classic' Speyside malts – took out an injunction to prevent Gordon & MacPhail from bottling their whisky without authorisation, and the following year the owners of Bunnahabhain Islay malt repeated the action against the same company.

The Scotch Malt Whisky Society of Leith successfully overcame distillers' sensitivities to buy and bottle single casks which it offers to members, though very few distilleries allow their names to be used on the society's labels. (See *single cask*). The Edinburgh firm of Signatory now bottle a range of single malts for the general public, but they have gone one step further than either Cadenhead or Gordon and MacPhail by including on their labels the cask number or numbers from which bottlings are taken, and each bottle is allocated its own number.

The adjective *bottled*, meaning *drunk*, is first recorded in 1927, and is still current. 'The crowd were worked up and many were well bottled' (*Daily Telegraph*, 25 January 1993). Apart from the most obvious implication of having consumed bottles of liquor, a possible derivation for this meaning of bottled comes from the sense of resembling a bottle, protruberant, swollen, first attested in 1594. Bottle as a synonym for bravery or 'guts', first recorded in 1958, would seem to derive from a sense of valour achieved through the consumption of alcohol – *Dutch courage*.

bottle of smoke Picturesque slang synonym for a bottle of whisky, derived from the smoky nature of the contents, current in Scots and Irish usage. Morton writes, 'There will always be an idiot prepared to pay £50, or £80, or even £500 for a *bottle of smoke* so strong it'll dissolve your teeth . . .' (p.67).

Bourbon Along with *rye* and *Tennessee Sour Mash*, *Bourbon* is one of the principal styles of whiskey distilled in the United States. According to Michael Jackson, 'It is the American classic' (*World Book*, 140). In common with nearly all American whiskies, Bourbon is produced in *column* stills. Bourbon is distilled principally from corn, and takes its name from Bourbon County in the state of Kentucky, which is still the principal state of production, being home to more than half the Bourbon distilleries in the United States.

According to legend, the spirit was first made in 1789 by Revd Elijah Craig, a Baptist preacher, though Craig did not distill in Bourbon County but in neighbouring Scott County. Another contender is John Ritchie, who is said by one source to have successfully produced a corn-based whiskey near Bardstown in 1777. In fact, American whiskey historians find it impossible to say exactly when and by whom the first really drinkable whiskey was distilled from corn, though one Evan Williams was perhaps the first man to distill whiskey in the Louisville area from 1783.

During the American War of Independence the French gave the rebel colonists significant aid, and once the war was over gratitude was expressed by using French names for many new settlements and administrative areas. When the-then Western Virginian county of Kentucky was subdivided in the 1780s, one new county was named in honour of the French royal house of Bourbon, and Kentucky became a fully fledged state in its own right in 1792. The name of Bourbon County became associated with the shipping of whiskey through the port of Maysville on the Ohio River. The modern Bourbon County is much smaller than the original, and ironically it has no distilleries and is officially 'dry'.

Kentucky probably developed as a 'whisky state' from the time when Thomas Jefferson, Governor of Virginia, granted to settlers sixty acres of land in the County of Kentucky on which they could grow corn. Sixty acres of corn takes a lot of eating, and turning the grain into whiskey was a logical way of producing a form of 'currency' which improved with time rather than deteriorated. Corn grows well on the limestone soil of Kentucky, and it is no coincidence that most of the other whiskey-producing states of America – past and present – such as Maryland, Pennsylvania, Tennessee and Virginia partly overlie the same limestone shelf. Limestone also produces good spring water, free from discolouring minerals, and American distillers maintain that the calcium content in water that flows through limestone aids enzyme action during the *fermentation* process.

By law, Bourbon must be produced from a *mash* of not less than 51% corn grain, and is usually made from between 70% and 90% corn, with some *barley* malt and rye or wheat. It is bottled at between 80° and 101° *proof*, with the characterful Wild Turkey from Lawrenceburg, Kentucky being the best known 101° proof Bourbon. Though the appellation Bourbon Whiskey has been used since the early nineteenth century, it was only by a resolution of Congress in 1964 that Bourbon was officially defined in terms of content.

The spirit is matured in new white-oak barrels that have been charred, or thermally degraded, and Jackson stresses the importance of the charring process. 'In Bourbon the defining characteristics are the tones of vanillin and caramel that the whiskey takes from the wood. It is the charring that permits the whiskey ease of entry into the wood' (*World Guide*, 155). Popular myth has it that Revd Craig accidentally discovered the positive effects that charring the barrels had on maturing Bourbon, though charring is known to have been used as a means of disinfecting casks in the early nineteenth century.

The principal centres for Bourbon production are Bardstown, Frankfort and Louisville in Kentucky, with Jim Beam, Old Crow, and Old Grandad being among the best known and most respected brands.

bracer In its nineteenth and twentieth century sense, a *bracer* was a tonic medicine, something which braced the nerves, and the first attestation occurs in 1740: 'Bark *Bitters*, and Steel and such Astringents and Bracers'. That application is long obsolete, but the transfer of use from standard English to the modern slang term for stiff drink to brace the nerves – first recorded in the United States *c*.1860 – is a natural one, bearing in mind that a tonic in colloquial use can be taken to mean a drink, particularly an appetizer.

'I chanced to encounter Mr Fink-Nottle in the garden, sir, while you were still in bed, and we had a brief conversation.'

'And you came away feeling that he needed a bracer?'

'Very much so, sir.' (P.G. Wodehouse, *Right Ho, Jeeves*, 1922)

brewing   From the Old English *brēowan*, probably with Germanic origins. The first attestation of the verb *brew* occurs in *c*.893, and *brewing* in 1467. 'I will that the seid Denys haue here esement in the bakhows in lawfull tyme for bruynge.' Lovett notes that 'Brewing, using malted cereals such as *barley*, was common in the Bible lands, and the ancient Egyptians even had a hieroglyph for brewer' (p.8).

Brewing is the process which follows *malting* in the production of malt whisky, and consists of *mashing* and *fermentation*, though in Irish distilling circles it is usually taken to mean just mashing, with fermentation being considered as a separate, successive operation.

As the brewing stage of whisky production is very similar to the process of brewing beer, it is not surprising that a common vocabulary has evolved, with much of the jargon used in whisky-making having its origin in the earlier craft of beer-making.

brown-bagging   According to Dunkling, this is 'an American term for taking one's own alcohol to a club or restaurant that is otherwise "dry"' (p.17). The expression obviously relates to the concealment of the illegal drink. Writing of the Jack Daniel distillery in *The Mail on Sunday* magazine (30 August 1992), Rodney Tyler notes 'Lynchburg is what they call a brown-baggers' town.'

burnt ale   Also known as *pot ale* or *spent wash*, this is the high-protein waste liquor left in the *low wines still* after the first *distillation* has taken place. The term *burnt* is used because *burnt ale* is the residue which remains after heating has taken place.

According to Daiches, 'it is sometimes turned into fertilizer or, evaporated and dried, into animal food...' (*Scotch Whisky*, 15). Neil Wilson recalls that in 1847 Donald Johnson of Laphroaig distillery on Islay was popularly believed to have drowned in a vat of burnt ale.

In common with its Islay neighbours of Lagavulin and Ardbeg, Laphroaig still discharges its burnt ale into the sea, and distillery manager Iain Henderson maintains that this has altered the ecological balance of the area of the southern shore where the three plants are sited: the largest crabs and lobsters in the greatest profusion caught of the island are to be found close to the distilleries. He points out that, according to Islay lore, the only time there has been a falling off in size and quantity of the local shellfish was during World War Two, when the three distilleries were *silent*.

See also *grains* and *spent lees*.

butt A *cask*. *Butt* has its origins in the same Late Latin noun *butta* as *bottle*, and is first attested in 1443: 'Rhenish 1 butt = 36 gals'. In terms of capacity, the butt had increased by the early eighteenth century to between 108 and 140 gallons, and is now taken to be approximately 110 gallons or 500 litres.

As a whisky cask the butt is the second largest – after the *puncheon* – and the most widely employed of the various sizes generally used in the storage and consequent *maturation* of Scotch and Irish spirit. It has twice the capacity of the *hogshead* and is usually made of Spanish oak. See also *barrel*, *octave* and *quarter*.

Campbeltown The smallest of the four recognised malt Scotch whisky regions, the others being *Highland*, *Islay* and *Lowland*. The term *Campbeltown* defines not just a geographical region of production but also a distinctive style of whisky, which remains to this day, though Grindal writes that 'Recently, because only two Campbeltown distilleries remain in operation, blenders have tended to drop Campbeltown malts as a category and treat the two whiskies from that area as Highland malts' (p.32).

Issue could certainly be taken with McDowall's assertion that 'the Lowland and Campbeltown malts are milder [than Highland and Islay malts] and now very much alike. Their differentiation probably had its origin when there were very many distilleries in Campbeltown producing a strongly flavoured whisky' (p.9). Skipworth observes that 'Such was its importance that even to this day the name of Campbeltown is used to describe a style of whisky, though virtually all the distilleries have gone' (p.35). He is inclined to place Campbeltown whiskies above Highland malts and below Islay in terms of 'heaviness'. Alfred Barnard dismissed Campbeltown whiskies as 'generally thin, useful at the price', though Daiches takes the more usual historical overview of their status when he echoes Macdonald's 'Deepest-voiced of all the choir' opinion, saying 'Campbeltowns have in the past had something of the strength and body of Islays, and are indeed traditionally regarded as the most manly of whiskies' (*Scotch Whisky*, 23).

Jackson remarks that relatively light peating is a perhaps unexpected characteristic of Campbeltown whiskies. 'This leaves especially unmasked in the Campbeltown malts a quite different taste element: a fresh, salty aroma and palate' (*World Guide*, 34). Jackson argues that this saltiness is almost certainly acquired during *maturation* from the sea mists which are such a feature of the narrow peninsula.

In the nineteenth century malts were divided into regions or classifications for the first time, initially Campbeltown, *Glenlivet*, Islay, Lowland, and *North Country*, though the Campbeltowns and Islays were sometimes categorised as *West Highland Malts*. The proper noun Campbeltown underwent a rank-shift so that it came additionally to have adjectival status as the region developed

26

as a whisky-making centre and its product gained its own stylistic identity, just as happened with the other producing regions.

The Royal Burgh of Campbeltown which gives its name to the eponymous classification of whisky has a population of 6,000 and lies at the southern end of the Kintyre peninsula in Argyllshire, the longest peninsula in Scotland. The name *Kintyre* comes from the Gaelic Ceann-Tire, meaning 'land's end', and by the time Thomas Pennant paid a visit to the area in the summer of 1772 illicit distillation was a notable feature of the local economy. Moss and Hume note that 'The illicit distillers in Kintyre . . . developed an extensive trade with Glasgow and its neighbouring towns, where their more peaty whiskies were preferred to those of the Lowland distillers' (*Making of Scotch Whisky*, 62). Pennant took some exception to the area's illegal whisky-making, stating, 'Notwithstanding the quantity of bear [*bere*: a kind of barley] raised, there is often a sort of dearth; the inhabitants being mad enough to convert their bread into poison, distilling annually six thousand bolls of grain into whisky.'

Campbeltown was founded as a burgh in 1609 by Archibald Campbell, seventh earl of Argyll, and by the time of the compilation of the *Statistical Account of Scotland* in 1794 there were twenty-two operational distilleries in the town and a further ten in the surrounding countryside. The Revd Mr John Smith who wrote the Campbeltown entry noted that 'Next to the fishing of herrings, the business most attended to in Campbeltown is the distilling of whisky . . .'. Overall, distilling has been documented as taking place at a total of thirty-four different locations in the town. 'The Campbeltown distillers were quickly able to corner the Glasgow market, a city with which there had been a good smuggling trade', according to promotional literature produced by Eaglesome's of Reform Square in Campbeltown.

From the middle of the nineteenth century until the 1920s there remained about twenty distilleries in Campbeltown, but by 1925 only twelve were operational and by 1934 just three existed. In 1934 Rieclachan closed, leaving only Glen Scotia and Springbank as representatives of the regional style, though they too had their periods of silence during that troubled decade.

Such was the scale of distilling in Campbeltown in the late nineteenth century that Alfred Barnard described it as 'The Whisky City' after a visit to the area in 1887, when he inspected twenty-one distilleries. In 1885 total output for the twenty-one plants in operation in Campbeltown was 1,938,000 gallons, with more than 250 men being directly employed in distilling. Hazelburn, the largest of the town's distilleries, boasted an output of

192,000 gallons and employed twenty-two people.

One school of thought holds that the craft of whisky-making was brought to Kintyre from Antrim in Northern Ireland, and it is interesting to note that the Campbeltown distilleries are actually slightly closer to the Bushmills operation on the northern Antrim coast than they are to the closest Islay distilleries of Laphroaig, Lagavulin and Ardbeg.

Jackson says, 'If the art of distillation did emerge from the mists of the West, as some believe, then it is reasonable to accept the notion that it arrived first in this part of the country, as has been argued' (*World Guide*, 32). The remoteness of Kintyre and the local availability of barley and peat made it a natural place for illicit distillation, and the existence there of the only coal mine in the Western Highlands was an additional factor in the growth of commercial whisky-making on the peninsula. 'Success, however, contained the seeds of destruction', as McDowall points out (p.40), in that while satisfying the blenders' voracious appetite for malts at the turn of the century, the quality and consistency of Campbeltown whiskies suffered appreciably. Several Campbeltown distillers also supplied quantities of *bootleg* whiskies to the United States during the period of *Prohibition*.

With the financial slump of the late 1920s, Campbeltown lost much of its business and its reputation suffered from the poorer-quality distilleries. Some became bonded stores, others were pulled down, and by the mid-1930s Gunn described the area as 'practically derelict'. No doubt the relative geographical remoteness of Campbeltown and poor road links to the distribution centres in Glasgow also played their parts in the region's distilling demise, along with the fact that by the 1930s the local coal mine had become worked out.

An idea of the Campbeltown distilleries that have passed into history can be gained from a verse of Aeneas Macdonald's ingenious rhymed guide to the distilleries of Scotland, written in the late 1920s.

> Last port seen by westering sail
> 'Twixt the tempest and the Gael,
> Campbeltown in long Kintyre
> Mothers there a son of fire,
> Deepest-voiced of all the choir.
> Solemnly we name this Hector
> Of the West, this giant nectar:
> Benmore, Scotia, and Rieclachan,
> Kinloch, Springside, Hazelburn,
> Glenside, Springbank and Lochruan,

Lochhead. Finally, to spurn
Weaklings drunk and cowards sober,
Summon we great Dalintober.

Now only Springbank and Glen Scotia malts are available, though since 1973 Springbank has also produced an excellent old-fashioned single malt called Longrow (the name dates back to 1874) made from entirely peat-dried malt and marketed at sixteen years of age. After periods of silence during the 1970s and 1980s, both surviving distilleries are back in production at the time of writing.

Springbank distillery dates from around 1828, and Glen Scotia from c.1832, when it was built on the site of an illicit still. Jackson describes Glen Scotia as having 'a smooth salty *palate*; and a warm finish' (*World Guide*, 34), whilst Wilson reckons it to be 'a rich, full, robust and peaty whisky with a slight suggestion of the oiliness of Irish whiskey...' (*Malt Whiskies*, n.p.).

Milroy calls Springbank 'a malt drinker's dram' (p.41), and Jackson describes it as a 'big, profound whisky', pointing out that it is 'generally regarded as the regional classic' (*World Guide*, 33). At Springbank the *foreshots* and *feints* are re-distilled in a separate still, instead of being put back into the *low wines still* as is usually the case, an operation which may account for some of the 'charm and elegance' Milroy identifies in this malt. Twelve-year-old Springbank achieved the rare distinction of being unanimously voted 'Premier Grand Cru Classic' by a panel of experts during a blind tasting for *The Times* in 1983. The distillery is still owned by descendants of its founders, the Mitchells, who are reputed to be Scotland's oldest distilling family, and there are associations with the Cadenhead bottling and merchandising company. The Springbank distillery boasts the unusual feature of its own bottling line, at which it fills malts for the Cadenhead range. It is one of only three Scottish distilleries still bottling at source, the others being Glenfiddich and the Spanish-owned Lochside at Montrose. Springbank has found favour in the lucrative Japanese market, where it is one of the best-selling single malt whiskies.

cask   The word apparently derives from the French *casque*, an adaptation of the Spanish *casco*, 'a caske or burganet, also a head, a pate, a skonce, an earthen pot, sheard or galley cup', according to the OED. 'Casco' may derive from 'cascar', to break into pieces, with the original sense of 'something broken, sherd'. The origins of 'cask' in the sense of 'barrel' are unclear, and this application only occurs in English, first being recorded between 1526 and 1556.

The fact that storage in casks improves the quality of spirits was probably first discovered in the seventeenth century, and the discovery was almost certainly made by accident. A period of *maturation* in wood began in time to supercede the use of blackberry, juniper and raspberry flavourings to disguise the harshness and unpleasant flavour of new spirit.

Cask is a general term in the whisky industry for the containers of varying capacities in which spirit is stored during maturation, also sometimes known as the *wood*. The cask is important in respect of size and any previous contents it may have had or artificial treatments it may have received.

The capacity of the cask is one factor which governs the rate of maturation, and it is a general rule that the smaller the cask the faster the whisky will mature. The contents of the cask when initially filled is stencilled on both ends, formerly being recorded in gallons and now in litres. As Cooper explains, 'In a 110 gallon butt only 48 square inches of wood comes into contact with each gallon of whisky, in a 55-65 gallon hogshead the area is larger – 60 square inches of benign oak through which the spirit can evaporate its less desirable elements' (*Century Companion*, 28).

Oak is the only material used in the construction of whisky casks as it is a hard wood with the porousness which enables the spirit to 'breathe' during maturation. American white oak and Spanish oak are generally considered to be the best varieties for whisky casks, as other varieties tend to be too porous.

As long ago as the early eighteenth century it was accepted that the use of sherry casks improved maturing whisky, and in 1864 William Sanderson – who went on to achieve fame by producing the Vat 69 blend – wrote on the subject of casks: 'it is well known that whisky stored in Sherry casks soon acquires a mellow softness which it does not get when put into new casks; in fact the latter if not well seasoned, will impart a woodiness much condemned by the practised palate. In Sherry casks the spirit likewise acquires a pleasing tinge of colour which is much sought for.' A cask that has previously contained pale sherry will naturally give a paler colour to the whisky than one that has held dark sherry, as it is the sherry soaking back from the wood into the whisky that colours the clear spirit. Whilst no distiller wishes his whisky to taste unduly of sherry, there can be little doubt that the different flavours of, for example, fino and amontillado sherries can be detected in two samples of the same whisky which have been matured in different types of sherry cask. Indeed, the Scotch Malt Whisky Society bottles samples of whiskies which vary only in terms of having been matured in different kinds of sherry wood for purposes of comparison by the discerning palates of its members.

In addition to its role in the process of maturation, the sherry cask is also an ideal size for whisky, being a *butt* with a capacity of 110 gallons or 500 litres.

The Macallan, one of Scotland's most highly regarded whiskies, is the only single malt which is still matured exclusively in sherry casks, generally those which have previously contained oloroso. A progressive shortage of sherry casks due to modern bulk transport methods of shipping sherry and the voracious demands of the whisky industry led the proprietors of The Macallan to take the unique step of commissioning their own sherry casks in Jerez in Spain; they are shipped to Scotland after being used to hold sherry for three years. One advantage of sherry casks is that their initial contents removes a considerable amount of tannin from the wood, leading to a smoother flavour in the opinion of The Macallan's owners.

Not that sherry casks find universal favour in distilling circles. The proprietors of the Glenmorangie distillery at Tain in Ross-shire have found by experimentation that their use masks the distinctive delicateness of Glenmorangie single malt, and instead prefer to use only former *Bourbon* casks, as do the owners of Laphroaig on Islay. Several of the tasters taking part in a malt whisky tasting session for *Decanter* magazine in February 1993 expressed concern at what they considered the over-sherrying of a number of malts, feeling that the sherry was smothering other valuable characteristics. Grindal makes the point that 'Some people in the trade argue that American oak is in fact better than sherry wood, for whisky matured in it is lighter in colour and less sweet, and for this reason more suited to what they see as changing public taste' (p.96).

As a result of the shortage of genuine sherry wood, many malts have been matured in new casks which have been treated with Paxarette, a sweetening and colouring wine developed for sherries and made from the Pedro Ximénez grape. Paxarette, however, has now been banned in the Scotch whisky industry and caramel is the commonly used alternative. The concept of the 'wine-treated' cask was developed by William Lowrie in the late nineteenth century, originally using a dark, sweet sherry. Plain and 'second-fill' casks – those which have previously contained malt whisky – are also used in many instances, along with ex-Bourbon casks. It is also not unknown for former brandy casks to be recycled for purposes of whisky maturation, and in 1991 a small quantity of Springbank whisky which had been matured in ex-rum casks was released on to the market.

Until comparatively recently, Bourbon and *rye* whiskies had, by law, to be matured in charred oak casks which could only be

used once, and which give Bourbon its typical vanilla palate. The
Japanese mature their whiskies in former sherry or Bourbon
casks, or new, charred oak casks. The country's largest whisky
producer, Suntory, imports some sherry wood and wine-treated
wood from Spain, and also wine-treats both American and
Japanese oak on its own premises.

(See also *fillings*.)

cask strength See *single cask*.

charger Each distillery contains two *chargers*, the *wash* charger
and the *low wines* charger. Moss and Hume write that after fermentation has been completed 'the wash is then pumped into the
wash charger and from there into the first pair of pot stills, the
"wash still", which separates the alcohol from the water and waste
matter in the wash... The distillate from the wash still, called
"low wines", is collected in a receiver, the "low-wines charger".'
Subsequently, 'The low wines are then pumped from the charger
...into the low wines or spirit still...' (*The Making of Scotch
Whisky*, 20). Though the charger is sometimes known as a
receiver, it takes its name from its function as a loading or filling
vessel: the chargers charge the stills. Moss and Hume write that
after distillation is completed 'The still is then recharged and the
process begins again' (p.24).

The Middle English *chargeour* may represent the Anglo-French
chargeour, that which loads, or it may be the Old French *chargeuior*
on the Latin type *carricā tōrium*, a utensil for loading. The senses
of both a platter and a vessel for liquids exist, in the latter case,
according to the OED, specifically 'a large flat vessel for the wort
in brewing'. As a vessel, charger is first attested in 1496 – 'Item
for ij dowbill platis of quhit irne to be gun chargeouris' – but its
first use regarding its role in the production of alcohol is not
recorded until 1880, 'Fermenting backs and wash chargers'.

chaser From the Old French *chaceür*, *chaceour*, Modern French
chasseur. The oldest of the English senses of chaser and the one
from which the drink usage derives – one who pursues – is first
attested in 1375, 'The chassaris...ourtuk sum at the last'. The
drink-related usage is probably of Scottish origin, though now
more widely employed, and it is defined in the *Dictionary of Drink*
as 'The name given to a measure of spirits (usually Scotch whisky)
consumed before a glass of beer. Both are purchased together,
eg, "Bitter and Whisky *Chaser*".' In the United States such a
combination is known as a *boilermaker*. The Scottish practice of
following a glass of whisky with a beer chaser leads to the order
for a 'half and half', while in Ireland 'a pint and a half' usually
refers to Guinness and Irish whiskey.

Chill-filtering The process of refrigerating whisky and finely filtering it to ensure that it retains its clarity in the bottle and when water is added by the consumer. *Chill-filtering* is frequently omitted when preparing *single cask* whisky, as it is considered to detract from the taste of the finished drink.

chwisgi Welsh for whisky, sometimes also *whisgi*. The word is borrowed from the English form, first being attested in 1784 as *whisci*, by which time a native whisky industry had been established in Wales. Professor Derec Llwyd Morgan of Old College, Aberystwyth, University of Wales explains, 'Welsh developed *chw-* from the *wh* (*hw*) of English; . . . but in South Wales dialects the *chw-* becomes *hw-*, invariably spelt *wh-*. That is why you have chwisgi and whisgi' (personal letter to the author).

In May 1990 The Welsh Whisky Company Limited, or Cwmni Chwisgi Cymreig Cyf, was formed by Dafydd and Gillian Gittins in Brecon, Powys as part of their attempt to revive production of the distinctive Welsh whisky/chwisgi, which was reputedly first distilled by monks on Bardsey Island off the Lleyn Penninsula in North Wales as early as AD 356, the process of basic *distillation* having been brought to them by Greek merchants.

These monks, in common with many early distillers in other parts of the world, found that adding honey and herbs to the new *spirit* made it considerably more palatable in the days long before the virtues of *maturation* were known, and a herbal infusion has remained a defining characteristic of Welsh whisky ever since.

The first commercial whisky-making operation in Wales was founded in the early eighteenth century by Evan Williams of Dale in Pembrokeshire, with the Daniels family of Cardigan also producing the spirit from the mid-eighteenth century. These two families later emigrated to Kentucky, where they were involved in developing the American whiskey industry.

Between 1887 and 1906 a large distillery operated at Bala in what is now the county of Gwynedd, but the strong temperance movement of the early years of this century led to Wales becoming virtually 'dry' and to the demise of the Bala enterprise.

The origins of the present Welsh Whisky Company date from 1974, when Dafydd Gittins and Mal Morgan began blending Welsh whisky, using Scotch as a base, before going on to produce a ten-year-old *single malt* which they first marketed in *vatted* format as Prince of Wales Welsh Whisky in 1986. Prince of Wales is actually an unspecified *Highland malt* from Speyside which is bought as *fillings*, but the 'product of Wales' marketing tag is considered acceptable as the whisky is processed in the Principality.

Gittins' operation moved to a new distillery – the first to be built in the country this century – at Parc Menter, Brecon in August 1991, and the native Welsh distilling tradition was restored when production of whisky commenced in the spring of 1992. The distillery is fully equipped with plant from Brittany, where the Welsh Whisky Company went to obtain specialist advice and equipment for their new venture. Initial production from two stills was around two *hogsheads* per day (110 gallons/500 litres), and while the new native Welsh whisky is being used in the company's existing whiskies and their Merlyn *liqueur* the intention is to bottle it at three years old as a single malt. According to Dafydd Gittins the herbal infusion, which takes place during filtration, 'gives the whisky a Cognac "nose" and a smooth, very rich flavour. Also unlike most Scotch whiskies we do not freeze filter, a process which we feel strips the whisky completely.'

cocktail   Partridge (*Historical Slang*) is specific in dating this term in a drink-related context – 'A whisked drink of spirits, occ. wine, with bitters, crushed ice, etc' – to the United States in 1809, when it appears in the writings of Washington Irving. 'They lay claim to be the first inventors of those recondite beverages, cock-tail, stone-fence, and sherry-cobbler.' Dunkling quotes an American periodical of 1806 as offering the first attestation of 'Cock tail', making the point that early references 'suggest that cocktail was originally the name of a particular drink, not a generic term' (p.217). Anglicisation of *cocktail* took place during the 1870s, and the first attestation of the expression 'whisky cocktail' occurs in 1862.

An Irish-American tavern-keeper and revolutionary soldier's widow by the name of Betsy Flanagan is often credited with inventing the cocktail during the American War of Independence, when she reputedly stole tail-feathers from a pro-British neighbour's cock and used them as decorations in drinks.

Another suggested origin of the word is from the English 'cock-ale', an eighteenth-century mixture of spirits fed to fighting cocks and also consumed by successful gamblers, who would place one tail-feather in their drinking vessels for each ingredient included, according to *The Dictionary of Drink*. Dunkling is dismissive of this particular definition of cock ale, maintaining that it was '. . . ale mixed with the jelly or minced meat of a boiled cock, plus other ingredients' (p.105).

A third possibility, and one given credence by Samuel Johnson, is that the cocktail has its origins in the equine world where non-thoroughbred animals were referred to by turf enthusiasts as cock-tails, due to the practice of docking the tails of hunters and coach horses, leaving them with a stump which stuck up like the tail of a cock. Hence, the argument goes, a cocktail is a 'non-thoroughbred' drink. Whatever the origins of the name, 'It was the jazz age that passed the cocktail into folk history, as a disguise for bootleg liquor', according to Jackson (*Pocket Bar Book*, 91), and considering the quality of much *moonshine* produced during *Prohibition* anything that masked the spirit base of a drink must surely have been welcome.

Harry Craddock of London's Savoy Hotel can be credited with popularising cocktails on the British side of the Atlantic Ocean. Jackson considers that the term cocktail is properly applied 'to a short aperitif (and therefore a dry drink) based on a predominant hard spirit. In such drinks, the base spirit should be tasted, and usually accounts for at least half the content' (*Pocket Bar Book*, 91).

The best known whisky cocktails include the *Highball*, the *Manhattan*, the *Mint Julep*, the *Old Fashioned*, the *Whisky Mac*, and the *Whisky Sour*. Dunkling makes the point that the 'word is now metaphorically used of almost any kind of mixture', offering 'prawn cocktail' and 'Molotov cocktail' as examples (p.217).

Coffey still   Also known as the *continuous* or *patent still*, the invention of the *Coffey still* (patented in 1830) which produces *grain* whisky revolutionised the spirits industry and led directly to the development of whisky *blending*.

Ironically, Aeneas Coffey, the man who invented the new still which brought boom times for Scottish distillers largely at the expense of Irish whiskey producers, was himself an Irishman. He was born in Dublin *c.* 1780, entered the Excise service as a *gauger* at the age of twenty, and rose through the ranks to become Inspector-General of Excise in Ireland. He resigned from the service in 1824 to run the Dock Distillery in Dublin, where he installed and developed his continuous still, though some of his experimentation was also carried out at the now *silent* Port Ellen distillery on the southern shores of the Hebridean Isle of Islay.

Coffey's original intention was probably to sell the comparatively pure grain spirit produced by his apparatus for industrial purposes rather than for domestic consumption. He proceeded to manufacture stills to his own design, selling them to several Scottish whisky and London gin distillers, the latter finding the strong neutral spirit of the *Coffey* still ideal for their product. The basic design of the still remains unchanged.

Coffey was not alone in seeking to improve on the traditional *pot* still in terms of rapidity and quantity of spirit distilled, with an additional advantage being that almost any type of grain could be used in the process. In 1826 Robert Stein, who owned the Kilbaggie distillery in Clackmannanshire, once the largest in Scotland, had invented a patent still which produced grain whisky far more quickly than pot stills, and his cousin John Haig soon adopted the same process at his Cameron Bridge distillery in Fife. Like Coffey, Stein did some of his pioneering work at Port Ellen distillery, then owned by John Ramsay, Member of Parliament for Stirling and a prominent businessman with extensive whisky interests.

column still   The American equivalent of a *Coffey, continuous* or *patent still*. This alternative name derives from the shape of the apparatus, which usually consists of two copper columns, some forty to fifty feet in height. According to Magee, 'The first column, called the analyser, separates the spirit from the wash, and the second column, the rectifier, further concentrates the spirit by removing unwanted fusel oils' (p.18). Up to five columns may be used, depending on the degree of purification required.

congenerics   Also known as *congeners* and in the United States as *congeries*. Jack Daniel distillery publicity material notes that 'the Charcoal Mellowing process removes the unpleasant congeries and harsh fusil oils...'. Dictionary definitions along the lines of 'allied in nature or origin', stressing the Latin derivation of the word, are unable to offer any clear explanation as to why the term has come to be applied to what the OED describes as 'by-product giving distinctive character in whisky etc.'.

Daiches describes congenerics as 'the aldehydes, esters, furfurol and other compounds of hydrogen, oxygen and carbon formed in the process of distilling the *wash*...' (*Scotch Whisky*, 15).

Neil Wilson writes: 'The chemistry of the low wines is complex, since there are literally hundreds of compounds along with some which have yet to be identified. They all appear, to a greater or lesser degree, in the whisky which we drink from the bottle. These compounds are collectively known as the congenerics and are responsible for the distinctive *nose* and flavour of the island whiskies – they help give Laphroaig that hint of seaweed for which it is famous, Bowmore that rich peaty-smoky bouquet and Jura that subtle, Highland freshness' (pp.30-31).

(See also *cutting, feints* and *foreshots*.)

continuous still   A *Coffey, column* or *patent still*. Its name derives from the fact that its operation is continuous, rather than being a 'batch' process as necessitated by *pot* stills. Jackson considers the *continuous still* 'A mixed blessing, since its talent for the light-bodied or even tasteless spirit, its efficiency and economy, and its ability to produce the same product irrespective of location or surroundings, place a terrible temptation before liquor producers and marketers' (*Pocket Bar Book*, 44).

cooking The process of breaking down the cellulose walls between starch molecules by heat in order to extract fermentable sugars in unmalted grains such as *corn*.

Cooking as action of the verb *to cook* is first attested in 1645, when it is used in a figurative rather than literal sense, 'It is man's perverse Cooking who hath turn'd the bounty of Good into a Scorpion.' The verb cook occurs in Old English as *cōc*, adapted from Latin *coquus*, Late Latin *cocus* – cook. As a transitive verb – to prepare or make ready food, to make fit for eating by application of heat – the first attestation of cook occurs in 1611: 'There is cold meat i' th' Caue, we'l brouz on that Whil'st wghat we haue kill'd, be Cook'd'.

In the production of some American whiskies, the unmalted grain may have rye added to it immediately after cooking, along with ground malted *barley* and hot water. As Daiches explains, 'As with the making of malt whisky, the enzyme diastase of the malted barley converts the starch in the cereal into maltose, producing the liquid wort' (*Scotch Whisky*, 57).

copita A rosebud-shaped sherry glass, which some experts recommend for sensitive *nosing* and *tasting* of *single malt* whiskies. The glass is large enough to satisfactorily swirl the whisky around in, and the narrow neck of the *copita* retains the vapours of the whisky. According to the OED, copita is the Spanish diminutive form of *copa*, cup. 'A tulip shaped glass, traditionally used in Spain for drinking sherry.' It is also used in the sense of 'a glass of sherry'. The word is first attested in 1841, 'the señor and the señora must drink a copita.' The Spanish phrase *tomarse unas copitas*, means to have a drink or two.

cordial In the United States cordial is a common synonym for *liqueur*, but 'In Britain a cordial is a flavoured *spirit* with little or no alcoholic content' (Jackson, *Pocket Bar Book*, 61). According to *The Dictionary of Drink*, cordial is also a Scots 'nickname for whisky'. The word is adapted from the Medieval Latin *cordiāl-is* (perhaps immediately through the 14th century French *cordial*). *Cordiālis* appears to have been in origin a word of medicine.

There are various heart-related senses of the word cordial, such as heartfelt or warm and friendly, but there is also the medicinal sense of something stimulating or invigorating to the heart, something reviving or cheering. With the meaning of a comforting or exhilarating drink, often sweetened spirit, cordial is first attested by Chaucer *c*.1386, 'For gold in Phisik is a cordial . . .' (See *uisge beatha*.)

corn   The term *corn* in the United States refers specifically to
maize, being a shortened form of Indian corn, whereas in general
British usage corn can be any cereal such as *barley*, oats, rye or
wheat. In this context corn has its first attestation in 1697, 'A
Fleet of Pereagoes laden with Indian Corn, Hog, and Fowls,
going to Cartagene'.

Corn whiskey is a generic term, defined by Jackson as 'An
American rural whiskey containing not less than 80 per cent corn,
and aged in uncharred barrels' (*Pocket Bar Book*, 45). It is variously described as 'fiery' and 'unsophisticated', and is generally
thought to improve very little with ageing. Corn whiskey was a
favourite *moonshine* product, and the story is told of a well-known
North Carolina moonshiner by the name of Quill Rose, who when
asked whether ageing was beneficial to the *liquor* she made is
supposed to have replied, 'Your Honour has been misinformed.
I have kept some for a week one time and I couldn't tell it was a
bit better than when it was new and fresh'.

Most *Bourbons* contain between 70% and 90% corn, along with
rye and barley malt. Legally they only have to contain a minimum
of 51% corn and, unlike corn whiskey, they must be aged in
charred barrels.

The growth in production of corn whiskey dates back to the
years following the imposition of the first tax on spirits in North
America in 1791, and the subsequent 'Whiskey Rebellion' of 1794
by distillers and their supporters, who refused to pay the tax,
assaulted *excise* officers and marched on Pittsburgh in protest.
The rebellion came to an end after 13,000 troops were assembled
and marched down the Monongahela River, under the command
of the future president General George Washington – himself a
Virginian distiller.

Many disgruntled distillers of predominantly rye whiskey
moved south and west from the eastern states of Maryland,
Pennsylvania and Virginia into Indiana, Illinois, Kentucky and
Tennessee. As these were great corn producing states, it was
inevitable that this migration led to a growth in whiskeys made
from corn rather than rye.

couch   During distillery *malting*, 'The barley is first soaked in a
large vessel called a "steep" for two to three days. It is then placed
in another receptacle called a "couch" to drain before being spread
out to germinate on the malting floor to the depth of about 30
cm, when it is known as the "piece"' (Moss, *Chambers Scottish
Drink Book*, 74).

The OED considers the *couch* to be not only a receptacle, but
also a term applied to 'the bed or layer in which the grain is laid

to germinate after steeping'. Couch is derived from the thirteenth century French word *couche*, in Old French culche, formed on the French *coucher*, and earlier *colcher, culcher*, Latin *collocāre* – to lay in its place, to lodge.

Relating to malting, couch is first attested in 1615, 'When . . . for want of looking to the Couch, and not opening of it . . . it come or sprout at both ends'; in use as a verb, with the sense of 'to lay or spread grain after steeping on a floor to promote germination', couch is first recorded in 1562, 'No brewer . . . Dare couch malte and water, in house togythere.' Couching – as one of the four processes of malting along with steeping, flooring and kiln-drying – is first attested in the 1876 edition of the *Encyclopaedia Britannica*.

crackerjack   For blending purposes, malts 'are graded into different classes, the very best being known as *"crackerjacks"*,' according to Morrice (p.39). The OED defines *crackerjack* as a slang expression meaning 'exceptionally fine or expert (thing or person)', first attested in 1895. The *Oxford Dictionary of Modern Slang* considers crackerjack to be 'A fanciful formation on *crack* verb or *cracker* noun'.

cream of the barley   See *barley*.

creature   What the OED describes as a 'humorous usage' of the word is as a metonym for intoxicating liquor, especially whisky. According to the OED it was applied after the Biblical usage '"every creature of God is good", to food and other things which minister to the material comfort of man . . . The "Irish" pronunciation is represented by the spellings *cratur, crater, crathur* etc.'.

The first recorded use of the word with this sense is in *c*.1570, 'The creature (wine) of the proper kinde Was good, though use offenden therewithall'. The first usage with an 'Irish' spelling which clearly relates to whisky occurs in 1772: 'He seems to like a bit of the good cratur as well as other folks'. The word occurs in both contemporary Irish and Scots usage as *cratur*, with Morton writing, 'What I'd really like is to taste the real cratur. You know, like from one of the illicit stills, like the one that used to be out at Melvaig . . .' (p.18).

cups, in one's   While drinking, during a drinking bout. Now almost obsolete. First attested in 1406, 'For in the cuppe seelden fownden is, þat any wight his neigheburgh commendith'. Partridge *(Historical Slang)* suggests that by *c*.1720 this colloquialism had become standard English. The plural use of cup is transferred from the sense of cup as a drinking vessel and ultimately the vessel and the liquid it contains. Partridge also offers *cup man* for a drinker (1830-1900), *cup-shot* for *tipsy* (late 16th C. – early 19th C.)

and *cup too much*, have got or had a, (mid-17th C. – 19th C.) for the act of being *drunk*. '[I]f I am to believe a report of the proceedings subsequently shown us, I must have become polyglot in my cups', Frederick Blackwood, 1st Marquess of Dufferin and Ava (ed. Bold, 31).

cut   Drunk. The adjective is first attested with the sense of being drunk in 1673, 'He is flons'd, fluster'd, Cup shot, cut in the leg or back', and from the late eighteenth century to the mid-nineteenth the phrase 'a little cut over the head' connoted mild inebriation. Perhaps the use of cut in these colloquialisms was meant to imply a staggering gait, as if wounded, or in the case of 'cut over the head' a state that would cause a headache, though the origins of the expression remain obscure. *Punch* in 1859 has, 'He goes on the Loose, or the Cut or the Spree'. The now more frequently used term *half-cut* – for partially drunk – dates from *c.*1860.

cutting   The *distillation* from the *spirit still* consists of three parts, namely *foreshots*, *middle cut* and *feints*, and division of those parts takes place in the *spirit safe*.

Where the stillman 'cuts' his distillation – when, in other words, he decides the time has come to start collecting whisky – has a profound and irreversible effect on the finished product ... All distilleries have their own formulae for fractioning or dividing the distillation into its three parts – two unwanted, one precious. Generally speaking the whisky comes over at 25° to 26° over proof and while it is being collected it decreases in strength perhaps down to 5° over proof. Some distilleries cease collecting the spirit when it is 8° over proof, others at 5°. If you cut low down you'll produce a heavier whisky because the heavier compounds will come over; if you cut high up, say at 12° over proof, you'll produce a lighter whisky. (Cooper, *Century Companion*, 25.)

It may be that the word cutting came to be employed in this context from the sense of making an incision, as the stillman mechanically cuts into the flow of spirit to divert it into various receptacles. (See also *congenerics*).

Cutting can also mean mixing with water, diluting, as in Martin Moodie's verdict in a *Wine* magazine whisky tasting (January 1993) on the Irish whiskey Black Bush, 'You wouldn't need to cut this'. The term is also used in relation to drugs such as cocaine and heroin, which can be cut with benign substances like talcum powder to increase their bulk and therefore dealers' profits.

cytase   See *diastase*.

Dark grains   See *grains*.
 de luxe   French 'of luxury'. The OED dates its first recorded usage in English to 1819 and the *Edinburgh Review*. 'The paper used for printing, except in what are emphatically called *les éditions de luxe* is very inferior to ours'. The OED also notes that early English use of the expression tended to relate to phrases such as that given above and *train de luxe* before acquiring a more general currency. The term *de luxe* when applied to blended whisky indicates a product containing a higher percentage of *malt* to *grain* whiskies than is usual in standard blends, and also a higher retail price.

The first use of 'de luxe' and similar spurious qualifications designed to connote rarity and high quality occurred during the last quarter of the nineteenth century when the advertising of whisky began in earnest, with the advent of *blending* providing a product which would sell beyond the traditional Scottish markets for whisky.

A feature of many de luxe whiskies is a statement of *age* on the label; anything from ten to fifteen years, and, exceptionally, twenty-five years. The higher costs incurred in producing and maturing malt whisky as opposed to grain whisky can be seen to justify the distillers' pricing policy, but there is perhaps an unnecessary element of expense involved in producing de luxe whiskies of considerable vintage, as not only do all the constituent malts in the blend have to be as old as the age statement on the label, but also the grain whiskies which are used. This seems a little pointless as grain whisky is generally considered to have reached full maturity after four or five years.

Derek Cooper made a plea for the creation of a 'National Whisky Office' to monitor and regulate the Scotch whisky industry, noting that 'the whisky industry has been in the habit of putting almost anything it likes on a label. I'm thinking of words such as de luxe, old, very old, rare old, old matured, VVO, special, extra special, supreme, three star, antique, liqueur and private cellar. Such descriptions have no legal sanction and no regulatory authority' (*Scotland on Sunday*, 3 November 1991).
 deoch an doruis   Also *dochan doris*, though since the last spelling

41

reform the final word is properly *dorais*. The expression is a translation of the Gaelic for 'a drink of the door', a stirrup cup. John Lamond (*Connoisseur's Book of Days* ... p.36) describes it as '... a Gaelic term for "one for the road"...'. The phrase has been in use from the late eighteenth century to the present day, and is widely understood by both Gaelic and non-Gaelic speaking Scots.

According to Philip Mackie's *Compleat Imbiber*, 'Everybody knows the phrase for the last drink of whisky, which Sir Harry Lauder (1870-1950) popularised in song, "Just a Wee Deoch an Doruis". The phrase is pronounced Joch and Dorish ... The real point is that "A Drink at the Door" is quite non-committal. It does not state on oath that it is positively the last drink. It leaves room for equivocation, and equivocation is the life-blood of the Gael, apart from whisky' (Cooper, *A Taste of Scotch*, 97).

The noun *deoch* – drink – also occurs in Irish where it has the sense of 'a small amount of Poteen offered to a possible business dealer to encourage him to quote a fair price' (Edwards, 349).

diastase   Daiches clearly explains the nature of *diastase* during his treatment of the subject of *malting*.

> In the course of germination the barley-seed develops two enzymes (an enzyme is an organic substance produced by living cells which acts as a catalyst), the enzyme cytase, which breaks down the cellulose enclosing the insoluble starch cells and so makes the starch accessible for growth, and the enzyme diastase, which converts the insoluble starch which the action of the cytase has made available into dextrin, a soluble form of starch. The diastase also changes the dextrin into maltose, a readily soluble sugar. It is the sugar which eventually produces alcohol. (*Scotch Whisky*, 9)

The term diastase was coined in 1833 by two French scientists, Payen and Persoz, and is an adaptation of the Greek word for separation. It was first used in English by T. Thomson in *Chemistry of Inorganic Bodies* (1838).

distillation   From Latin *distillāre* or *dēstillāre* – to drop or trickle down.

The OED describes *distillation* as, 'The action of converting any substance or constituent of a substance into vapour by means of heat and of again condensing this by refrigeration into the liquid form, by means of an alembic, retort and receiver, or a still and refrigeratory; the extraction of the spirit essence or essential oil of any substance by the evaporation and condensation of its liquid solution; and, in a more generalised sense, the operation of separating by means of fire, and in closed vessels, the volatile parts of any substance from the fixed parts, in order to the collection of the products'.

The first English usage occurs in 1390, 'First of the distillation Forth with the congelation, Soluction, disention', though Aristotle had recorded the same phenomenon in his *Meteorology* more than seventeen hundred years previously.

Distillation follows *fermentation* in the process of whisky production: 'Distillation is the process characteristic of whisky making, indeed of all spirit making. In distillation the alcohol is separated from the wash by heating it. The alcohol is more volatile than steam and comes off first' (McDowall, 104).

The early history of distilling remains a matter for conjecture. Tradition ascribes it to Osiris, the great God, and, perhaps, the first king of Egypt', Ian MacDonald records (p.9), though rival claims favour the Chinese. It is generally believed that the Egyptians practised the art of distillation in the time of Diocletian (AD 284-305), and are said to have passed on their knowledge to the Babylonians and Hebrews, from where it travelled to Spain and Gaul. 'The Arabians excelled as distillers', according to Sillett 'being the first to cool the tube leading from the still-head with water' (p.1), who suggests that the art of distillation was introduced into Europe in about 1150, 'supposedly by the Moors of Spain'.

Historians of whisky-making in Wales, however, are of the opinion that during the fourth century one Reauilt Hir adapted the process of distillation introduced to the remote Bardsey Island off the North Wales coast by Greek merchants in order to distil the ale made by monks on the island and produce a kind of whisky, later called in Welsh *chwisgi*. Marshall Robb writes that 'Irish settlers came over into Pembroke and established distilleries in the time of Henry VIII, and others reached the islands off the south-west coast of Scotland' (p.7).

Ian MacDonald says, 'shortly after the invasion of Ireland by Henry II in 1170 the English found the Irish in the habit of making and drinking *aqua vitae*' (p.17). Inevitably, an Irish legend has it that Saint Patrick introduced distillation to the Irish people during the fifth century, though it is thought that they did not manage to produce alcohol by distillation for another six hundred years due to the difficulty of condensing the liquor. Magee prefers the less legendary theory that 'the art of distillation was brought by Irish missionaries from the Mediterranean region about 500 or 600 A.D.' (p.7).

It is believed that Irish monks carried the secret of distillation to Scotland in the late fifteenth century, though some sources would say it had crossed the Irish Sea several centuries previously. An early centre for distilling in Scotland would logically be the remote western peninsula of Kintyre. (See *Campbeltown*). Gunn offers a typically original and imaginative theory about the accidental discovery of the 'miracle' of distillation by a member of a Scottish tribe whilst making ale: 'the fermented liquor was then boiled, and as the steam came off it was by happy chance condensed against some cold surface'. The piece is sufficiently interesting as to merit reading in its entirety (*Whisky and Scotland*, pp.3-15).

What can be said with certainty is that the first recorded reference to whisky distillation in Scotland occurs in the Scottish Exchequer Rolls for 1494 (see *aqua vitae*). The first attempt to restrict the distillation of whisky in Scotland occurred in 1579, and then only on the grounds that grain was scarce. The first duty levied on Scotch whisky was in 1644 by the Scottish parliament to help finance their rebellion against King Charles I, though, as McHardy points out, 'From as early as 1609 central government had attempted to restrict the manufacture of spirits in Scotland. Over the next two hundred years the government, first in Edinburgh, then in far away London, consistently tried to stop the common people having access to distilled spirits. Most of these restrictions were relatively ineffective, but they were universally resented all the same' (*Tales of Whisky*, 6).

The first *excise* tax of 4d per gallon on whiskey production was imposed in Ireland by King Charles II in 1661. 'In Ireland it was totally ignored. One hundred years later the Crown tried again. In the year 1760 the law was changed. Private distillation, unless licensed by the State, became a "crime". Overnight a large proportion of the Irish population became "criminals"' (McGuffin, 9).

Inevitably, once any form of duty was imposed the history of whisky distillation took on two areas of operation, one legal, the other illegal. Equally inevitably, all the best whisky stories concern the illegal trade, and there are enough anecdotes of illicit distilling in Scotland, Ireland and the United States to fill several volumes. Indeed several volumes have been filled in precisely that way. See also *gauger*, *innocent*, *moonshine*, *mountain dew*, *peatreek* and *poitín*.

distillery The place of production for distilled spirits. First recorded in 1759, 'A community which not only imports great quantities of... spirits from abroad, but employs such an extensive distillery at home on that subject'.

Although *distillation* is just one of a series of processes which combine to produce whisky, albeit a defining process in the production of all spirits, the term *distillery* is applied to the plant where the entire business of spirit production occurs. In addition to the buildings used in whisky production, distilleries usually comprise a range of warehouses where the spirit can be stored during *maturation*. Human judgement and instinct still count for much even in a modern distillery, where, as Cooper puts it, 'technology has made life easier, ironing out the uncertainties, shortening the odds against failure . . .' (*Century Companion*, 15).

Traditionally *barley* went in at one end of the distillery and barrels of whisky came out at the other end, though in recent years rationalisation policies have meant that floor *maltings* have ceased to operate in all but a handful of Scotch whisky distilleries. Instead ready-malted barley is brought to the site and the process of producing whisky begins with *mashing* in the mash house, followed by *fermentation* in the tun room and finally distillation, which takes place in the still house. The kiln houses where barley was dried during malting have usually been preserved, however, on account of their distinctive pagoda-like chimneys; almost a trade-mark of distilling in the eyes of the public. Distilleries which have been constructed or reconstructed during the last few decades tend to lack such chimneys, though when the Braes of Glenlivet distillery was constructed in 1973, a purely 'cosmetic' pagoda was incorporated into the design.

The decline of distillery-based malting along with increased automation of the other processes has inevitably led to lower levels of employment in what Cooper describes as 'the least labour intensive industry in Scotland'. According to The Scotch Whisky Association's official figures for 1990, just over 16,000 people were directly employed in the country's whisky industry in that year, of whom only 574 were employed in the Highland Region and 1,742 in Grampian Region. Most worked in bottling, blending and distribution operations in the Lowlands rather than in individual distilleries.

Although some historic, rural distilleries remain, much whisky is distilled in industrial, urban surroundings. In Scotland there are currently some 90 malt distilleries and half a dozen grain distilleries in production, though in 1980 114 malt distilleries were active, a number of new plants having been constructed during the 1960s and 1970s. The highest number of operational distilleries in Scotland this century was 153 in 1905, though by the end of the First World War only 8 were still working. In the early 1920s this figure had risen once again to 130.

During the mid-1980s the Distillers Company alone closed a total of twenty-one distilleries, several of which – such as Glen

Mhor and Glen Albyn in Inverness – have since been demolished.
Some have found other uses, while the remainder are currently
silent. In early 1993 the Guinness subsidiary United Distillers –
which incorporates the old Distillers' Company – announced the
closure of a further four malt distilleries and one grain, with the
eventual loss of at least 700 jobs. About a dozen of the distilleries
which closed for a time during the 1980s due to the whisky *loch*
created by over-production have since re-opened, including the
two *Campbeltown* distilleries of Glen Scotia and Springbank, and
Ardbeg on *Islay*.

In Ireland all whiskey-making had become concentrated on
two major sites until 1987, when the entrepreneur John Teeling
bought a former chemical plant which had been used for the
production of industrial alcohol on the Cooley Peninsula near
Dundalk, and proceeded to convert it into a grain distillery,
adding a malt whisky plant two years later. Of the two large Irish
distilling operations, Bushmills on the North Antrim coast in
Northern Ireland is reputedly the oldest distillery in the world,
having first been licensed by King James I in 1608, while the
second is near the village of Midleton in County Cork in the Irish
Republic. By contrast with Bushmills, the modern Midleton complex only dates from 1975, and it contains a uniquely flexible
arrangement of *pot stills* and *column stills*, all under one roof.

With the exception of Cooley Distillery, the entire output of *Irish
whiskey* is in the hands of Irish Distillers Ltd, itself a subsidiary of
the giant French-based drinks company Pernod-Ricard, who also
own three distilleries in Scotland, including the country's smallest
distillery of Edradour in Perthshire. Edradour turns out some six
hundred gallons per week, or forty-eight casks, and as Jackson
points out, 'It produces as much malt whisky in a year as some
distilleries can make in a week...' (*Malt Whisky Companion*, 79).

In Scotland very few distilleries remain in the hands of native
companies, with Guinness, Allied Lyons and Grand Metropolitan
now controlling more than seventy percent of the domestic whisky
business.

The Canadian company Seagram also has substantial whisky
interests in Scotland, while the Japanese are relatively recent new-
comers to the ranks of Scottish ownership. They are now in
possession of three plants, including Tomatin in Inverness-shire,
Scotland's largest malt distillery with no fewer than twenty-one
stills, and one of the largest anywhere in the world. The old 'Long
John' distillery of Ben Nevis at Fort William belongs to Nikka
Whisky Distilling, and much of the malt whisky produced there
is shipped to Japan for blending with domestic whisky for the

Asian market. The Japanese also have a significant interest – through Suntory – in the Morrison Bowmore company, owners of Auchentoshan and Glen Garioch distilleries, as well as the 'flagship' Bowmore distillery on Islay, and they have close ties with Allied Distillers, proprietors of the Laphroaig operation on Islay. Suntory is Japan's largest whisky producer, being responsible for more than 70 per cent of the nation's whisky, and owning five domestic distilleries.

It is instructive to consider the locational factors that have produced the 'whisky map' of Scotland. The first and almost certainly the most important factor that influences any distiller in his choice of site is the guaranteed supply of clean, fresh *water*. The importance of this element in the successful production of spirit can hardly be over-emphasised. A second factor in Scotland has traditionally been the ready supply of *peat*, for drying the barley during malting and for firing the stills. Centralised malting and the use of steam and oil to heat stills has rendered the convenient supply of peat irrelevant in most modern distilleries, though it is worth noting that one locational factor which contributed to the development of Campbeltown as a major whisky centre in the nineteenth century was the discovery there of sizeable reserves of coal suitable for heating the stills.

Modern Irish whiskey production does not rely on peat at all, as the malt is dried in sealed vessels using coal as a heat source in order to prevent the peaty flavour so prized by many Scottish malt-whisky makers from 'contaminating' the delicate Irish spirit.

In days when roads and transport were primitive and travel very time-consuming, relatively local sources of peat and of barley were essential to a distiller, and the distribution of distilleries on the 'whisky map' reflects those necessities. One classic example of an area providing all the requisite locational advantages is *Glenlivet* on Speyside.

One other apparently essential component if your distillery was operating outside the law – whether in Kentucky, Donegal or Glenlivet – was remoteness. As Cooper puts it, 'There are... historical and practical reasons why the early distilleries were built in unpopulated glens and on the shores of remote lochs; in the days of smuggling, out of sight was out of the gauger's eye' (*Century Companion*, 15). Not all illicit distillation took place in geographical isolation, however. In 1777 the *Excise* authorities calculated that whilst there were eight legal distilleries in Edinburgh, the Scottish capital probably concealed some four hundred illegal ones! Historically, Irish prisons have also been places where spirit is produced for the diversion of inmates. In terms of the importance of the water supply in determining distillery locations, it is not surprising that a considerable number of present day distilleries occupy the tried and tested sites of one-time illicit operations. Ardbeg on Islay, Glenturret in Stirlingshire – the oldest Highland distillery in production – and Highland Park on Orkney are such examples.

In terms of the island distilleries, whether on Islay, Jura, Mull, Orkney or Skye, one important factor in determining the site for operations was a coastal location for ease of transport by sea of barley, coal and other vital ingredients, as well as for the convenient export of the finished product.

Compared to malt whisky distilleries, the location of grain whisky plants is appreciably less dependent upon climatic considerations and the availability of peat and water in large quantities, as the *patent still* process is much more economical in terms of such resources. It is therefore possible to site grain distilleries conveniently in the urban Scottish Lowlands where there are good transport links – and often significant port facilities – for the import of the large quantities of grain required and for distribution of the finished product. All the Scottish grain distilleries currently in production are situated in the Lowlands, with the exception of Invergordon which is located north of Inverness.

One enduring mystery of whisky making is just how spirits which, on the basis of location, ingredients and technical details, should be almost identical can vary so much. Maurice Walsh, one-time *exciseman* and Kerry-born popular novelist of the 1920s and 1930s, and a friend of fellow *gauger* Neil Gunn, wrote about the whisky centre of Dufftown on Speyside in this context. 'The seven distilleries were in one mile of Highland river; they used the same water, peat, and malt, and the methods of brewing and distillation were identical, yet each spirit had its own individual bouquet. One, the best, mellowed perfectly in seven years; another, the least good, not a hundred yards away, was still liquid fire at the end of ten years' (quoted by Cooper, *Taste of Scotch*, 30).

It has been suggested that neighbouring distilleries differ in the manner of neighbouring vineyards. Obviously variables such as the barley, the way it is malted, the design of the stills in which distillation takes place and the skill of key members of the distillery staff such as the *stillman* will affect, however subtly, the finished product, along with water and peat. Jackson claims that in addition, what he terms the micro-climate affects the character of the spirit:

   although similar yeasts . . . are used throughout the malt distilling industry, each tun room (fermentation hall) produces its own characteristics. This may vary according to the material from which the fermenting vessels are made, with wood perhaps harbouring its own resident microflora, but it is also influenced by the micro-climate in and around the distillery.

A cold location makes for low temperature spring waters. When very cold water is available for use in the coils that condense the spirit, and the ambient temperature is low, that seems to produce an especially rich, clean, whisky. Distilleries in shaded, mountain, locations are noted for this characteristic. (*Malt Whisky Companion*, 11)

(See *Glenlivet*). It is also true, of course, that the temperature and the atmosphere in which whisky *maturation* takes place can significantly affect the final product.

dog Amongst distillery workers on Speyside, a *dog* is a 'primitive retrieval device', according to Cooper, in which newly made whisky is smuggled out of the plant for future consumption or sale. 'In one famous distillery I was shown a small museum of dogs ranging from slim bottles to beautifully fashioned copper tubes for slipping down the trouser leg. Other trophies included inconspicuous body-shaped flasks which could be worn under the jacket to spirit the whisky past the gateman' (*Century Companion*, 26). The term is not confined to Speyside, but enjoys a much wider currency in distilling circles, though it is unclear why 'dog' is the noun used, unless Cooper's use of the word 'retrieval' is particularly significant, and dog here is, as in retriever, or possibly ratter, an animal which (perhaps illicitly) retrieves.

Morton writes of the practice once common in Scottish distilleries of 'dooking' or 'dunking', noting that ' "Dunkin' jars" were usually home-made from copper or some other soft metal, and could be easily concealed about one's clothing' (p.66). He also quotes John MacDonald, the manager of Dalmore distillery on the shores of the Cromarty Firth, who showed him 'a copper tube, about two feet long and an inch and a half wide. It is sealed at one end and has a leather thong at the other. "There you are", he says. "A dooker..."' Perhaps it is not inconceivable that dog could be a corruption of dook.

Writing of *Lowland* whiskies, Jim Murray described a dog on display in the Glenkinchie distillery museum, south of Edinburgh, and suggested that the slang term *hair of the dog* had its origins in these whisky-poaching vessels (*Observer*, 15 December 1991).

On the subject of *hangover* cures, Dunkling comments that 'since at least the 16th century they had been calling for a hair of the dog that bit them. In medieval times it was believed that a

wound caused by a dog-bite could be cured by laying a hair of
the same dog across it. When that belief was proved erroneous,
the saying seems to have been applied metaphorically to alcohol'
(p.48).

With reference to drink, the implication is that consuming more
alcohol is actually an aid to dealing with the alcohol which has
already caused damage to the system. The hair of the dog works
as a hangover remedy by replacing lost blood sugar, though
perhaps honey is a more sensible alternative. Floyd quotes the
Greek philosopher Antiphanes in translation, giving what he calls
'the first recorded hangover cure' (479 BC): 'Take the hair, it is
well written/Of the dog by which you're bitten/Work off one wine
by his brother/One labour with another' (*Floyd on Hangovers*, 44).

doubler still   See *spirit still*.

doubling   See *feints*.

draff   The OED defines *draff* as 'Refuse, dregs, lees – wash or swill
given to swine; hogs-wash; spec. the refuse or grains of malt after
brewing or distilling'. In early Middle English *draf* probably represents the unrecorded Old English *dræf*, corresponding to Middle Dutch and Dutch *draf*. In Irish and Scots Gaelic, *drabh* means
grains of malt, probably from the English, according to the OED.
Draff is first attested in *c.* 1205, 'He gon ȝesten draf and chaf and
aten'.

The expression *hogs-wash* or *hogwash* 'contemptuously applied
to weak inferior liquor or any worthless stuff' (OED) is first
recorded in 1712. 'Your butler purloins your liquor, and the
brewer sells you hogwash'. In his song 'In Praise of Claret', William Hamilton of Gilberfield (1665-1751) refers to inferior whisky
as 'The dull draff-drink', the implication obviously being that
this is poor spirit which would seem to have been made from draff.

One of the first recorded uses of 'draff' in specific relation to
whisky production occurs in a public statement made by the Scots
distiller James Haig in 1784, when his Canonmills distillery was
threatened by a mob, and he issued the assurance that far from
using roots such as potatoes which could otherwise be used as
cattle food as well as consumed by the rioters themselves, his
distillery at Canonmills actually provided for cattle 'the grains or
draff, and by that food alone they are fattened for the market'.

Neil Wilson defines draff specifically as 'The spent grist left in
the mashtun after mashing is completed. Excellent cattle food'
(*Scotch and Water*, 7). The initial processes of whisky production
are geared to the removal of starch and enzymes from grain, and
what is left over at the end of these processes has a high protein
content which makes it ideal fodder for cattle. It can either be fed

to cattle straight from the distillery or stored in the same way as silage for use at a later date.

One great advantage of this particular animal feedstuff is that it is entirely natural, being of vegetable origin, and this has become a valuable source of raw materials used in animal foodstuffs in the light of BSE or 'mad cow disease'. Clearly draff is not only nutritious but also a very palatable animal feed, as an old distillery worker at Lagavulin on Islay recently confirmed with the words, 'The cattle are just daft for it'.

The processing of draff into animal feedstuffs has increased considerably during the past two decades, partly due to more stringent pollution controls which have in many cases ended the time-honoured practice of dumping distillery by-products in rivers and seas, and partly due to a new awareness in the distilling industry of the desirability for 'good housekeeping', an awareness initially stimulated by dramatically rising oil prices during the 1970s. By-products of distillation were being converted into animal feed by Thomas Borthwick of Glasgow as long ago as the 1860s, and they are still active as the animal-feeds subsidiary of United Distillers. 'Campbeltown distillers co-operated in running a draff refinery or grain-drying factory, run after the liquidation of the Scottish Grains Company Limited in 1892 by the Campbeltown Distillers' Association. Wet grains or draff was sold locally at 4d a bushel, dried grains were shipped in frequent cargoes to Rotterdam to feed the horses of the German Army!' (Newton).

What is relatively new in re-cycling, however, is the production of *dark grains* from burnt or *pot ale* and draff, and the way in which whisky producers have developed methods of using waste heat from their production processes to convert the by-products of distillation. Something in the region of 50 per cent of the original tonnage of grain used in whisky making can be recovered in the form of animal feeds. A recent project undertaken by the Scottish Agricultural College and backed by United Distillers has concluded that on the islands of Skye and Islay – both of which have distilleries – draff is now the most cost-effective feed available to farmers. It is also a notably versatile feed, being used to replace concentrates as well as hay or silage.

This interest in conservation and re-cycling has also led to generally increased energy efficiency in many distilleries. At Glen Garioch otherwise waste heat has been utilised in more than one and a half acres of glasshouses, as well as in drying barley in the plant's own maltings. At Bowmore on Islay waste heat is also now utilised to dry barley, as well as to help heat a community swimming-pool which has been established in a disused warehouse.

dram Defined by *The Dictionary of Drink* as a Scottish slang term for 'a measure of spirits (usually whisky)'. Usage is principally Scottish, but has now become synonymous with a *nip* of whisky in any geographic location. It is frequently used with the diminutive 'wee' as a prefix, as in *goldie* and *sensation*.

Daiches, like most commentators, considers the word *dram* to be of Greek derivation, coming from *drachma*, one-eighth of an ounce or sixty grains in apothecaries' weights. In the sense of liquid it was originally one-eighth of a fluid ounce of medicine, and ultimately 'a small draught of cordial, stimulant, or spiritous liquor' (OED). Although 'dram' is now used almost exclusively with regard to whisky, it used to have a more general sense. Even in Scots usage dram could apply to other spirits; James Boswell recorded in his 1785 *Journal of a Tour of the Hebrides* drinking a dram of brandy. As a fluid, dram is first attested in *c.* 1590, 'Thou shalt see me take a dramme...shall cure the stone', and occurs a couple of years later in *Romeo and Juliet*, 'let me haue A dram of poyson'.

The first written use of dram in a specifically whisky-related context probably dates from a 1752 edition of the *Scots Magazine*, 'They went in and drank some drams'. Neil Wilson, writing of the late eighteenth century says, 'the public's thirst for whisky remained unquenched and dram drinking (a dram being one third of a pint of whisky containing 60% alcohol by volume) was now a popular habit...' (p. 16). Moss holds the opinion that a dram then was actually a whole *gill*, i.e. a quarter of a pint *(Chambers Scottish Drink Book)*. Dr Johnson's description of a Hebridean breakfast from his tour of 1774 seems to suggest, however, that 'dram' already had the sense of 'a small draught of...spiritous liquor' rather than one of a specific quantity: '...no man is so abstemious as to refuse the morning dram, which they call a skalk'.

The Scotch Whisky Association claims 'A dram can only apply to a measure of Scotch Whisky, the size of which is determined by the generosity of the pourer', though in some areas of northern Scotland a dram is taken specifically to mean a quarter gill. Begg writes that whilst the term now has an imprecise definition in terms of quantity, 'in most Scottish bars a dram is usually, but by no means always, a "large", or "double", measure of whisky' (p.20).

One of the very few commentators to question the Greek derivation of dram in relation to Scottish usage is Neil Wilson, who defines the word in the glossary of his *Scotch and Water* as 'In Gaelic – A drink'. When writing of the liqueur Drambuie, Dunkling notes '"Yellow or golden drink" is the literal meaning of

Gaelic *dram buidhe. An dram buidheach*, in the same language, is said to mean "the drink that satisfies"' (p.13). It therefore seems plausible that parallel to the development of the word 'dram' from its Greek origins in more general usage, there was a separate, coincidental and specifically Scottish development from the Gaelic source. This could explain the survival of the word in relation to Scotland and its national drink long after it had become obsolete in other countries and with regard to different drinks.

A series of compounds was derived from 'dram', for example *dram-bottle, -cup* (first recorded in 1674), *-dish* (1722), *-glass* (1716), *-house* (1752), *-pot* (1691), and *-shop* (1793). The phrase *dram-drinker*, 'One addicted to drinking drams, a tippler' dates from 1744, whilst *dram-drinking*, 'tippling', is first recorded in 1772.

The best-known dram shops were those founded in Glasgow by William Teacher, who opened his first in 1830 when he was just nineteen years old. Teacher's dram shops were strictly run places which won guarded approval from temperance-minded folk for their refusal to allow the purchase of rounds of drinks in order to cut consumption. Drunkenness and smoking were not allowed, and Teacher soon became the largest single licence-holder in Glasgow, with eighteen dram shops to his name, the last of which survived until 1960.

Dram is first used as an intransitive verb, 'To drink drams, to tipple', (OED) in 1715, 'Habitual drinkers, drammers, and high feeders', and in 1752 Horace Walpole writes in a letter, 'Melancholy. . . is not strong enough, and he grows to dram with horror'.

The verb application of *dramming* is first attested in 1771, 'Whether they discover'd his dramming by his breath, or by his behaviour'. The word is still current in a specific context within the Scottish whisky industry. Lockhart describes the now illegal practice of dramming in some detail when reminiscing about his childhood on Speyside, where his family owned the Balmenach distillery. 'When I was a boy, the distillerymen at Balmenach were "drammed" three times a day. In my innocence I assumed that this gift of free whisky came from my uncle's generous heart . . . I was of course mistaken. The free "dramming" was instituted for one purpose only; to counteract a temptation which existed then, exists to-day, and is apparently irresistible' (*Scotch*, 50).

The motive of preventing whisky pilfering by supplying free drams may seem reasonable enough, but David Duncombe of HM Customs & Excise is not persuaded, as he makes clear in his book *The Call to Duty*, where he explains that in addition to their regular drams once or twice a day, some distillery workers received additional measures of whisky for performing dirty jobs and 'sometimes for performing little more than normal duties. The manager appeared to see this practice as being good for morale, whilst most wives and local publicans took a different view'. A distillery worker at Glenmorangie recalls that the staff were 'drammed' at lunch-time and tea-time, and that although the times were fixed the measures were not. 'It all depended on what tune the head brewer was in'. Dramming ceased during the 1970s due to the implementation of new Health and Safety regulations.

drunk   The past participle of the verb *to drink*. Relating to alcohol, *drunk* has the sense of having consumed intoxicating liquor to an extent which affects steady self-control; intoxicated, inebriated. The OED considers that 'The degree of inebriation is expressed by various adjectives and adverbs, as *beastly, blind, dead, half,* etc'. The first attestation of drunk with this meaning occurs in *c.*1340, 'Drunke he lay & slept bi his one'.

Drunk as a drinking bout is first recorded in 1862, 'a "general drunk"', and as an intoxicated person in 1882, 'Such a brave display of disorderly drunks'. Partridge defines a drunk as 'a debauch', suggesting the term had this colloquial usage from *c.*1860, rather surprisingly two decades before coming to mean 'a tipsy person'. *Drunkard*, one addicted to drinking, one who habitually drinks to excess, an inebriate, first occurs in 1530, '*Yuroynge*, a man *droncarde*'.

The state of drunkenness offers a vast array of euphemisms and other slang expressions. Dunkling points out that in 1772 Benjamin Franklin published a list which contained no fewer than 228 synonyms for drunkenness which he claimed to have heard in tavern use (p.44). Many of the euphemisms developed because drunkenness was socially unacceptable, or, in the case of a modern example such as 'tired and emotional', because to have stated in less ambiguous terms that the prominent political figure in question was drunk could have led to legal action.

The social unacceptability of drunkenness is nicely reflected in the declension offered for a *New Statesman* competition, '*I* am sparkling; *you* are unusually talkative; *he* is drunk'. Writing in 1682, Richard Lawrence (*The Interest of Ireland...*) observed, 'We have a story of a young man that was long tempted by the devil to commit one of three sins: either to kill his father, ravish his mother, or be drunk, he chose the last as most innocent; but when drunk committed both the other'.

Needless to say, the literature of whisky is filled with stories of drunkenness. In both Ireland and Scotland, some of the most colourful stories of whisky-related drunkenness inevitably concern

social functions such as weddings and funerals, with death apparently providing the greater incentive for really dedicated imbib-
ing. Cooper records that at the funeral of Flora Macdonald in
Skye three thousand mourners drank a total of three hundred
gallons of whisky, and he goes on to write that 'At the funeral of
the Hon. Alexander Fraser of Lovat a few years later, several of
the hearse bearers, unbalanced by grief and whisky, fell into the
grave; brawls, mayhem and even violent death were not uncom-
mon at a really convivial interment' (*Century Companion*, 7). The
same author quotes Revd Charles Rogers (*Social Life in Scotland*,
1884) on the subject. 'The funeral expenses of Hugh Campbell
of Calder, in 1616, amounted to £1,647 16s 4d. This expenditure
included a charge for whisky equal to one-fourth of the amount'
(*Taste of Scotch*, 106).

Sir Archibald Geikie (*Scottish Reminiscences*, 1904) writes that
'Strangers are often astonished at the extent of the draughts of
undiluted whisky which Highlanders can swallow, without any
apparent ill-effects'. He goes on to quote Edmund Burt (*Letters
from a Gentleman in the North of Scotland to his friend in London*,
1754) who observed that Highland gentlemen could drink 'even
three or four quarts at a sitting, and that in general the people
that can pay the purchase, drink it without moderation'. Elizabeth
Grant (*Memoirs of a Highland Lady*, 1797-1827) was unequivocal
in her condemnation of the amount of whisky consumed in the
Highlands in her time: 'Whisky-drinking was and is the bane of
that country; from early morning till late at night it went on'. She
is, however, forced to conclude that 'except at a merry-making
we never saw any one tipsy'.

From drunk comes the slang American term *drunk tank*, first
attested in 1947, and defined by the *Oxford Dictionary of Modern
Slang* as 'A large prison cell for the detention of drunks'. The
expression *drink-taken* to connote drunkenness also exits, principally in Irish usage. 'If the Local Government Board had any
notion of the knowledge and wisdom that takes a hould of me
when I have the drink taken, d'ye know what they'd do?' (Henry
Robinson, *Further Memories of Irish Life*, 1924).

Innumerable similes based on drunk occur, as noted by the
OED, and perhaps the best known of these is 'drunk as a lord',
where a serious degree of inebriation is implied. Unlike many
drunk similes such as 'drunk as a rolling fart' (*c*.1860) or 'as a
wheelbarrow' (1709) – both of which are recorded by Partridge
(*Historical Slang*) – 'drunk as a lord' does have a genesis based
on obvious reality, in that members of the aristocracy were popularly conceived as spending much of their time in a drunken and

debauched state. Partridge dates the simile from 1670, noting that it developed from the expression 'drink like a lord', meaning to drink hard. The earliest recorded drunk simile occurs in c.1386, 'We faren as he þat dronke is as a mous'.

Dutch courage   False courage acquired by the consumption of alcohol. Partridge *(Historical Slang)* explains that due to trade rivalry and naval jealousy in the seventeenth and early eighteenth centuries, 'Dutch', both as noun and adjective, acquired in Britain a derisive and opprobrious sense. Thus, *Dutch courage* is false or coward's courage. The term probably also owes something to the fact that imported Dutch gin was the most popular working-class drink during the eighteenth and early nineteenth centuries. Dunkling suggests that Dutch courage may not have developed as 'an intentional insult to the Dutch', pointing out that 'It is said that English soldiers serving in the Netherlands induced it by drinking Dutch gin' (p.26).

The first recorded use occurs in Sir Walter Scott's *Woodstock* (1826), 'Laying in store of what is called Dutch Courage'.

E **astern malts**   A classification occasionally used for those whiskies from the eastern area of the *Highland* whisky region. As Daiches writes, 'I have in fact seen Highland malt whisky classified simply as Eastern Malts and Western Malts' (*Scotch Whisky*, 23).

excise   Can be any toll or tax, but specifically, according to the *Encyclopaedia Britannica* it is 'A duty charged on home goods, either in the process of their manufacture or before their sale to the home consumers'. Dr Johnson in his *Dictionary* recorded that 'The taxes levied under the name of Excise by the Ordinance of 1643 included certain duties imposed, in addition to the customs, on various foreign products, it was not until the present century that the actual use of the word became strictly conformed to the preceeding definitions.'

The Dutch apparently first had the courage to tax alcohol, but the parliamentarians of England rapidly took up the idea – actually to finance the army in 1643. Scotland followed the next year and levied a duty of 37½p per English gallon of *aqua vitae*, the strength, however, not being specified. For a period the tax on Scotch whisky appears to have lapsed but it was reimposed in 1693. The Board of Excise was set up in 1707 and has levied duty ever since. (McDowall, pp. 133-4) McDowall's assertion that Holland was the first country to tax alcohol is not quite accurate, as the imposition of duty on spirits for the high moral purpose of controlling excessive consumption whilst conveniently raising revenue dates back to fourteenth-century Europe, where immoderate brandy-drinking in Germany led to heavy taxation in 1360.

The word *excise* apparently comes from the Middle Dutch *excijs* or *exziis* (1406), which in turn is probably an adaptation of the twelfth-century Old French *acceis*. In its specific sense of referring to an imposition of duty on domestic products, excise is first used regarding the Dutch in 1596, by Edmund Spenser, and in respect of the British situation in 1642: 'Aspersions are by malignant persons cast upon this House that they intend to . . . lay excizes upon . . . commodities'.

In the United States, Thomas Jefferson wrote in 1789, 'Excise is a duty . . . paid in the hands of the consumer or retailer . . . But in

Massachusetts they have perverted the word excise to mean a tax
on all liquors, whether paid in the moment of importation or at
a later moment, and on nothing else.' A. Delmar in *Johnson's
New Universal Encyclopaedia* (1875) says, 'Excise . . . in the US . . .
is confined to the tax on the production or sale of spiritous or
fermented liquors, or the productive capacity of liquor stills,
revenue from liquor stamps, etc.'

Once excise duty was imposed on whisky, there were people
who chose to evade it for various reasons, particularly in parts of
Ireland and the Scottish Highlands where families had distilled
as they liked for generations. Not that illicit distillation was
restricted to Ireland and Scotland. The art was certainly practised
in parts of Wales and rural Lancashire, and legal production of
whisky now occurs in Brecon and Wigan respectively. *Moonshining* also occurred in areas close to the Scottish border such as
Cumberland, Westmorland, and Northumberland, where the
product of illegal stills was known as *innocent*.

After the Act of Union in 1707, the Scots perceived excise
impositions as English in origin, and avoidance became something
of a point of honour. The not unreasonable argument ran along
the lines: 'If a southern English farmer can make cider from his
own apples without paying duty on it, why should a Scottish
farmer not distill whisky from the barley he has grown in the
same manner?'

Dr John Mackenzie *(Highland Memories)* makes the following
observation about the Highland perception of excise laws relating
to illicit whisky in the 1820s. ('Smuggling' usually refers to the
whole business of producing and distributing illegal spirits, rather
than having the more specific sense it enjoys today.) 'Laws against
smuggling are generally disliked. People who if you dropped a
shilling would run a mile after you with it, not even expecting
thanks, will cheerfully break the law against smuggling. When I
was young everyone I met from my father downwards, even our
clergy, either made, bought, sold, or drank cheerfully, smuggled
liquor'. Excise legislation has done much to shape the economic
and social history of whisky production, and the development of
major commercial distilling in the Scottish Lowlands followed
the passing of the Gin Act in 1736, which imposed heavy excise
duty on gin in an effort to curb drunkenness while exempting
whisky.

One man who enjoyed a unique position as a legal distiller
without any burden of excise duty to pay was Duncan Forbes of
Ferintosh in Ross-shire, who enjoyed this peculiar privilege from
1690 until 1784.

During the 1770s the licensed distillers sought to undermine illicit production by flooding the market with cheap whisky, and in 1781 the government banned private distillation and allowed the excise authorities to seize whisky, whisky-making equipment and later even horses and vehicles used in the transportation of illicit spirit. A premium of one shilling and sixpence was offered to anyone handing in an illicit still to the authorities, though this measure rather backfired in that many shrewd smugglers gave up old, worn-out pieces of equipment and bought new ones with the 'reward' money!

In 1784 the Wash Act reduced duty and simplified regulations regarding the production of legal whisky, as well as establishing a precise geographical line between the *Highland* producers and *Lowland* producers for excise purposes, as one aim was to stimulate legal distilling in the Highlands and reduce smuggling. Accordingly, lower rates of excise duty were applied to small-scale distilleries north of the line which used locally produced barley, though their product was banned from being exported into the Lowlands a year later in order to protect Lowland distilleries from unfair competition.

A very significant increase in legal distillation in the Lowlands came about as a result of the Wash Act, accompanied by large-scale exports of whisky into England, though this was effectively ended by the imposition of prohibitively high levels of duty on spirits crossing the border into England in 1786. This, plus over-production – not for the last time in the Scotch whisky industry – led to disaster for the major legal concerns, with the five largest Scottish distillers who were responsible for producing almost half the country's whisky going bankrupt. Trebling of duty in 1793 to help pay for war with France hardly improved the situation, and this led to Lowland whisky being produced quickly, the quality of the product suffering significantly as a result.

In the Highlands matters were generally much better, because the small-scale stills produced a comparatively high quality product, and illegally distilled *Glenlivet* whisky was even enjoyed by King George IV and his courtiers. The not unreasonable notion that illicit Highland whisky was superior in quality to the legal Lowland spirit dates back to the years following the extension of the English malt tax to include Scotland in 1713. In order to minimise the amount of malt tax which had to be paid, legal distillers used as little malted barley as was feasible with a high percentage of raw grain.

Until 1795 the Highland region of whisky production included *Campbeltown*, which by that time had become the centre for the whisky industry in the West, but in that year legislation was introduced which incorporated Campbeltown into the Lowland classification, obliging the district's distillers to pay duty at the higher Lowland rate. This initiative, along with the generally high rates of duty which kept on rising, led to a growth in the illicit trade once again, with the superior Highland product entering the Lowland area in such quantities as to prove a serious threat to the legal Lowland operations.

The government's response was the 1816 Small Stills Act, which abolished the 'Highland Line' for purposes of excise and reduced duty throughout Scotland. The use of stills of less than five hundred gallons' capacity had been outlawed two years previously in an ill-advised move to extend English distilling regulations to Scotland, a move opposed by the Scottish Board of Excise, who realised the obvious implication of increased illicit distilling. The Small Stills Act reduced the minimum still capacity to a much more realistic forty gallons, and as a result forty-five new legal distilleries opened in the Highlands in the first three years following the Act, taking the total to fifty-seven.

Highland landowners had tended to turn a blind eye to illicit distilling on their land, as the money made by their tenants through this trade was often the only way they could pay their rents. In 1820, however, a number of Highland lairds, including the Duke of Gordon – whose estates included the great whisky-making centre of Glenlivet – offered to support increased measures aimed at stamping out the illegal trade in return for a better deal for licensed distillers. The advantages were perceived as being more revenue for the government, despite the lower level of duty, and opportunities for the lairds to make money out of the new distilleries that would surely be built as a result of the proposed legislation.

In 1822 the Illicit Distillation (Scotland) Act was passed, which introduced harsher penalties for anyone involved in making, supplying or drinking illicit whisky. The following year an Excise Act dramatically cut duty to two shillings and threepence per gallon, with a distilling licence costing ten pounds, and the export market to England was made significantly more attractive. The Act also made it compulsory for every distillery to provide accomodation for a resident *exciseman*. The complexities of excise legislation relating to Scotland become apparent when it is discovered that between the first imposition of excise duty in the seventeenth century and the 1822 Act more than thirty changes had been made regarding the production of whisky.

The effects of the two new Acts were very soon obvious. The

number of licensed distilleries in Scotland doubled in two years, and production of duty-paid whisky rose from two million gallons to six million gallons per annum. Illicit distillation fell dramatically during the next few years, with an astonishing 14,000 detections being made in 1823 – clearly just the tip of an enormous alcoholic iceberg – but only 692 in 1834, and six in 1874. The 1823 Excise Act was clearly doing its work, and Cooper observes that 'this notable piece of legislation founded the whisky industry as we know it today' (*Century Companion*, 12).

The history of excise legislation and its effects in Ireland roughly parallels that in Scotland until 1823, with a levy on spirits having first been imposed in 1661, although that and several subsequent pieces of excise legislation were almost universally ignored. As in Scotland, passing an Act was one thing but enforcing it in often wild, remote and inhospitable country, where a vast majority of the local population was openly opposed to the excise officers, was quite another.

The governmental tool of excise duty has continued to be used for various purposes during the nineteenth and twentieth centuries both in Ireland and on the British mainland, including the reason for their first imposition in Britain, that of raising revenue to fight wars. Even in 1939 duty was increased as war with Germany became an inevitability. Lloyd George – no friend of the distillers – increased duty on whisky by a third in his famous 'People's Budget' of 1915 in an attempt to cut alcohol consumption, and from 2s. 6d. (12½p) for a bottle of standard blended whisky in 1909 the cost had risen to 33s. 4d. (£1.67) for the same article by 1948, with more than three-quarters of the price representing excise duty. As Morrice puts it, 'The trend was established and there was no doubt in anyone's mind that the Exchequer had developed a bad habit which it would never be able to kick' (p.73).

The Scotch Whisky Association provides statistics which show that whisky fares badly in terms of taxation when compared with sherry, wine and beer. The Association points out that 'The only reduction in the Excise duty since the last century was made in 1973, when the rate was lowered to compensate for the extra taxation which resulted from the introduction of Value Added Tax. By contrast, during the last few years more than once there have been reductions in the duty on high strength wines such as Sherry and Port, on sparkling wines, on beer and on British wines which are made largely from imported grape juice' (*Questions and Answers*, 32). Taxation accounts for between 75 per cent and 80 per cent of the selling price of a bottle of whisky, and, according to the Association, 'The Excise Duty paid on mature spirits is the same regardless of whether they are produced in this country or abroad. Scotch Whisky is not protected in any way against competition from spirits produced overseas, even those from the countries which themselves discriminate against imports of Scotch Whisky' (ibid.).

It seems that Neil Gunn's declaration in the 1930s that 'this discrimination against whisky is so manifestly unjust that it does have the appearance of being deliberately vindictive' (p.190) can still be said to have some validity.

Writing in 1967, R.J.S. McDowall described the price of whisky as 'a scandal', and lamented the fact that the Scottish national drink had been priced out of the reach of many Scots, though the novelist Martin Amis pointed out in a *New Statesman* article in 1975 that a bottle of whisky actually cost half of what it did in the 1930s. Derek Cooper seeks to illustrate the same point by comparing the price of whisky with that of Penguin paperbacks. He remarks that when the first five titles were originally published by Penguin in the 1930s, they were priced at 6d. per copy, at a time when a bottle of whisky cost 12/6. In 1985 Penguin reissued the five books at a total price of £15.90. 'If the whisky industry had decided that it was entitled to a similar rate of inflation a bottle today would cost £75!', declares Cooper (*Taste of Scotch*, 58).

exciseman 'An officer employed to collect *excise* duties and prevent infringement of the excise laws', according to the OED. The term is first used in 1647, 'the Corruption of Committee Men and Excisemen'. Dr Johnson left no one in any doubt of his opinion of the *exciseman* and his work with his *Dictionary*'s definition: 'Wretches, hired by those to whom excise is paid'.

Properly called Excise or Revenue Officers, but usually known in Scotland and Ireland as *gaugers*, revenue men, and keg-hunters, excisemen performed a difficult, often dangerous and generally fairly thankless job in the days when illicit distillation was a way of life for so many people in Scotland and Ireland.

Preventing 'infringement of the excise laws' was much easier said than done in remote parts of Galway or Glenlivet, and, as Philip Morrice notes,

> The exciseman's lot was not a happy one. He was working against a highly motivated, hostile and sometimes desperate section of the population, whose activities were either supported or connived at by a majority of the rest. He was often working in unfamiliar territory and was obliged to do so to a rule-book, whereas his adversary had none. Like all tax collectors in history, he had no natural allies, save the government

of the day which left him to execute its unpopular policies. In fact and fiction he was portrayed as heavy-handed, humourless, dim-witted and not always honest.

The other side of the story, that of the exciseman's should not be forgotten. He was expected to make his living from the proceeds of the take which he shared with the exchequer, and from which he had to meet all his expenses, including sometimes costly legal fees. (*Schweppes Guide*, 48)

It was hardly surprising that excisemen sometimes succumbed to bribery to make ends meet, and John Mackenzie (*A Hundred Years in the Highlands*) recalled that 'Excisemen were planted in central stations as a terror to evildoers, but they seemed to stay for life in the same localities, and report said they and the regular smugglers of liquor were bosom friends, and that they even had their ears and eyes shut by blackmail pensions from the smugglers.'

The totally unsatisfactory nature of their means of remuneration is perhaps most graphically illustrated by the tragic and well-documented tale of Malcolm Gillespie, or 'Gillespie the Gauger' as he was more usually known. Gillespie was a Highlander who joined the excise service in 1799, soon proving himself to be one of its most dedicated and successful officers when it came to countering the illegal production and distribution of whisky in Aberdeenshire. Despite his successes – taking and destroying an astonishing 25,000 gallons of spirit during his career – his financial situation, largely caused by the necessity of paying substantial sums of money for information leading to seizures of whisky, finally drove him to falsify returns for spirit which he had seized, and he was executed for the capital crime of forgery in December 1827. Excisemen sometimes lost their lives on 'active service', and the physical dangers of their job were underlined when Gillespie indicated on the morning of his execution the scars on his body from no fewer than forty-two wounds incurred in the line of duty.

The makers and distributors of illicit whisky used their detailed knowledge of local terrain to construct smuggling bothies which were frequently undetectable to even the sharpest exciseman's eye. At least one still was set up in a cave behind a waterfall so that the tell-tale smoke from distilling appeared as spray, and in other cases chimneys were constructed from bothies to nearby cottages where they linked up with domestic fires. At one stage even the clock-tower in the centre of Dufftown on Speyside concealed an illicit still, with smoke travelling up a narrow chimney which resembled a lightning conductor. The local Supervisor of Excise passed the clocktower on his way to and from work every day but never suspected anything. If the smell of whisky seemed strong at times it would obviously appear to come from one or more of the seven stills then operating in the town.

The smugglers could be just as clever and resourceful when it came to outwitting the excisemen. Feigned death was a useful tool for the whisky smuggler, and one famous example recorded by former exciseman Steve Sillett comes from Orkney, concerning Magnus Eunson, a Church Officer who operated an illicit still on the site on the outskirts of Kirkwall where Highland Park distillery now stands. Eunson often hid his spirit beneath the pulpit, but on one occasion when he discovered that the excisemen were about to raid his church he transferred the whisky to his house, laid a coffin lid and a white cloth over it, and muttered 'small-pox' when the excisemen finally arrived after a futile search of the church. Needless to say, they did not stay long.

Women frequently took on the role of couriers for illicit whisky, hiding bladders of spirit beneath their skirts, and in the government's *Fifth Report of Revenue arising in Ireland* of 1823 there is the observation that, 'some women have pockets made of tin, and a breast and a half moon that goes before them, and, with a cloak around them they will walk with six gallons and it shall not be perceived'. Caesar Otway (*A Tour in Connaught and Sketches in Ireland*, 1839) tells of a distiller having a tin vessel made 'with the head and body the shape of a woman which he dressed to resemble his wife'!

Robert Burns is almost certainly the most famous of all excisemen, serving at Dumfries from 1789 until his death in 1796. His celebrated song 'The Deil's Awa' Wi' The Exciseman' may seem at odds with his calling, and is often assumed to have been written before he joined the service. In fact it dates from 1792, and according to Burns's biographer, Lockhart, it was composed when the poet was on duty watching a suspected brig in the Solway Firth. The song was the result of Burns's impatience at having to wait in a salt-marsh for what he considered an unnecessarily long time, and is written in a somewhat tongue-in-cheek manner. His poem of 1785, 'Scotch Drink', in which he mourns the loss of *Ferintosh*'s tax-free privilege contains the lines: 'The curst horse-leeches o' th' Excise,/Wha mak the whisky-stells their prize!' This reference seems to have been intended more in the passionate spirit of his oft-quoted pronouncement from 'The Author's Earnest Cry and Prayer' (1786), 'Freedom and whisky gang thegither'.

If Burns is the most famous exciseman, then Aeneas *Coffey* must surely rank as the exciseman who was most influential in the history of whisky, as his invention of a *continuous* still revolutionised the entire industry. He served as an excise officer from around 1800 until his resignation in 1824, by which time he had risen to become Inspector General of Excise in Ireland.

With the gradual decline of illicit distilling during the nineteenth century, the exciseman's role changed appreciably. As James Bramwell puts it, 'nowadays the outlaw is tame and the exciseman has become a probation officer camped beside the distillery in a neat office and able to keep an exact check on the amount of whisky distilled'. Bramwell was writing in 1939, and at that time the amount of actual on-site work to be done by the exciseman was not always too onerous. Burns was not the only literary exciseman, as both Neil Gunn and the Irish novelist Maurice Walsh filled the same role for several years. Gunn found time to write six novels and *Whisky and Scotland* between 1923 and 1937, when he was excise officer at Glen Mhor distillery in Inverness before leaving the service to write full-time. 'Long experience has created an almost perfect system of supervision, interfering so little with practical operations and producing such figures of liability or accountancy as distillers unhesitatingly accept, that normally the relations between the Excise official and the distiller are pleasant and charged with mutual respect' (Gunn, 145).

When Maurice Walsh was working as an exciseman at Forres on Speyside and took leave, Gunn would sometimes be sent in his role as 'unattached officer' – for a decade from 1911 – to act as his relief. The two became great friends, and Gunn recalled later writing to Walsh in advance of his visits, urging him to get all the necessary paperwork done before his arrival so that the pair could spend Walsh's vacation fishing, hunting and generally having a good time together.

Such experiences were used by Walsh in his first and best-known novel *The Key Above The Door* (1926), and the Kerryman recalled later in life that when he and other young excise officers used to gather on Speyside for what was then the distilling 'season' from October to May there was a great deal of friendliness and companionship between the distillery staff and the 'revenue men'.

Writing in 1967, McDowall defined the exciseman's role as 'the watch-dog of the Government': 'it is his job to see that all alcohol made is recorded in order that duty may be paid . . . Control begins as soon as the worts go into fermenting vats – the wash backs. From the volume of the contents and its sugar content the amount of whisky which is to be produced can be estimated' (p.129). At the conclusion of *distilling*, 'the exciseman confirms his earlier calculations as to the amount of excisable spirit to be

produced from a given quantity of wash', according to Morrice
(p.29). Supervision continued through the period of warehouse
maturation.

Since McDowall and Morrice described the duties traditionally
carried out by the distillery exciseman, liberalisation has taken
place using modern computer technology to the extent that since
April 1983 the distillery manager has been responsible for measuring all yields and submitting returns to Customs and Excise
regarding the amounts of wash and spirit. There is no longer a
resident exciseman in each distillery to hold one of the keys previously needed to open the *spirit safe*, formerly one of the most
tangible examples of the exciseman's position of authority. Padlocks on the safe are still sealed, however, and may only be opened
in the presence of the manager or brewer, and the reason for
opening them must be recorded. Skipworth writes that 'The role
of the Excise is more as auditors, though spot-checks on distilleries
are made. Symbolic of the distilleries' new responsibilities is the
demise of the Crown Locks. These locks, good and solid, were
to be found at the spirit safe and the warehouses where the whisky
is matured. The distillers now provide their own locks . . . (p.70).
Iain Henderson, manager of Laphroaig distillery on Islay, outlines
the practical changes that have occurred since 1983. 'Before the
changes there were thirteen excisemen on Islay, and now there
are only four, based in an office in Bowmore. We don't call them
excisemen anymore, just customs officers, because they also have
other duties, including VAT and drugs-related work.'

Feints The OED defines *feints* as 'The impure spirit which comes over first and last in the process of distillation', but in whisky-making circles they are now usually considered to be only the 'lasts'. Feints are also sometimes referred to as 'after-shots' or the 'tail', with the *foreshots* correspondingly being known as the head, and the *middle cut* as the *heart*. Some distillers combine the terms and talk of 'the foreshots and the tails'.

The plural is always employed, and the spelling variant of 'faints' also occurs historically, as in the first recorded use of the term in 1743: 'Is it not a great Fault among Distillers, to allow any of the Faints to run among their pure Goods?' 'Feints' is in use by 1816, but both variants occur during the 1880s. Alfred Barnard, in his 1887 *Whisky Distilleries of the United Kingdom*, favours the spelling in modern usage.

Being in derivation a substantive plural of *faint*, the term seems in its application to distilling to have the sense of 'wanting in strength', 'weak' or 'feeble'.

After the initial process of malt whisky distillation has taken place in the *wash still*, the *low wines* are transferred into the spirit or low wines still for the second distillation. 'This time very great care has to be taken to retain only that part of the distillate which has the appropriate alcohol concentration and character for what is now the new whisky. The first part of the distillate, the fore-shots, which are too strong and impure, and the last part, the feints, are discarded by turning them into a feints receiver for redistillation in the next batch. No alcohol is wasted' (McDowall, pp.106-07).

The skill and experience of the *stillman* determines just when *cutting* takes place, and the existence of feints and foreshots is detected by tests he carries out in the *spirit safe*. One test is to add distilled water to the spirit, and if it turns cloudy then impurities are present.

According to Neil Wilson, 'The feints consist of the heavier compounds and less volatile constituents of the low wines such as fusel oil, which although undesirable compared to the purer ethanol of the middle cut appear (with some elements of the foreshots) in small quantities in the final product, helping to contribute to the character of each malt whisky' (p.30).

67

From feints comes the adjective *feinty*, and Grindal, writing of
the rare occasions on which distillers can be persuaded to speak
ill of their rivals' products, notes that 'the most common criticism
of a malt whisky will be that it is "too feinty" – in other words
the collection of the spirit has been allowed to continue for too
long' (p.43).

Irish pot still whiskey production involves triple distillation,
which means that even more of the feints and foreshots are
removed during the third distillation, ensuring, in the words of
Irish Distillers, 'maximum purity of the spirit'. The company is
not correct, however, in its assertion that 'no other whisk(e)y in
the world is distilled more than twice', as a number of Scottish
malts are triple distilled, including the *Lowland* whiskies Auchentoshan and Rosebank, and more surprisingly the *Highland*
Speyside malt Benrinnes. Springbank from *Campbeltown* is effectively distilled 'two and a half times', as two spirit stills are used
in its production, one for the low wines and the other for re-
distilling the feints and foreshots.

In American *moonshine* circles and amongst *poitín* distillers in
Ireland, low wines are often known as *singlings*, and the second
distillation is the 'second' or 'doubling' run. In the United States
the equivalent of the Scottish spirit still is known as a 'doubler
still'. Feints are referred to as 'backings', and as in professional
distilleries they are usually re-distilled with the next batch of
singlings.

Terms such as 'backings' and 'singlings' are never used in Scottish distilleries, not even in a colloquial 'shop floor' sense, where
the jargon words of production such as *draff*, feints, foreshots,
low wines, *mash*, *wash*, *wort* etc are now officially designated by
Customs and Excise.

(See also *congenerics*, *run*.)

Ferintosh A village near Dingwall in Ross and Cromarty, north-
east Scotland, and subsequently the name given to a kind of
whisky produced there during the eighteenth century. A *Ferintosh*
distillery, also sometimes known as Ben Wyvis, operated in
Dingwall from 1879 until 1926. According to Robert Forsyth
(*The Beauties of Scotland*, 1805), Ferintosh whisky 'was much
relished in Scotland; it had a strong flavour of the smoke of the
peat with which the malt of which it was made was dried; but
this was considered as one of the marks of it being genuine.'

As the anonymous editor of Nimmo's 1867 edition of *The Complete Works of Robert Burns* wrote in his illustrative note to the
poem 'Scotch Drink', 'as Ferintosh whisky was cheaper than
that produced elsewhere, it became very popular, and the name

Ferintosh thus became something of a synonyme for whisky over the country'. It was to retain that apparent synonym until the early years of the twentieth century, as is illustrated by Ian Mac-Donald's observation in *Smuggling in the Highlands* (1914) that a London spirits dealer was at that time still supplying a brand of whisky called Ferintosh. 'This alone is sufficient to show how highly prized Ferintosh whisky must have been', wrote Mac-Donald.

Prince Charles Edward Stuart – 'Bonnie Prince Charlie' – is reputed to have drowned his sorrows in Ferintosh whisky after the Jacobite defeat at nearby Culloden in 1746, and Sir Walter Scott was a great admirer of the product, writing to the poet and dramatist Joanna Baillie in December 1813 that he had 'plenty of right good and young Highland Ferintosh'. It is interesting to note that 'young' was clearly not a pejorative adjective to apply to whisky at that time.

The Ferintosh story is unique in Scottish distilling history, as the Forbes family of Culloden who owned the operation were granted exemption from payment of normal *excise* duties between 1690 and 1784. Duncan Forbes was a staunch supporter of the Protestant King William III who deposed the Catholic James II in 1688, and his estates were laid waste during the Jacobite rebellion in favour of James the following year, with damage valued at £5,400 Scots or £4,500 sterling being caused to Ferintosh distillery. By way of compensation, the Scottish parliament granted him the right to distill at Ferintosh in perpetuity on payment of 400 marks Scots per year, a perk which lasted until 1784, when it disappeared with the introduction of new excise legislation. The amount of monetary compensation – £21,580 – was decided upon by a jury before the Scottish Court of Exchequer; despite the fact that the Forbes family was satisfied by the outcome, Robert Burns, for one, was not. His poem 'Scotch Drink' (1785) and 'The Author's Earnest Cry and Prayer' of the following year articulate his feelings at the loss of the Ferintosh privilege and the repressive state of the excise laws relating to whisky in general:

> Thee, *Ferintosh*! Oh, sadly lost!
> Scotland lament frae coast to coast!
> Now colic grips, and barkin' hoast
> May kill us a';
> For loyal Forbes's charter'd boast
> Is ta'en awa'!

fermentation Adaptation of Latin *fermentātiōn-em*, first recorded in 1601, 'Some used to put therunto (the juice out of mulberries) myrrhe and cypresse, setting all to frie and take their *fermentation* in the sun.' As a verb, however, *ferment* dates from 1398, 'Soure dough hyghte fermentum, for it makyth paast ferment and maketh it also aryse'. Fermentation was first used figuratively – in the sense of being excited by emotion or passion – in *c.*1660, 'A young man in the highest fermentation of his youthful lusts'.

The *brewing* process consists of *mashing* and fermentation, with the latter changing *wort* to *wash* in the *washbacks* with the addition of yeast, although in Irish distilling circles fermentation is usually considered as an entirely separate process from brewing.

After leaving the *mash tuns* in the *tun room*, the wort is cooled before being pumped or gravity-fed to the washbacks, where living yeast is added to induce fermentation, the temperature being maintained at 20° – 32°C to keep the yeast active.

Yeast, for all its extraordinary capacity to set things seething, is really a delicate plant of a rather low order whose minute cells grow by a process of budding, yet in prime condition amidst prime wort it causes the liveliest commotion that I know of in nature. It needs oxygen to breathe, and as the oxygen of the air is kept away from it in the wash back, it turns upon the sugar to take the oxygen out of that, and in the process decomposes it into alcohol and carbonic acid. That anyway and roughly is Pasteur's theory of what takes place. (Gunn, 136). The production of carbon dioxide causes the wash to bubble and froth, often with some violence. 'I have heard one of those backs rock and roar in a perfect reproduction of a really dirty night at sea,' Gunn recalls. Generations of distillery workers have taken a delight in opening the lids of washbacks and inviting unwary visitors to sniff the contents. The presence of carbon dioxide and lack of oxygen means that 'the effect on nostrils and lungs is as sharp as an electric shock on the fingers and much more unpleasant' (Gunn, 138). The process of fermentation lasts for some forty-eight hours, and the resultant wash of no more than 10 per cent alochol is similar to strong beer.

Fermentation is generally considered to be just as important a stage of whisky-making as the process of *distillation* which follows, in terms of the effects it can have upon the finished product. As Gunn puts it, 'It might please Rabelais to reflect that the more rousing the life, the surer is the brewer of a generous quantity of spirit. Not but that a slower, gentler fermentation may produce a more saintly spirit. There is always an ideal in those things. But where so much can go wrong, the brewer is always happy to see a merry ferment' (ibid.).

If fermentation takes place too rapidly and the temperature of the wash rises above 33° or 34°C the spirit to be distilled can be adversely affected, as the coarse acids, alcohols and aldehydes that will give harshness to the final whisky are created at high temperatures.

As the first stage of whisky production during which alcohol is created, fermentation is where *excise* supervision traditionally commences.

fillings New whisky. 'Having settled on the formula for its blend, the blending company must buy the necessary quantities of new whiskies from the different distilleries and allow it to mature. The custom of the trade is that the blending company buys new whisky as "fillings" and provides the casks to be filled. The whisky is then allowed to mature in the distillery warehouses until, in the opinion of the blender, it is ready to be added to his blend' (Mackinlay, 75, 78).

Cooper points out that 'Nowadays many large firms remove their fillings as soon as they have been put in casks and mature them in their own warehouses' (*Century Companion*, 32), while Marshall Robb writes, 'Grain whiskies, sometimes called silent spirit or just "fillings", although they now cost about two-thirds of the filling price of malts, do not respond so much to ageing beyond about four years...' (p.42).

A whisky cask which has already been used once for storage and *maturation* of the spirit is known as a 'second fill' cask. In this case the type of whisky which the cask has previously held is taken into account. Obviously a *filling* of an assertive *Islay* malt would influence the finished flavour of a delicate *Lowland* malt, just as different types of sherry affect the first and subsequent whisky fillings of the cask. Casks can be re-used for whisky several times, although the maturing effect of the cask diminishes with each filling.

finger First used as a measurement – the breadth of a finger – in *c.*1400, 'Nere a foot lang and v. fyngers on brede'. *Finger* was also sometimes taken as a specific measurement: three-quarters of an inch.

It is first recorded in slang usage relating to a *nip* of alcoholic liquor in the United States in 1888, where the *Newport Journal* reported the following conversational snippet between two farmers: '"Which is correct, spoonfuls or spoons-ful?" "In Denver we say fingers".' The French *doigt* is used in the same context.

'Take a small, thimble-shaped "shot" glass, hold two fingers horizontally alongside it, and fill it with whiskey to that level... You now have two fingers of whiskey' (Jackson, *World Guide*, 136).

finish Along with terms such as *body*, colour, *nose* and *palate*, *finish* is part of the vocabulary used to create a profile of a specific whisky. The finish of a whisky – or any other drink – is the after-taste left in the mouth, but Jackson considers it to be more than just an after-taste in a malt whisky. 'It is a crescendo, followed by a series of echoes. When I leave the bottle, I like to be whistling the tune' (*Malt Whisky Companion*, 23).

'Short' and 'long' are the two most common words used to describe the finish of a whisky, but there are many variants; Lamond, for example, describes the finish of Glen Garioch as 'Good, smooth, delicate', whilst Tobermory 'Finishes smokily and rather woody' (*The Malt File*).

With the nominal sense of 'the final stage, the conclusion, that which gives completion', 'finish' is first attested in 1793.

firewater   An essentially colloquial term for any strong and fiery liquor, sometimes hyphenated to *fire-water*, and most frequently applied specifically to whisky. It is originally attributed to the North American Indians, and Partridge *(Historical Slang)* suggests the name derives from the fact that if one applied a match to the liquor it would catch fire. A more plausible view is that it derives from the pronounced burning sensation that the clear and apparently innocuous liquid gave when swallowed. Partridge also notes the now obsolete expression 'liquid fire', which he defines as 'bad whisky'.

'Fire-water' is first recorded by J.F. Cooper in *The Last of the Mohicans* (1826): 'His Canada father…taught him to drink the fire-water, and he became a rascal', and it had become anglicised, according to Partridge, by *c*.1850, achieving the status of standard English by 1890. In that year it is used without the hyphen by J. Hughes in *Tom Brown at Oxford* – 'Awful firewater we used to get' – but Lockhart hyphenates it as 'the fire-water of the illicit stills of the cities…' (*Scotch*). In current usage the hyphen is usually omitted: 'And all those lemonade bottles of firewater you buy for a fiver must come from somewhere' (Morton, 67).

first run   Usually refers to the production of *low wines*, which, according to Gunn 'is weak, impure spirit, offensive to the nostrils, and quite undrinkable' (p.144). See *run*.

foreshots   'The first raw runnings of the second distillation of the Low Wines', according to Cooper *(Century Companion)*. The term is initially recorded in *The British Medical Journal* (1893): 'The alcohol which had not passed over in the "fore-shots" and the "clean spirits"'. *Foreshots* are also known as the *head* of the distillation, when the *middle cut* is the *heart* and the *feints* are the *tail*. The hyphenated 'fore-shots' rarely appears in modern usage, and though Gunn writes of 'the foreshot', the plural form is usually employed as in 'feints'. *Fore* has the sense of 'before' or 'in front of', though the use of *shot* or *shots* in relation to production of spirit is obscure. The noun, however, has the sense of a rush or flow of water from *c*.1400.

'The first flow,' (during secondary *distillation*) 'known as the foreshots, is strong and oily, containing as it does an excess of esters, aldehydes and acids – it is this unwanted spirit which when mixed with water turns cloudy', according to Cooper (*Century Companion*, 24). As with the feints, the volatile compounds of the foreshots which boil off first during distillation are re-distilled along with the next batch of low wines, and their presence in small quantities is also important to the character of the finished whisky.

The expression 'foreshots and feints' is sometimes used colloquially to signify less important or less substantial items, 'bits and pieces'. The Malt Whisky Association's newsletter, *The Malt Letter*, contains a page of news snippets under that heading.

(See also *congenerics, cutting, first run*.)

fou' Also *fu*. Colloquial Scots variation of 'full', i.e. full of drink, *drunk*. The apostrophe is optional, and the adjective is now frequently used with qualifications such as 'blin' (blind), 'roarin', and in phrases such as 'fou as a puggie' ('puggie' being Scots for jackpot, the 'bank' in a card school). Partridge *(Historical Slang)* also recognises 'greetin' fu' ', literally 'crying drunk'.

First recorded usage dates from 1535, in Sir David Lyndsay's *Ane Pleasant Satyre of the Thrie Estaitis*: 'Na he is wod drunkin I trow; Se ʒe not that he is won fow?' Lyndsay's spelling variant had become obsolete by the early nineteenth century, being replaced by the current *fou'*, with *fu'* also in use from the late eighteenth century.

'I amna fou' sae muckle as tired – deid dune' – Hugh MacDiarmid (*A Drunk Man Looks at the Thistle*, 1926).

fusel oil Adaptation of German *fusel* – bad brandy or other spirits, German *fuseln* – to bungle. 'A term for a mixture of several homologous alcohols, chiefly amylic acid, and especially applied to this when in its crude form'.

The first use of *fusel oil* is in 1850: 'Being abundantly obtained during the distillation of potatoes . . . the name of the oil of potato spirit, or fusel oil, has been assigned to it'. In 1868 it is noted that 'A particularly foetid oil, termed "fusel oil", is formed in making brandy and whisky.'

(See also *feints* and *first run*.)

Gauger One who *gauges*, specifically an *exciseman*. The Old French word *gauge* (Central Old French and Modern French *jauge*) is of unknown origin, and is not found in the other Romance languages. It occurs along with the related verb *gauger* in the thirteenth century, the earliest sense appearing to be 'action or result of measuring'.

The first recorded use of *gauger* in English occurs in 1483: 'All the Vessels of Wine...shall...be well and truly gauged by the King's Gauger', though it had been recorded in French 130 years previously. 'Gauge' as a verb with the sense of measuring capacity or contents of *casks* or other containers also has its first English usage in the above quotation.

Marshall Robb records that 'Legislation...passed in 1657 was the foundation of the excise control of manufacture, various powers were given to officers, including the power to gauge vessels' (p.21).

Gauging-rod (an exciseman's instrument on the principle of the slide-rule for measuring capacity or contents of a cask) is first attested in 1656, though *gaging* rod occurs in 1570. *Gauging*-rule/ruler/stick are also recorded.

In relation to whisky, the term 'gauger' was regularly employed in a colloquial and not always respectful sense in both Scotland and Ireland from the early eighteenth century. Though now largely confined to historical usage, it is still sometimes heard in conversations between older distillery workers. 'Culloden was to bring in its train an invasion of excisemen, known locally as gaugers, because their main task is to gauge the amount of spirits produced, and a mass of crippling legislation including a rise in the duty' (Lockhart, *Scotch*, 10).

gill A liquid measure of one quarter of a standard pint. The word is an adaptation of the Old French *gille, gelle* in Medieval Latin, *gillo, gellus,* the name of a vessel or measure used for wine. The first recorded use of *gill* occurs in 1275: 'Mensuræ quæ vocantur schopinas et gilles', 'measures which are called schopinas and gills'.

The variant spelling of *gyll* also occurs in the late sixteenth century, whilst the current 'gill' is first recorded in the early 1700s. The first specific reference to whisky and the gill occurs in

74

Burns's 'Holy Fair' (1785), 'Be it whisky gill, or penny wheep, Or any stronger potion'.

Historically a gill could also be a vessel holding a gill of liquid, usually alcoholic, first attested in c.1440, 'Gylle, lyttle pot, gilla, vel Gillus', and attributively compounds such as -glass (1673), -house (1728) and -stoup (1820) also occur. According to Partridge *(Dictionary of Historical Slang)* the term 'gill-ale' had a colloquial currency c.1670-1750. 'Since a gill is only one-quarter of a pint, (it) would seem to mean medicinal ale (? stout).'

The Dictionary of Drink (p.458) gives the modern northern-English colloquial use of gill as referring to a half-pint of beer, and to further confuse matters it is often taken in Yorkshire to mean one-third of a pint. The Tap & Spile Traditional Alehouse at Glasgow Airport is the only place in Scotland currently serving beer in one-third pint measures, and the Leeds-based Pubmaster company which runs the bar officially describe their one-third pint as a *nip*, which would seem likely to lead to some misunderstandings.

The gill is currently the standard bar measure for spirits in Britain and Ireland, with three fractional measures having been laid down in the Weights and Measures Act of 1963, their 'generosity' frequently depending on geographical location. The standard English measure is usually one-sixth of a gill ($^5/_6$ fl.oz. or 20ml), while in Scotland it is one-fifth (1 fl.oz. or 25ml). The Irish measure is the most bountiful of all, usually being 1¼ fl.oz. or 35 ml, i.e. one-quarter of a gill.

'In Scotland in former times the "glass" and "nip" of whisky were respectively one-half and one-quarter of a gill. In England the corresponding measures were, as far as I am aware, fractions of the Quartern, which is one-quarter of a pint, i.e. a gill of five fluid ounces' (Marshall Robb, 70). The terms 'glass' and 'nip' to signify double and single measures of whisky respectively are still current in most areas of Britain, though in Ireland 'small' usually connotes a single measure.

Robb recalls that by 1920 a 'small' whisky or nip had been reduced in volume to one-fifth of a gill, and that it generally remained that size in Scotland until 1948, when some publicans reduced it to one-sixth of a gill. At the time when Robb wrote *Scotch Whisky* (1950) some London publicans were serving measures of whisky as small as one-seventh of a gill. Ivor Brown asserts that 'The true Scottish measure is a half-gill or a quarter-gill and such should be demanded. A good innkeeper will serve them. The half-gill is almost double one of the debased English "doubles"' *(Summer in Scotland*, 1952).

In January 1995 the gill will become a redundant term for practical purposes as metric legislation has decreed that by then all British bar measures will have to be either 25ml (between one-fifth and one-sixth of a gill) or 35ml (just less than one-quarter of a gill).

glass   From Old English *glæs*. Made by fusing sand (silica) with soda or potash (or both), usually with the addition of one or more other ingredients, especially lime, alumina, or lead oxide. *Glass* as a substance is first recorded in *c*.888, and in the sense of a drinking vessel made of glass in 1392-3, 'Pro glases et verres'.

The first figurative use of *glass* to imply the liquor contained rather than the vessel itself seems to occur in 1757, 'It is common for a number of them, that have got a glass in their heads, to . . .'

In relation to whisky, glass has both the sense of a drinking vessel and a specific quantity of spirit. In bars an order of a 'glass of whisky' will often produce a double measure, twice the size of a *nip*. (See also *gill*.)

The Scotch Whisky Association states that 'whisky does not require any specific shape [of glass] to enhance its delights and no rigid convention has grown up in this connection' (*Questions and Answers*, 39). For purposes of analytical *nosing* and *tasting*, however, a tall-stemmed, tulip-shaped glass is usually used, as the narrow neck helps to contain the vapours which give the whisky its *nose*. Fleming considers that such a glass could also be used to serve 'a good after dinner malt' (p.40).

Phillip Hills regards a *copita* as best for analytical purposes, though he maintains that a small brandy glass is an acceptable substitute. The Austrian designer George Riedel recently produced a revolutionary malt whisky glass with a flared lip, which appeared to contradict all accepted wisdom in terms of nosing and tasting. In a 'test drive' for *Wine* magazine (January 1993), however, a panel of experts unanimously voted it better than the copita, *snifter* or tumbler. As Gordon Brown explains, 'The design includes a small lip to direct the spirit on to the tip of the tongue, to bring out the latent creaminess of top quality malt'.

'The traditional whisky glass, the cut-crystal tumbler with a wide neck and tapering sides, is quite useless', says Hills. 'It was devised in the nineteenth century and was for drinking blended whisky out of. Since the whisky was being mixed with ice and soda it had no nose to speak of'. The tumbler is, none the less, the standard whisky glass, particularly where water or mixers are to be added, and if the drink is to be served *on the rocks*. Fleming says that 'Bourbon ought to be drunk from a large tumbler, Irish from a small tumbler . . .' (p.40). In Scotland the quarter-pint straight or thistle-shaped tumbler is popular, whilst American drinkers tend to prefer the seven-ounce tumbler for whisky on the rocks and the ten-ounce *Old-fashioned* glass. *Dram*, *shot* or *tot* glasses which contain a single measure of whisky are also used, usually only if the spirit is to be drunk neat.

When serving whisky *cocktails* a variety of glasses are used as appropriate for the style of drink in question. The six-ounce Old-fashioned glass is used for cocktails such as the formidable *blue blazer* and for any cocktail served on the rocks, like the *rusty nail*. Jackson says that it 'also doubles for whisky, though the typically chunky old fashioned glass is less attractive for that purpose than the cut-crystal and faintly tapered tumbler traditionally used for Scotch' (*Pocket Bar Book*, 23).

The eight-ounce *highball* glass is used for the cocktail of that name and also serves as a general purpose cocktail glass, while a *whisky sour* is served in a five or six-ounce stemmed sour glass. The *mint julep* comes in a long glass, probably a ten-ounce Collins, and *whisky toddy* in what Jackson describes as 'fireproof glasses with handles' (*Pocket Bar Book*, 23).

The art of glass-making was known to the Egyptians and Syrians before 1500 BC, and glass had been used for practical and decorative purposes in Britain by the Romans, though it was imported from the continent. The domestic glass industry only dates from the early sixteenth century, when Venetian glassmakers who had fled to Antwerp in Holland arrived in Britain as refugees. If drinking glasses were in use by the fourteenth century, the art of making satisfactory glass bottles and their widespread use really only dates from the early seventeenth century.

Dunford says that 'The earliest recorded instance of a Scots glassworks was in 1610, when one was established at Wemyss. This does not mean that no Scotsman used a glass for his whisky before then. No doubt some would have been imported over the Border...But it was not until well into the 18th century that glasses were in common use' (n.p.).

Gunn observes that Adamnan, ruler of Iona, refers to the Picts as using drinking glasses some thirteen hundred years ago, though wood and subsequently pewter were usually the staple materials for drinking vessels, with ram's horn and scallop shells also sometimes being used to dispense whisky. Boswell describes an occasion on the island of Coll when he and Dr Johnson were served whisky in a shell, 'according to the ancient Highland custom'.

Probably the most interesting historical examples of glasses which would be used for whisky drinking are those of the eighteenth century with obvious Jacobite provenance. Some displayed exquisite craftsmanship, being engraved with roses and verses dedicated to James II or his son Charles Edward Stuart, occasionally with a teardrop set in their stems. (See also *quaich*.)

Stemmed glasses or goblets were regularly used for whisky drinking during the eighteenth and nineteenth centuries, and Skipworth advocates their use even now, on the grounds that the goblet is 'bowl-shaped to concentrate the smell and it has a foot and a stem which make it easier to pick up and swirl around, thus bringing out the aroma' (p.76). The tumbler, he thinks, 'is altogether too crude for a drink that is often very delicate'.

The adjective *glassy* occurs as a synonym for 'drunk', perhaps deriving from the sense of having consumed too many glasses, but also from *glassy-eyed*, an all too obvious sign of advanced inebriation. 'Scandinavian deckhands glassy with Younger's Ales', (David Craig, 'Looking After Herself' in Craig, ed., *Fresh Starts*, 1992, p.90). 'Glass' can also take on a slang verb sense, with *to glass*, the action of *glassing*, meaning attacking an opponent in a pub fight using a glass as a weapon, with the usual intention of inflicting facial injuries.

Glenlivet   Set in the heart of the Banffshire Highlands of north east Scotland, *Glenlivet* is fourteen miles long and some six miles broad. With regard to whisky, in the words of Neil Gunn, 'Historically speaking, Glenlivet is a synonym for "the real stuff"' (p.181). In 1951 Lockhart wrote 'in many countries (Glenlivet) is even today regarded as a synonym for Highland whisky' (*Scotch*, 28).

The first recorded use of Glenlivet in the sense given by Gunn occurs in 1822, in *Noctes Ambrosianae*, a series of articles published in *Blackwood's Magazine* between 1822 and 1835, many of which were the work of John Wilson, writing under the pseudonym of Christopher North: 'I never drank better Glenlivit'. Five years later the geographically correct spelling was employed by North in the same publication, when he attributed to James Hogg one of the most famous references to Glenlivet, 'If a body could find oot the exac' proportion and quantity that ought to be drunk every day and keep to that, I verily trow that he might leeve for ever, without dying at a', and that doctors and kirkyards would go oot o' fashion.' The 'correct' spelling eluded Sir Walter Scott, too, as he uses the variant 'Glenlivat' in *St Ronan's Well* (1824), where the character Dr Quackleben declares the liquor to be 'Worth all the wines of France for flavour and more cordial to the system besides'.

If Scott was partial to a *dram* of (illegal) Glenlivet – calling the glen's distillers 'cunning chemists' – then so was his monarch,

King George IV, whose visit to Scotland in 1822 was stage-managed by the writer. Elizabeth Grant of Rothiemurchus recalled in *Memoirs of a Highland Lady* (1898) that 'Lord Conyngham, the Chamberlain, was looking everywhere for pure Glenlivet whisky; the King drank nothing else.'

During the nineteenth century Glenlivet was one of the five officially recognised classes of malt whisky, along with *Campbeltown*, *Islay*, *Lowland*, and *North Country*. When Alfred Barnard made his epic exploration of all the distilleries in Scotland and Ireland during the 1880s, he wrote of Glenlivet in his subsequent book, *The Whisky Distilleries of the United Kingdom* (1887), 'This neighbourhood has always been famous for its Whisky. Formerly smuggling houses were scattered on every rill, all over the mountain glens, and at that time the smugglers used to lash the kegs of spirit on their backs, and take them all the way to Aberdeen and Perth for disposal'.

It was estimated that some two hundred illegal stills were operating in and around Glenlivet at the end of the eighteenth century, which begs the question as to why this was such an optimum area for the production of whisky. One obvious answer in respect of illicit distillation was its geographical remoteness and inaccessibility, which provided an element of security from the unwelcome attentions of the *excisemen*, but the glen also enjoyed ready supplies of the other ingredients essential to successful distilling, such as an abundance of clear spring water, locally available *peat* and high quality *barley*. Its mountainous location – the current Glenlivet distillery is one of the highest in Scotland – also contributed to successful *distillation*, as cold water made for more efficient condensing of spirit, an activity also best undertaken in a cold climate. 'It might almost be thought that Nature had conspired to provide the perfect conditions for distilling whisky', as the anonymous author of The Glenlivet distillery's official history (1982) puts it.

In his *Malt Whisky Companion*, Jackson writes that 'What Grand Champagne is to Cognac, the glen of the river Livet is to Speyside. The only whisky allowed to call itself "The Glenlivet" is historically the most famous Speyside malt (p. 120).

The history of The Glenlivet is a fascinating one. The farmer and illicit distiller George Smith of Upper Drumin, a tenant of the Duke of Gordon, decided to legitimise his operation in the wake of the 1823 *Excise* Act which made legal distilling a more attractive proposition in the Highlands. The Smith family had been 'out' with Charles Edward Stuart during the Jacobite rising of 1745, prior to which its surname had been Gow, and the subsequent anglicisation was doubtless a prudent precaution against reprisals. George Smith himself was not an average Banffshire farmer, having been trained as an architect.

The Glenlivet was the first distillery to be granted a licence under the new Act in 1824, and not surprisingly the far-sighted and courageous Smith, who realised the advantages of conducting his business in an open and lawful way, became extremely unpopular with his old smuggling colleagues, who saw him as the worst kind of traitor. As Smith himself put it, 'I was warned by my civil neighbours that they meant to burn the new distillery to the ground and me in the heart of it. The laird of Aberlour had presented me with a pair of hair trigger pistols worth ten guineas, and they were never out of my belt for years'.

Three other distilleries were started up in Glenlivet, but they were forced out of business by the smugglers, though George Smith's son-in-law, Captain William Grant, built a distillery in the 1840s at Auchorachan in the glen which survived. It is interesting to note that in 1849 Grant was advertising in the national press that only his and his father-in-law's distilleries were in the glen and were therefore entitled to use the name Glenlivet. Clearly nobody took much notice of such oft-repeated declarations, and as the reputation of The Glenlivet whisky grew so the temptation also grew for other distillers to 'arrogate to themselves some of The Glenlivet's stature', as John McPhee puts it (p.117) by using the Glenlivet name. It was not only a question of gaining some reflected glory from The Glenlivet, it was also a matter of selling whisky to city spirits merchants for whom Glenlivet was the first specific producing district they knew by name.

Such was demand for The Glenlivet whisky that in 1850 the Smiths built a new plant called the Cairngorm distillery at Delnabo, near Tomintoul, but demand so outstripped production that in 1858 another new and much larger plant was constructed at Minmore in Glenlivet, capable of producing six hundred gallons of whisky per week. Both the old Upper Drumin and Cairngorm distilleries were subsequently scrapped. Andrew Usher of Edinburgh was The Glenlivet's energetic agent, largely responsible for the dramatic growth in sales during the next few decades. Usher is credited with a founding role in the *blending* industry as a result of his launching of one of the first branded blends, Usher's Old Vatted Glenlivet.

By 1880 so many whisky-makers throughout Strathspey were using the name Glenlivet alongside their own names on the pretext of vague stylistic or geographical similarities that it was jokingly referred to as 'the longest glen in Scotland'. George Smith's son,

John, had taken over control of The Glenlivet distillery from his
father and in 1870 he registered the name Glenlivet at Stationer's
Hall in an attempt to protect its exclusivity. Ten years later he
felt the need to take a test case to establish whether, in the words
of Lockhart, 'Glenlivet whisky [had] to be made in the glen in
order to justify the title of Glenlivet or could any distillery in the
neighbourhood usurp the name? (*Scotch*, 25). The result was only
a partial victory for Smith, as Lockhart recounted. 'The court
decided that only The Glenlivet Distillery was entitled to label
its whisky "Glenlivet" without qualification. The other distillers,
however, were not restrained from hyphenating Glenlivet with
their own name'.

At one time no fewer than twenty-eight distilleries used the
Glenlivet suffix, though many no longer feel the necessity to do
so, The Macallan being a notable example of a whisky which is
now thought to have enough cachet of its own without any hyphenated embellishments on its label. Aberlour, Glenburgie, Linkwood, Longmorn, Milton Duff, Tamdhu and Tormore are some
of the whiskies which still employ the Glenlivet suffix, and as
Cooper points out, regarding the Perthshire malt whisky
Edradour, 'they also bottle it, vatted with one other Highland
malt, under the name of Glenforres-Glenlivet, despite the fact
that there is no such place as Glenforres and Edradour itself is
nearly fifty miles away from Glenlivet' (*The Whisky Roads*, 99).

Memories of the 1880 Glenlivet court case were rekindled in
1991, when the Scotch Whisky Association successfully objected
to the use of the name Glen Gold by John Teeling of Cooley
Distillery in Ireland, on the grounds that 80 per cent of purchasers
of the cut-price product thought they were buying Scotch whisky.
Not only was Glen Gold not Scotch, but it was not whisky as
defined by EC regulations, as it contained only 10-15 per cent
whisky mixed with *alcohol* distilled from molasses. It is difficult
to understand how the Association could logically object to the
use of the word 'glen', however, as Scotland does not have a
monopoly of geographical features with that appellation, as resi-
dents of Glencolumbcille in Donegal or the Glens of Antrim would
testify. Somehow distillers on the Isle of Man get away with producing a whisky called Glen Kella, which even uses the Irish
spelling of whiskey. As a prefix for brands of Scotch whisky, both
blended and malt, 'glen' enjoys great popularity, with more than
120 different permutations currently in use.

For many years The Glenlivet was the only operational distillery
situated in the glen, but in 1966 Tamnavulin distillery was built
at the hamlet of Tomnavoulin, and in 1973 Seagram, subsequently

owners of The Glenlivet, constructed a new plant called Braes of
Glenlivet, the produce of which has yet to be bottled as a single
malt. Also in the parish of Glenlivet, though actually situated on
the river Avon, into which the Livet flows en route to the Spey,
is Tomintoul distillery, which dates from 1964. The Glenlivets
are sometimes known generically as 'The Glen Whiskies', though
this is usually taken to mean not just those produced in the glen
itself but any whiskies of similar style eligible to carry the Glenlivet
suffix.

In 1977 The Glenlivet distillery was acquired by Seagram, and
the whisky is generally considered to be as good as its history and
the use of the definite article would suggest, with tasters unanimous in praise of its quality, using such terms as 'delicacy', 'deep
mellowness' and 'honeyed sweetness'. The Glenlivet is currently
the best selling single malt whisky in the United States.

golden square/golden triangle   On almost every 'whisky map' of
Scotland there is a small area in the North-East which boasts such
a concentration of distilleries that it is marked with an inset square
and treated in detail away from the main map. This is the *golden
square* of Scotch whisky-making, and the term – which implies
something of a centre of excellence – has given its name to a brand
of blended whisky bottled in Berwick upon Tweed.

Some writers, such as Derek Cooper (*Whisky Roads of Scotland*,
8), refer to the area in the counties of Banffshire and Morayshire
as a 'golden triangle in the north-east corner of Scotland centred
on Elgin, Rothes, Keith and Dufftown', and it also includes the
historically famous distilling centre of *Glenlivet*. Writing in the
Scots Magazine in November 1986, Tom Weir refers to entering
'the golden triangle where whisky-making was a cottage industry
when there was enough corn to produce it, and before restrictions
on folk's freedom to do so.'

In essence the golden square or triangle is the area which is
home to an unofficial sub-division of the *Highland* classification
of whiskies known as 'Speysides', all of which share certain stylistic similarities and are produced in some proximity to the River
Spey. The Spey is Scotland's fastest flowing and second longest
river, rising in the high country of Badenoch, south-west of The
Cairngorm, flowing by Aviemore, Grantown and Rothes to the
sea between Elgin and Buckie.

The *water* of Speyside 'is the parent of the region's thorough-
bred whiskies', according to Jackson (*World Guide*, 61); 'the
clean, mountain water picks up enough of the region's peat to
impart the smokiness that is their particular characteristic'. He
describes the Spey valley as 'the backbone of the region' (*World*

Guide, 63), which can be defined as extending from the River Findhorn in the west to the River Deveron in the east, and as far south as the latitude of Aberdeen. It is 'the great heartland of Highland Malt whisky', according to David Daiches.

The golden square or triangle of Speyside production is home to around 50 per cent of all malt whisky distilleries in Scotland, and Jackson considers that more than fifty of the sixty distilleries in what is basically the Grampian administrative region – 'the world's greatest whisky-making region', according to Jackson (*World Guide*, 61) – can be categorised as 'Speysides'. Stylistically the Speysides are characterised by their 'smoky and firm' character and 'with more than a hint of sherryish sweetness, they are the most complex of whiskies, and the most elegant' (Jackson, *World Guide*). The same writer claims that the valleys' mild climate helps to create a Speyside character.

Some of the best known malt whiskies produced in the golden square or triangle include Glenfarclas, Glenfiddich, Glen Grant, Knockando, The Glenlivet, and The Macallan.

goldie Affectionate Scots term for a glass of whisky, obviously with reference to the drink's colour, and often prefixed with the diminutive 'wee'. Morton notes that at Edradour distillery in Perthshire, when *dramming* was still practised, each worker received 'a daily ration of three drams, all raw, white spirit straight from the still, and a final, going-home dose of matured, golden whisky. This was known as "three whites and a goldie"...' (p.177).

grain Seed, seed of cereal plants, corn, Old French *grain, grein* (Modern French *grain*). Latin *grānum*, a grain, seed.

The first written record dates from some time in the fourteenth century, 'Vch gresse mot grow of graynez dede', and the earliest attestation of *grain* whisky occurs at the surprisingly late date of 1887, 'Grain whisky, i.e. made of barley in the grain stage, and not of malt'. Grindal declares that 'The name grain whisky is in any case a misnomer. All whisky is made from cereals, in other words grain' (p.105).

The fact that whisky is distilled in Scotland from grain owes much to climatic factors. As Jackson explains, 'Warm countries like France grow grapes to produce a fermented drink, wine, and a distilled one, brandy. Colder climes grow grain; their fermented and distilled drinks are beer and whisky respectively' (*World Guide*, 5).

The 1887 definition is not quite accurate in respect of what is considered to be grain whisky today, as unmalted barley is only one type of grain which can be used, with *corn* (or maize as it is usually known in Europe), rye and wheat all being permissible within the accepted modern definition. Jackson says 'Though most American whiskey is produced from maize (corn), the distillers also use this grain to produce neutral spirit for the purpose of blending. Some of this is aged and bottled as grain whiskey' (*Pocket Bar Book*, 51). Grindal notes that in the United States 'blended whisky may contain up to 80 percent of neutral spirit' (p.106).

It is important to note that the production of grain whisky does require a malt input; McDowall states that around 15 per cent of malted barley is usually added to the *mash* in order to provide the *diastase* necessary to convert the starch of the maize or other grain to maltose. Maize was first used to make grain whisky in Scotland in 1865, and there and in Ireland it is now the principal grain employed.

Most Irish whiskey was made only from malted and unmalted barley until well after World War II, when the fulness of its flavour was perceived to be a negative factor with regard to export sales, and an element of grain whiskey was therefore introduced to lighten the *spirit*. Whiskey for both the export and domestic markets now contains grain spirit, and because the Irish prize their *pot still* whiskey made from malted and unmalted barley so highly they distil their grain spirit almost to neutrality. As Jackson writes, 'its job is merely to lighten the body of the whiskey. The Scots distil their grain slightly less thoroughly, with a view to their making a definite, if small, flavour contribution' (*World Guide*, 103).

Dr Philip Schidrowitz concurred with this view of Scottish grain whisky in the *Encyclopaedia Britannica* (1911), stating that the products of the *patent still* 'possess a distinct flavour which varies at different distilleries, and analysis discloses the fact that they contain very appreciable quantities of the "secondary" products which distinguish potable spirits from plain alcohol'. Lockhart also considers grain whisky to be more characterful than neutral spirit, describing it as 'lighter in weight and less distinctive in taste than malt whisky'. He makes the point that 'it does not improve in cask in the same manner or to anything like the same extent as malt whisky' (*Scotch*, 60). The Scotch Whisky Association says of grain whisky that 'Because of the rectifying element present in this process [patent still distillation] the distillate is generally lighter in aroma than most Malt Whiskies. It consequently has a milder character and requires less time to mature' (*Questions and Answers*, 46). None the less, like malt whisky it must by law be matured for a minimum of three years.

Maurice Walsh, writing in his foreword to Marshall Robb's *Scotch Whisky*, recalls his early days in the *excise* service before the First World War and time spent 'down amongst the raw grain distilleries about Alloa'. 'Cambus on the Forth', he writes, 'was held to be the best of the Patent distilleries, its only rival being Chapelizod on the Liffey. In those days patent spirit was no more than a by-product of yeast making; but Cambus, skimming no yeast, used malt and barley in the mash tun, and turned out a palatable drink, maturing in three to five years, and was as near a silent malt whisky as I have ever sampled in a strictly official way'.

Whatever the merits or otherwise of *straight* grain whisky, its principal value has always been as a blending agent, and the development of grain spirit and of blending grain with malt was responsible for transforming distilling in Scotland from a cottage industry into the multi-million pound business it is today.

Nowadays, grain whisky production takes place in *Coffey, continuous* or patent stills rather than pot stills, though Moss points out that

> Before the First World War, pot still grain whisky was produced in large quantities in Scotland. This was made from a mash consisting of unmalted barley and other *grains* and about five per cent *malt* – necessary to produce the diastase that converts the starches in the other grain into sugars. This pot still grain whisky was mostly sold straight from the still under the generic name Irish Whiskey, as it was and is the process most commonly used by pot distillers in Ireland. (*Scottish Drink*, 82)

The patent still production process is continuous as opposed to the 'batch' system necessitated by the pot still, which means that the amount of spirit produced over a given time is significantly greater. Grain whisky is much cheaper to produce than malt whisky, and the whole scale of grain whisky distilling is appreciably larger than malt whisky distilling, with 235.9m litres of alcohol being produced in Scotland in 1990. To take one example of scale, Allied's Laphroaig malt whisky distillery on Islay has a maximum capacity of 2½ million litres per year, whilst the same firm's Strathclyde grain plant has an annual capacity of 37 million litres. Morrice makes the point that due to the continuous process, less skill is needed by the grain whisky distiller than his malt whisky-making counterpart, who is required to maintain 'the established standards and patterns peculiar to his distillery' (p.30).

The grain whisky distillery tends to be functional rather than aesthetically pleasing, both inside and out, and grain whisky production is, as Cooper puts it, 'just a highly efficient industrial process which can, as occasion demands, produce gin and vodka and all manner of industrial spirits' (*Century Companion*, 33).

The fact that grain whisky can be produced almost anywhere meant that when Barnard made his tour of the distilleries of the United Kingdom in the 1880s, he was able to visit four distilleries in England which were producing whisky, and he notes the existence of a further six making 'plain spirit' for rectifying and manufacturing purposes. In Bristol he toured the oldest distillery in England, built in the seventeenth century, and he records that it was certainly producing malt spirit in 1761. At the time of his visit the Bristol distillery was producing almost 640,000 gallons of both 'plain' spirit and grain whisky per annum, the latter being sent to Scotland and Ireland 'to make a blended Scotch and Irish whisky, for which purpose it is specially adapted and stands in high favour'. The Lea Valley distillery in Stratford, London was producing some 155,000 gallons of 'malt spirit' and 305,000 gallons of grain spirit per year, though Liverpool was clearly the leading centre for English whisky production, with the modern Bankhall distillery in Sandhills making one and a half million gallons of plain spirit, malt and grain whisky per year, though the output was predominantly of plain spirit. Liverpool's Vauxhall distillery had been founded in 1781 and in Barnard's time made an annual two million gallons of grain whisky which was sent to Scotland for blending purposes.

All but one of the grain distilleries currently operating in Scotland are situated in the urban Lowlands, and Irish grain whiskey production takes place at the large, modern Midleton plant in County Cork. As Irish Distillers put it in their promotional literature, 'In Midleton maize can be used as a raw material for the mash and a separate mashing system exists for this purpose. Spirit from maize is used primarily for Gin and Vodka production in Ireland, and maize is also used in a mash with malted barley to make lighter whiskey types'. Neutral grain spirit is also distilled at Invergordon, a large distilling complex constructed in 1961 by the Cromarty Firth in the Scottish Highlands, where it is made as 'a high strength pure spirit, without odour, or colour, but with the cereal character so prized by makers of gin and vodka'.

The first Scottish grain whisky was produced in 1828 at Cameronbridge in Fife by John Haig, and 'Choice Old Cameron Brig' endured as the only single grain whisky on the market for many years until it was joined by The Invergordon in 1990. Another early grain plant was Cambus near Alloa, the produce of which won a kind of praise from Maurice Walsh. While the

Royal Commission of 1908/9 was debating whether grain whisky could properly be called whisky at all – with all the implications that held for the burgeoning blending industry – the owners of Cambus, the Distillers Company Limited, produced a seven-year-old patent-still grain whisky which they described as 'light, delicate, exquisite'. Press advertisements proudly proclaimed that 'Cambus is not a pot still whisky', and made the claim – hardly tenable in these days of an Advertising Standards Authority – that their whisky produced 'not a headache in a gallon'. It was, they stated, 'a soft, round, natural wholesome stimulant, that ministers to good health and neither affects the head nor the liver'.

DCL funded the 'What is Whisky?' case, and its advertising campaign for Cambus anticipated the Royal Commission's findings that 'whiskey' was nothing more specific than a spirit obtained by distillation from a mash of cereal grains saccharified by the diastase of malt. Gunn writes of molasses being used in patent still distillation in Scotland in the 1930s, though the term 'whisky' could not legally be applied to the product, and more recently John Teeling of Cooley distillery in Ireland ran into problems with his Glen Gold whiskey which also features molasses among its ingredients. (See *Glenlivet*.) McDowall writes that 'The result of the "What is Whisky?" Case by which grain whisky could be called Scotch Whisky really set the company on the way to fortune' (p.50). Once the battle had been won Cambus reverted to its previous role as nothing more than a blending agent, despite the extravagant claims that had been made for it by its distillers.

The origins of the Distillers Company lie in the fact that much of the grain spirit produced in Lowland Scottish patent stills was sent to England where it was re-distilled and flavoured for gin. The leading Scottish grain distillers combined to protect their market share in the face of what could be seen as unfair competition from English distilling concerns, as an Act of 1848 allowed the English to use a wide range of raw materials – including molasses – in distilling, while the Scots were forced to use only grain.

Various groupings and trade agreements within the grain whisky industry took place from the 1850s onwards, with six of the leading Lowland grain producers finally forming The Distillers Company Ltd in 1877. By the time the company was acquired by Guinness in 1986 it owned almost half the malt whisky distilleries in Scotland, along with three operational grain plants which accounted for more than one third of the industry's grain output. It encompassed such household whisky names as Buchanan, Dewar, Haig, Johnnie Walker and White Horse, and boasted more than one hundred brands of blended whisky on sale through-out the world.

Regarding the character of grain whisky, it is interesting to note that Edinburgh's North British grain plant allows a higher than normal level of *foreshots* and *feints* into the finished whisky to enhance its character, and the company insists that its product improves with *ageing* for up to at least six years. Daiches remains unpersuaded that it is a product to rival malt whisky, however, and to him North British had 'little or no body, but all surface flavour, and that flavour of a pungent sweet sharpness that makes one think more of a chemistry laboratory than a bar' (*Scotch Whisky*, 60). Choice Old Cameron Brig earned from Daiches the verdict 'Clear and sharp in taste, almost antiseptic indeed, with nothing at all of what I would call whisky character'. McDowall found the same whisky 'surprisingly reasonable to drink, with a slight malt flavour' (p.49). Prudently he concluded that it is 'certainly better than no whisky, a little reminiscent of D.Y.C., the Spanish whisky'. Daiches sums up grain whisky in general with the nice remark 'not a whisky to drink by itself, nor can it compare as a drink with a pot-still malt whisky. But it is clearly not just "silent spirit"; indeed, it is rather noisy'.

Invergordon Distillers would doubtless point out that Daiches made that observation before sampling their single grain whisky, launched in 1990 with a dynamic promotional campaign after they had identified and targeted an entirely new market for grain whisky. Research has revealed that whisky in general has the image of being a middle-aged man's drink, and Invergordon decided that at ten years old their grain whisky had enough character to stand against malts, yet was also sufficiently light and *mellow* to appeal to younger drinkers and women of all ages. It was, they discovered, perceived as more of a 'white' spirit (like vodka) than a 'brown' spirit, and white spirits have greater popularity with the younger age group. The Invergordon ten-year-old single grain whisky has a *nose* which suggests surgical spirit, but a pleasing flavour of honey and vanilla. It is marketed as being 'Too special to be hidden in a blend'.

Grain or grains can also have the same sense as *draff*: the refuse left after *brewing* or *distilling*. It is first recorded for certain with this sense in 1595, 'No persons...shall sell any Draffe graynes or branne by any other measure than onlye by the measure that they by...theire corne bye'. In the early seventeenth century the practice of using the draff or grains as animal food was already in existence, 'There is also two other Foods...excellent for Hogges: the first whereof is Ale or Bere Graines' being recorded in 1616.

The first-known reference to distillery grains as opposed to those from beer-making occurs in 1718, 'The feeding Cows with Distillers Grains was a new custom'. In 1751 Dr Johnson writes in *The Rambler*, 'I met Miss Busy carrying grains to a sick cow'.

From grains comes the modern distilling term *dark grains* which refers to the cubes or pellets of animal fodder which are made by treating the *burnt* or *pot ale* with dried draff, also known as *light grains*. The pot ale evaporates into a dark brown syrup, hence the name, and light grains are then added. Dark grains have a much higher protein content – up to 24 per cent – than light grains. The process was pioneered in America and Canada, and first introduced into Scotland by Hiram Walker, who installed a dark grains plant at Dumbarton in 1964.

green malt   See *malt, green.*

grist   In general use, *grist* has the senses both of corn which is to be ground and corn which has been ground, and specifically related to beer and whisky making it is taken to be malt crushed or ground for *brewing*.

With this sense it is first attested in 1822, 'The water rises upwards through the malt, or as it is called, the grist', though in its more general sense as outlined above grist is first recorded in *c*.1430 with the spelling variant *gryst*. Old English *grist, gryst*, cognate with Old Swedish *grist* – in *gristgrimmo* – grinding of teeth. Grist is also employed in common phrases such as 'It's all grist to the mill', meaning everything can be put to good use, turned to account. It is first recorded in this sense in 1583, 'There is no lykelihoode that those thinges will bring gryst to the mill.'

After malting, the barley – or malt as it is then known – is 'dressed' to remove the rootlets and any other impurities in a dressing machine. Daiches writes that 'the combings (or rootlets) used to be sold as cattle food under the name of "malt culms"' (*Scotch Whisky*, 10). 'Once it has been ground into a rough floury meal or grist it is ready for mashing', according to Cooper (*Century Companion*, 22).

H **air of the dog** See *dog*.

Half Grindal writes, 'The "half and half", in other words a half-pint of beer and a small whisky, remains a traditional Scottish way of drinking...' (p.179). The expression 'half and half' was commonly used in Glasgow and the West of Scotland, and still survives, while in Edinburgh and the East 'a *nip* and a half' or 'a nip and a pint' was the more usual order, but is now fairly rare.

Jackson considers that the term 'half' as a pub order for a single measure of whisky probably occurs because 'The Scot, appreciating that reality can be mean, feels that the term "half" fairly describes a full single whisky' (*World Guide*, 15). Begg explains that 'In days when measures were generous a "half" was a half gill, but the Scottish phrase "hauf an hauf" literally means half (of a half gill of whisky) and a half (of a pint of beer)' (p.20).

Half is used in Ireland with the same sense, and Magee writes 'The standard Irish spirits measure is 2½ fluid ounces to the glass, or four "half-ones" to the gill...' (p.107).

half cut Partly drunk. See *cut*.

hangover Defined by Keith Floyd *(Floyd on Hangovers)* as 'The unpleasant symptoms that follow the drinking of too much alcohol. These include nausea, vomiting, intense headache, stomach pain and photophobia (sensitivity to light). The symptoms are caused by dehydration, irritation of the stomach lining and a degree of poisoning by the breakdown products of alcohol'. Dunkling notes that 'The word "hangover" has only been in use since the beginning of the 20th century, though we can be sure that many a hangover was experienced before that' (p.48).

The first attestation of the word with the sense of 'The unpleasant after-effects of (esp. alcoholic) dissipation' occurs in 1904: '*Brain*, usually occupied by the Intellect Bros., – Thoughts and Ideas – as an Intelligence Office, but sometimes sub-let to Jag, *Hang-Over* & Co'. The drink-related *hangover* is ultimately related to the verb *hang* in its sense 'to remain in...suspense...To remain unsettled or unfinished', first attested in the fourteenth century. By the end of the nineteenth century a nominal sense of 'A thing or person remaining or left over; a remainder or survival, an after effect' had also developed, leading to the current usage.

It is often said, with some justification, that there is no true 'cure' for a hangover except the passage of time, but many and very varied substances and practices have been tried over the centuries in an attempt to ameliorate if not cure the effects of alcoholic over-indulgence. The *hair of the dog* is perennially popular, with one such hangover remedy being attributed to Eddie Conlon, 'For a bad hangover take the juice of two quarts of whisky'. The hair of the dog can help to ease a hangover in that it replaces lost blood sugar, though honey may be a more sensible alternative. Floyd explains that 'Your monstrous headache may in part be caused by the sudden change in concentration of alcohol bathing the brain and a morning-after drink containing alcohol . . . can add just enough alcohol to make the change more gradual' (p.15). He recommends the vodka and tinned-beef consommé-based 'heavyweight reviver' 'The Bullshot' for particularly serious cases, but perhaps the best known hair of the dog hangover cure is the cognac-based 'Prairie Oyster'. James Boswell records in his *Tour of the Western Isles and Hebrides* drinking brandy as an effective morning-after headache remedy.

Floyd notes the consumption of soused herring and a glass of Pils as a hangover cure in Germany, while in Australia steak pies and tomato sauce accompanied by cold coca-cola are supposed to have the same effect. In all hangover remedies the aspect of dehydration has to be addressed, and one preventive practice is the consumption of copious quantities of water before retiring to bed, though this is not always such a sound idea if one sleeps at some distance from the nearest bathroom.

There is no shortage of ardent advocates of Kingsley Amis's patent hangover cure, which consists of a vigorous 'morning after' bout of sexual intercourse, though he is at pains to warn that 'guilt and shame' are prominent constituents of what he terms 'the metaphysical hangover', as opposed to the 'physical hangover' (*Kingsley Amis on Drink*, 1972).

In 1594 Sir Hugh Plat *(The Jewell House of Art and Nature)* recommended drinking 'a good large draught of Sallet Oyle' before going on a *bender*, and also suggests the more palatable alternative of milk, something which Sir Clement Freud echoes in his *Book of Hangovers*. Perhaps the most curious hangover cure is suggested by Robert Boyle in his *Medical Experiments, 1692-94*, where he writes, 'Take green Hemlock that is tender, and put it in your socks, so that it may lie thinly between them and the Soles of your Feet; shift the Herbs once a day'.

Addressing the psychological side of the hangover, Vernon Scannell writes, 'I have sometimes wondered if the hangover is not unconsciously desired by the boozer, that he feels a need for it just as some people gamble heavily because they crave the punishment of losing...' (*The Tiger and the Rose*, 1971). He considers the hangover and the gambler's losses to be experiences 'that offer parallels with, or perhaps parodies of, mystical states of consciousness...'.

hard stuff 'Whiskey and other strong liquors', according to *The New Dictionary of American Slang*. *Hard* is a common Germanic adjective, *heard* in Old English, and with reference to liquor – having the sense of harsh or sharp to the taste – the adjective is first recorded in 1581, 'Neither hard wine is pleasant to the tast, neither haughtie behaviour acceptable in companie.'

The colloquial American sense of intoxicating, spiritous, strong, first occurs in the *Boston Times* (1879): 'Before the court for selling hard liquor, when he had only a licence for selling ale'. Hard liquor is defined in its modern American sense as 'Whiskey, rum, gin, brandy, as distinct from wine and beer' *(American Slang)*. Five years later the first reference to *hard stuff* occurs, 'Two or three keep of the "hard stuff"', and whilst Partridge acknowledges the term's American parentage he also notes its use from *c*.1890 in Australia and New Zealand. Rather imprecisely, he defines hard stuff simply as 'intoxicating liquor'. Morton gives a modern Scots example of usage when he writes of Clynelish distillery in Sutherland that if the plant had not been there to buy *barley* 'Most crofters would otherwise have been selling mainly to illicit distillers, in a desperate attempt to make some money. Either that or making the hard stuff themselves' (p.62).

Sometimes, particularly in Ireland, the word hard is used by itself, as in 'Gunning's Word' by Tom Mac Intyre. 'He was never what you'd call a very resilient class of a man now, was he? Gunning will enquire, raising his glass of the (undiluted) hard, I certainly would never have used that word of him' (*The Word for Yes*, 1991, p.32).

head   See *foreshots*.

heart of the run   Also known as the *middle cut*. With the relevant sense of the innermost or central part of anything, *heart* is first attested after 1310, 'That ys in heovene hert in-hyde'. See *cutting*.

het pint   A traditional Scottish Hogmanay or New Year's Eve drink which was served hot and consisted of ale, whisky, eggs, sugar and nutmeg. The drink used to be carried through the streets and served from large copper 'toddy kettles', as well as being offered to warm 'first foots' at houses they visited. McNeill describes *het pint* as 'a sort of wassail bowl' (p.216).

The adjective *het*, which corresponds to the modern English *hot* or *warm*, is first recorded in *c.* 1375, 'With het chenʒeis, as fyre brynnand', and now only has localised usage in Scotland. J.G. Lockhart writes of Hogmanay being celebrated at Abbotsford 'with the immemorial libation of a het pint'.

A typical recipe for het pint would suggest putting four pints of mild ale into a saucepan with a teaspoon of grated nutmeg and then bringing almost to the boil. Four ounces of caster sugar are stirred in and allowed to dissolve. Three well-beaten eggs are gradually added, being stirred to prevent the mixture curdling. Half a pint of whisky is then added and gently heated, though it must not be allowed to boil or the alcohol content will fall.

highball A *cocktail* usually based on whisky, and the name given to a six-ounce or eight-ounce *glass* now used for serving a variety of cocktails. Jackson explains the origins of the drink's name as follows: 'It is said that some American railroads used a signal with a ball raised on a pole to indicate to the train driver that he was running late. A highball meant "hurry". It also came to mean a simple drink that could be fixed in a hurry' (*Pocket Bar Book*, 120).

Dunkling also notes the railroad usage, and refers to an article in *American Speech* (February 1944) by Professor I. Willis Russell: 'He compared French *rapide*, "express train", an argot term for *vin qui saoule rapidement* "wine which gets you drunk quickly"' (p.211). Dunkling also records that it has been suggested that 'highball is from a raised glass, resembling a train conductor's raised fist as a signal to depart'. The OED lists both the drink and 'A railway signal to proceed'.

Alan Reeve-Jones writes that a highball 'originally meant a tall, usually whisky, unflavoured spirit drink in the U.S.A. – as opposed to, say, a Julep. It is now indiscriminately used for various long iced spirit drinks topped with mineral or plain water' (p.98). However most highball recipes still specify whisky – usually 1½oz of American whiskey – served on ice in a straight six or eight-ounce highball glass, and in most recipes the drink is filled up with soda or ginger ale. 'He took the flowers out of a vase and poured the water out, and made himself the biggest highball he had ever seen. It did not last very long' (John O'Hara, *Appointment in Samarra*, 1935).

Highland Along with *Campbeltown*, *Islay* and *Lowland*, *Highland* is one of the four official regional classifications of Scottish malt whisky. For the purposes of whisky categorisation, Highland is now defined as an area north of a theoretical line which follows the old county boundaries between Greenock on the Firth of Clyde in the west and Dundee on the Firth of Tay in the east.

The term 'Highland' is first attested with regard to Scotland in *c*.1425 – being implied in *Highlandman*.

As well as being a specific geographic area of production, Highland can also be considered a generic term for a style of malt whisky, though there is unquestionably more stylistic diversity in this classification than in any of the other three. The Highland category of malt whiskies is the largest and most important in Scotland, with around 80 per cent of the country's operational distilleries being situated in this region, which includes the *golden square* or *triangle* of production where so many of Scotland's most highly prized malts are made.

The oldest Highland distillery is Glenturret in Perthshire, which was founded in 1775, and the classification embraces Highland Park and Scapa to the north in Orkney, Talisker on Skye to the west, the now *silent* Glenugie by Peterhead in the east and Glengoyne in the south. Glengoyne is situated just a dozen miles from the centre of Glasgow, and the distillery itself straddles the Highland line, though the Distillery Burn which provides its water is actually on the Highland side. By contrast, Auchentoshan and Littlemill distilleries are both geographically Lowland operations, though their water sources lie north of the Line.

Daiches makes the point that 'Campbeltown and Islays may also be regarded as Highland Malts from which the Highland Malts produced in the north-east of Scotland are often distinguished by being called Eastern Malts... I have in fact seen Highland malt whisky classified simply as Eastern Malts and Western Malts, the latter including Islays, Campbeltowns and Talisker' (*Scotch Whisky*, 23). Writing in the late 1940s, Marshall Robb divided malt whisky distilleries into three categories, namely Highland (of which he lists sixty-three), Lowland (ten), and West Highland, which included ten on Islay and four in Campbeltown, with Talisker being classified as a Highland malt. According to Cooper, 'In the nineteenth century malt whiskies were somewhat arbitrarily divided into five classes; Islay, Glenlivet, North Country, Campbeltown and Lowland' (*Century Companion*, 37). In other words, there was no such 'Highland' category as exists today.

The *Dictionary of Drink* describes Highland malts as 'Light and full flavoured whiskies', which is a necessarily sweeping generalisation. Oban, for example, is a West-coast malt described by United Distillers as being stylistically half-way between an Islay malt and a Highland Speyside malt, while Clynelish from Brora in Sutherland on the opposite coast is certainly closer in style to some Islay malts than it is to many Highlands. Such is the stylistic

range within the Highland category that, although there are no
official sub-divisions, many experts do sub-divide in order to
group similar malts together. Divisions such as Eastern Highland,
Island, Northern Highland, Perthshire and Speyside therefore
occur in the whisky industry. Grindal notes that many blenders
now classify the Campbeltown malts as Highland, and 'At the
same time it has become increasingly fashionable to divide the
Highland malts into two sub-divisions, Speyside malts and other
Highland malts' (p.32).

The great Scottish folklorist Calum MacLean, brother of the
poet Sorley, wrote in his excellent study of *The Highlands* that
the Highland area 'is divided from the Lowlands by a line which
is clearly observable on orographical maps and extends from
Stonehaven through Comrie and Aberfoyle to Helensburgh on
the west'. To the geologist this 'Highland line' is the 'Highland
Boundary Fault', with the Highland side consisting of older, harder rocks than are found in the Lowlands, but definitions of just
what is Highland vary considerably, with the inhabitants of parts
of the Grampian region and much of Caithness, for example,
certainly not considering themselves Highlanders.

The first official definition of the Highland area was made in
1784 when the Wash Act 'drew a formal distinction between the
Lowlands and the Highlands' as Daiches puts it, for the purposes
of differential *excise* legislation. Daiches points out that 'The
Highland line, which separated the two forms of duty, was pre-
cisely defined in the Act – the first time that a specified area of
Scotland was separated from the rest as the Highlands by Act of
Parliament' (*Scotch Whisky*, 33). Gunn picks out the main points
of the line as defined in the Act as follows: 'A certain line or
boundary beginning at the east point of Loch Crinan...Loch
Gilpin...Inverary, Arrochar, Tarbet, north side of Ben Lomond,
Callendar, Crieff, Dunkeld...Fettercairn...Clatt, Huntly,
Keith, Fochabers...Elgin and Forres, to the boat on the river
Findhorn...' (p.107). The Highland Line operated as a boundary
between two varying areas of excise operation until the introduction in 1816 of the Small Stills Act, and the whisky-making centre
of Campbeltown was originally included within the Highland area
for excise purposes, though in 1795 the definition was altered,
and Campbeltown distillers subsequently had to pay duty at the
higher Lowland rate.

Long before the Wash Act, the qualifying adjective 'Highland'
had been applied to whisky produced in 'the Highlands', however
imprecisely that term was used, rather than in the Lowlands.
Cooper points out that 'Ironically it was the invidious way in

which the duty was raised on the whisky produced in the legal distilleries in the Lowlands which gave the homemade Highland whisky its superior reputation. In order to avoid the pernicious Malt Tax of 1725 some of the Lowland distillers mixed unmalted *grain* with malted barley, sacrificing quality for quantity' (*Century Companion*, 9). By virtue of this fact – Burns called Lowland whisky 'a most rascally liquor' – the term Highland in relation to whisky frequently implied spirit of high quality. Cooper affirms that 'Historically the Highland malts were considered to be the finest of all, preferred in the early days of smuggling to the product of the licit Lowland distilleries which frequently used substandard wheat, unmalted *grain* and even oats and root crops in their *mash*' (op. cit., 37). He continues, 'The Highlands retained their reputation for good honest malt while the Lowland cities went on to become the great centres of grain distilling'.

hogshead   A large *cask* for liquids, the capacity of which traditionally varied according to the type of contents and the locality in which it was being used. A statute of 1423 prescribed the contents of a *hogshead* as fifty-one gallons of ale or beer, but in 1749 a hogshead of molasses was fixed at one hundred gallons, and for some contents it could have a capacity of up to one hundred and forty gallons.

The modern hogshead has a capacity of approximately fifty-five Imperial gallons or two hundred and fifty litres, and for the purposes of whisky storage and *maturation* it is usually made of American white oak.

The first use of hogshead is recorded in 1390, 'Clerico panetrie per manus Fyssher pro ij barellis et j hoogeshed vacuis per ipsum pro floure imponendo xviiid'. The current spelling first appears in 1674, and a number of variants are also recorded, such as *hoggeshedes* (1392), *hoggyshedys* (1467), *Hugshead* (1569), and *hogsed* (1578). Two Scottish dialect alternatives occur in *hogheids* (1577) and *hogheidis* (1634).

Hogshead also has the sense of a caskful of liquor, as well as being the name of the cask itself, and it can therefore be a liquid measure of fifty-five gallons or two hundred and fifty litres.

Boswell uses 'hogshead' figuratively in his *Journal of a Tour to the Hebrides* (1773) when he writes that 'This man is just a hogshead of sense'.

From an etymological point of view, 'hogshead' promises much, but sadly, as the OED points out, 'The reason of the name is uncertain'. The word *hog* 'originally had reference to the age or condition of the animal, rather than to either pig or sheep...'; further, the notion of 'yearling...runs through most of the uses'.

Perhaps, therefore, it may be conjectured that early applications of hogshead somehow referred to the vessel's use as a receptacle for young, immature spirit.

hooch   *The Dictionary of Drink* gives the colloquialism *hooch* simply as 'drink' in English usage, but specifies 'gin' in the United States, where the noun is chiefly used. It is usually, however, taken to mean alcoholic liquor in general, 'especially inferior or illicit' spirit, according to the OED.

The noun is used by McGuffin 'If the *hooch* was then watered down a man could easily turn his 5 dollars into 500 dollars' (p.55). 'Hooch' is an abbreviation of the Alaskan *Hoochinoo*, the name of a small Indian tribe renowned for liquor-making, and is first attested in the United States in 1897. According to Gyles Brandreth *(Modern Phrase and Fable)*, 'In the years of the Klondike gold rush at the end of the 19th century saloon-keepers there also distilled their own liquor, which acquired the same appellation'.

hot Irish   See *Irish, hot.*

I **nnocent** Illicitly distilled whisky, *moonshine* or *poitín*. The term was used in the Border counties of England and Scotland, and is recorded by R.W.F. Poole in the *Daily Telegraph* (11 July 1992); 'this area was once the haunt of Rory, one of the most notorious distillers of *"innocent"* (of *excise* duty, that is) whisky in the Borders'.

Irish *Irish* whiskey differs from *Scotch* in several important ways, not least of which is the use of the letter 'e', a characteristic shared with American whiskey, but strangely not with Canadian whisky.

By law, Irish whiskey has to be distilled and matured in Ireland for a minimum of three years, but as well as being a geographical definition 'Irish' is also a generic term for a distinctive style of spirit.

In their booklet *Irish Whiskey: The Water of Life*, Irish Distillers Ltd are more specific about the use of the word Irish, making the point that 'The Irish always order their whiskey by brand in a pub and you will never hear, except from a tourist, an order for "an Irish" or "a whiskey", but always "a Bushmills", "a Paddy" or "a Jameson".'

The first recorded use of 'Irish' relating to whiskey dates from 1893, 'Two bitters and a small Scotch . . . and a large Irish', though Partridge *(Historical Slang)* dates the term from *c.*1650, declaring it to be colloquial but very nearly standard English.

In distilling rather than linguistic terms, Irish whiskey is distinguished from Scotch in three principal ways. Despite the abundance of *peat* – or turf as the Irish call it – 'In the case of Irish whiskey, the malt is dried in a closed kiln retaining its own natural taste, whereas in Scotland it is dried over open peat fires which gives a smoky taste to the whisky' (Irish Distillers Limited promotional literature). Old Bushmills distillery, however, does briefly peat its malt, and this along with the fact that it uses only malt and no unmalted *barley* in its production means that stylistically its whiskey is a little closer to its Scotch neighbours across the water than are most Irish whiskies.

Jackson points out that 'In the matter of raw materials, Irish is unique among serious whiskies in that, as well as barley, an uncooked cereal is used. This is usually unmalted barley, though small proportions of wheat, rye, and, notably, oats have variously been employed' (*Pocket Bar Book*, 54). The barley distillate continues, however, to be the most significant in terms of the character of the finished whiskey. The use of unmalted barley dates back to the early eighteenth century and the introduction of the Malt Tax, and the ratio of malt to raw barley varies between 40:60 and 20:80.

In Ireland, this product is known simply as *pot-still* whiskey. Irish pot stills are usually larger than those found in Scotland, another factor which influences the difference in flavour between the two whiskies. Most Irish whiskies were straight pot-still whiskies until relatively recent times, but many are now the products of *blending* pot-still whiskies and continuous-still grain whiskies, the trend in recent years being towards producing a lighter spirit with a higher grain content. This progression has not been to everyone's liking, Jackson expressing the opinion that 'It would be not only Ireland's loss but also the world's if Hibernia settled for a bastard version of Scotch in order to meet an international taste for the light, the bland and the innocuous' (*Pocket Bar Book*, 55). The introduction in 1985 of Bushmills Single Malt would seem to offer hope to Jackson and his supporters, as would the production since 1989 of a malt whiskey at John Teeling's Cooley distillery in County Louth, the only legal Irish whiskey distilling operation outwith the control of Irish Distillers.

The triple distillation process is not unique to Ireland as is sometimes suggested (see *feints*) but it is certainly a characteristic of Irish distillation and very significant in shaping the ultimate style of the spirit. It gives Irish whiskey a purity and lightness of body, and the frequent absence of peat makes for a clean palate; Fleming describes it as having 'a mellow roundness and faint oiliness' (p.21). In 1755 Dr Johnson differentiated between Scotch whisky and Irish whiskey in his *Dictionary* on the basis that 'The Irish sort is particularly distinguished for its pleasant and mild flavour. The Highland sort is somewhat hotter...'.

With regard to the history of Irish whiskey, Cooper has no doubts that Irish came before Scotch, declaring that 'long before *uisge* was distilled in Scotland the art flourished in Ireland, where the oldest distillery in the world was established on the banks of the river Bush in 1608' (*Century Companion*, 150). Bushmills was certainly the first distillery to be granted a licence (in 1608), but there are references to Henry II's soldiers drinking whiskey in Ireland in 1170, and it is recorded that in 1276 Sir Robert Savage of Bushmills fortified his troops prior to battle with 'a mighty draught of *uisce beathe*', making it more than likely that a distillery of sorts existed on that part of the Antrim coast even then.

In his *History of Ireland* (1577) Raphael Holinshed wrote of the medicinal properties of what he termed *aqua vitae*, recording that the people of Ireland drank it to counteract 'distillations, reumes and flixes' caused by the wet and boggy nature of the country they inhabited. The long and extravagant list of claims for whiskey – which Holinshed says were originally made by Theoricus – includes the opinion that 'it sloeth age, it strengtheneth youth, it helpeth digestion, it cutteth fleume, it abandoneth melancholy, it relisheth the hart, it lighteneth the mind, it quickeneth the spirites...'. Not surprisingly, after much more of the same, Holinshed concludes 'truly it is a soueraigne liquor, if it be orderly taken'.

In 1604 the playwright John Marston wrote
> The Dutchman for a drunkard
> The Dane for golden locks
> The Irishman for uisca beatha
> The Frenchman for the pox

and Queen Elizabeth I was thought to have had a taste for Irish whiskey, probably being introduced to the spirit by Sir Walter Ralegh, who recorded receiving in County Cork 'a supreme present of a 32-gallon cask of the Earl of Cork's home-distilled uisce beatha'.

By the late eighteenth century some two thousand stills were making whiskey in Ireland, and it is thought that by 1823 up to two-thirds of all spirit sales in Ireland were of illegally distilled *poitín*. The late eighteenth century saw legal distilling grow into a serious industry with many new distilleries being constructed, notably in Cork and Dublin, and when Alfred Barnard visited Ireland in the 1880s there remained twenty-eight in production.

It is often forgotten that, until the early years of the twentieth century, Irish was far better known than Scotch as a drink in England, and indeed throughout the rest of the world. In the United States more than four hundred brands of Irish were on sale by the time of *prohibition*, and it was principally that particular piece of American legislation that brought about the downfall of the Irish whiskey industry. Not only did Irish whiskey lose a major share of its markets overnight, but its reputation in America suffered from the actions of unscrupulous *bootleggers* who sold all kinds of inferior spirits under the name of Irish whiskey. The Irish War of Independence (1919-21) and the subsequent trade war with Britain also prevented Irish whiskey access to English and Empire markets. For the thrusting entrepreneurs of blended Scotch this was a heaven-sent opportunity to increase sales on an unprecedented scale, and Irish whiskey never really recovered.

Long before prohibition was enacted, the blending industry

had already dealt Irish pot still whiskey makers a serious blow by 'adulterating' their product with large quantities of grain whiskey and marketing it in England under the name of 'Irish whiskey'. In many cases, as little as 20 per cent of the contents was what was generally recognised by that name, the rest being grain spirit, but the English public developed a taste for the light and easily mixed drink, to the understandable chagrin of the Dublin pot-still distillers.

Soon Irish distillers jumped on the bandwagon themselves, and before the turn of the century grain whiskey was being manufactured in Belfast, Cork, Dundalk, Limerick and Londonderry. The Dublin men enlisted the support of some powerful allies, including the medical journal *The Lancet*, which drew attention to the potential pitfalls of drinking what Magee describes as 'premature spirit of dubious origin'.

The controversy raged until the pronouncement of the Royal Commission of 1908/9 regarding what had become known as the 'What is Whisky?' case. This represented, of course, the ultimate triumph for the blending interests, with 'whiskey' being defined as 'a spirit obtained by distillation from a mash of cereal grains saccharified by the diastase of malt'. Irish whiskey was simply 'whiskey, as above defined, distilled in Ireland'. The effects of the 'What is Whisky?' case on the Irish pot distillers, along with the effects of prohibition in the United States and lost English and Empire markets, meant that many of Ireland's smaller distilleries were forced to close. Once prohibition was repealed in 1933, Irish distillers were unable to supply the renewed demand for their whiskey in the United States, and again the blended Scotch salesmen were only too happy to come to the rescue and assuage the thirst of American drinkers.

By 1968 only five Irish distilleries were still working, and in that year they combined to form the Irish Distillers Group. It was subsequently decided to concentrate most of their production in a new and very advanced plant at Midleton in County Cork, alongside the existing Midleton distillery, which re-opened in 1992 as a visitor centre and whiskey museum.

The new operation was fired-up in 1975, when it was the first distillery to have been built in Ireland for more than a century. By contrast the group's only other distillery which remains in production is Old Bushmills on the north Antrim coast, the oldest licensed distillery in the world. This plant produces a whiskey made from 100 per cent malted barley, marketed as Bushmills Malt, and it is also a principal constituent of the *de luxe* blend Black Bush and the standard Bushmills blend.

Midleton is a uniquely flexible distillery, with a dozen different *single* whiskeys being made under one roof, and these, along with the product of Bushmills, are the components of almost all Irish whiskeys. As Irish Distillers explain, 'Each of these is triple distilled through a different permutation of linked stills, pot or column. Each is produced from a different combination of malt and barley or grain. Each is matured for a different period in a different type of cask.' Midleton can produce 6.5m *proof* gallons of whiskey per year, while Bushmills, an old-fashioned pot-still distillery, has an annual capacity of one million proof gallons of whiskey per year.

The amalgamation of Irish whiskey interests into Irish Distillers Group (a subsidiary of Pernod-Ricard since that firm won a bitter takeover battle with Grand Metropolitan in 1988) brought together the great Dublin distilling names of Jameson and Power, along with the Cork Distilleries Company, manufacturers of the Paddy brand. Jameson is currently the world's largest selling Irish whiskey, and the firm's Dublin distillery was built in 1780 in Bow Street, where the Irish Whiskey Corner is now a museum dedicated to the history of the spirit, though distilling ceased there in 1971. The Irish are not always too quick to point out that the founder of the company, John Jameson, was actually a Scot! The writer and bon vivant Sir Clement Freud described Jameson as 'a hot cross bun of a whiskey' when writing in *Sporting Life* about the variety of liquid refreshment on offer at the Punchestown festival of National Hunt racing in April 1992.

If Jameson is the world's best selling Irish whiskey, then Power's Gold Label is the favourite in the domestic market. Like Jameson, John Power set up in business in Dublin – in 1791 – during what Irish Distillers describe as 'the golden age of Irish whiskey'. By the mid-nineteenth century there were four principal distilleries in operation in Dublin, and as Magee puts it, 'There were a dozen or more distilleries around the country, all of them regarded, it would seem, with a certain disdain by the metropolitan manufacturers as being of an inferior class' (p.21). Indeed, Dublin firms tended to spell their product with an 'e' to differentiate it from the spirits of their provincial competitors.

The second most widely drunk whiskey in Ireland is Paddy, formerly produced in Cork by the Cork Distilleries Company Ltd, and notably popular with younger drinkers, while Tullamore Dew is the lightest and most mellow of all the Irish whiskeys, and is therefore ideal for use in Irish coffee. In common with most brands of Irish it is also particularly suitable for *cocktails* because of its lack of peatiness. Formerly produced in the town of Tullamore,

County Offaly, by the firm of Williams, who now manufacture the popular *liqueur* Irish Mist, Tullamore Dew has a strong following in Europe.

Though likely to make the purist shudder, it is a fact that in recent years the international profile of Irish whiskey has been significantly raised by the part it has played in Irish coffee. This beverage is actually a variation on the traditional Irish drink of sweetened tea with whiskey, and usually consists of coffee, sugar, whiskey and cream. It was invented at Shannon airport on the West Coast of Ireland in 1952 by chef Joe Sheridan, who served it one cold evening to an American journalist who introduced it to the 'Buena Vista' on Fisherman's Wharf overlooking San Francisco Bay. The 'Buena Vista' now serves more than two thousand Irish coffees per day. Jackson considers that Irish whiskey has 'shoulders broad enough to shrug with compliant amusement when it is required to perform hot toddies, flirt with coffee, or be married to chocolate in "Irish Cream" liqueurs' (*World Guide*, 101).

Irish, hot   Colloquial name used in Ireland for a punch made with cloves and cinnamon, *Hot Irish* is popular in Irish bars during winter months and is often available at sporting events such as race meetings, where it can be invaluable as an aid to the thawing of extremities after watching your punts fall in a three-mile steeplechase at Fairyhouse or Clonmel. Irish Distillers' own recipe for Hot Irish is as follows: 'Stud a lemon with four cloves. Into a stemmed glass put one measure of Irish Whiskey, two teaspoons of sugar (preferably brown) and the lemon. Fill with boiling water and add a pinch of cinnamon.'

Islay   As with the other three recognised Scottish malt whisky classifications which have been generally accepted since the nineteenth century, *Islay* is defined both by geographical parameters and by stylistic cohesion. From at least the late eighteenth century whiskies produced on the island of Islay have been noted for their individuality of flavour, though Thomas Pennant observed when he visited Islay in 1772 that 'in old times the distillation was from thyme, mint, anise, and other fragrant herbs...'. Neil Wilson makes the point that fifty years prior to Pennant's visit only one-eighth of the grain grown on Islay was barley, and that distilling was a comparatively small-scale and croft-orientated activity (p.15). Jackson maintains that the island's 'geographical position suggests a longer history of distilling than records show' (*World Guide*, 41), which makes sense if the theory that distilling was introduced to the west of Scotland from Ireland is to be believed. The Antrim coast of Ireland is, after all, just a dozen miles from Islay. Barnard in 1887 recognised the Islay whiskies as comprising a distinctive classification, writing of Ardbeg that 'The make is pure Islay Malt'.

The name *Islay* is first recorded in *c*.690 as *Ilea*, and according to Johnston *(Place Names of Scotland)* is probably Old Celtic for 'swollen place'. The island has been settled since the Middle Stone Age. It is the largest and most southerly of the Inner Hebrides, with *peat* cover over some 25 per cent of its surface area. It has a population of four thousand and an economy largely geared to farming, fishing, tourism and distilling. The last named activity is still of major importance, and McDowall makes the point that 'No island in the world owes more to whisky than Islay and there are few blends which do not owe something to an Islay whisky' (p.43).

Seven distilleries – all with coastal locations – currently operate on the island, providing the government with around £150 million a year in duty, and it is interesting to consider why such a relatively large-scale distilling industry has survived on Islay – with only Lochindaal at Port Charlotte and Port Ellen distilleries having ceased production this century – compared to the former great whisky centre of *Campbeltown*, just a few miles to the east. The answer would seem to lie in the island's abundance of peat and the distinctive nature of the Islay malts, and consequently the crucial role that comparatively small quantities of them have always played in *blending*. When Alfred Barnard visited Islay he noted that 'ten years ago there were but few distilleries in Islay, but the increasing demand for this valuable make of Whisky for blending purposes, encouraged further enterprise in the extension of existing Distilleries and the erection of new ones' (p.35). Ardbeg, Lagavulin and Laphroaig are situated on the southern shore of Islay, the island's oldest operational plant of Bowmore is in the centre, Scotland's most westerly distillery is at Bruichladdich, and Bunnahabhain and Caol Ila are situated in the north-east.

Sometimes the *West Highland* category has been used to encompass Islay and Campbeltown malt whiskies, though this is now almost obsolete. Islays are, of course, 'island' whiskies – and some commentators lump them together with malts from Mull, Orkney and Skye in such an informal category – but they are worthy of their own classification on the grounds of stylistic similarities which are not shared, certainly not to the same degree at any rate, by the other island malts.

Hills writes that Ledaig malt whisky from Mull is 'an island malt for dwellers in a semi rather than a blackhouse' (p.189)! The

implication is that most Islay malts are best left to the more local
or certainly more experienced nose and palate, though as we shall
see the Islay category embraces a considerable range of whiskies.
It is basically true to say that Islay malt whiskies can be characterised as having the 'strongest' flavours of all Scottish malts;
they are the weightiest, most heavily peated and most pungent.
The implication that Islays are not for the novice malt-drinker is
echoed by most commentators, and even many experienced
whisky drinkers find them almost too much of a good thing.
Words such as 'uncompromising' are used to describe Islays, and
Jackson writes of their 'seaweedy, iodine-like, phenolic character'
(*Companion*, 16). It has been said that Islays can taste like TCP
or hospital gauze, though quite why anyone should have tasted
hospital gauze in order to make the comparison remains obscure.
Jackson considers Caol Ila 'so oily it reminds me of olives in brine'
(*Observer*, December 1991), which hardly seems to make the
whisky a marketing man's dream, though it must be said that in
other places Caol Ila has been described in terms that make it
seem more palatable, and if it is more difficult to find than it was
a century ago – when it was so popular that supplies had to be
rationed – it remains an extremely desirable drink, well worth
the search.

'A geographical accident, but not a bad one,' says the manager
of Laphroaig distillery, Iain Henderson, when asked why he considers Islay to be such a great whisky-making island, producing
such a stylistically unique product. Clearly two of the determining
factors of the Islay style are peat and the proximity of the sea.

The peat takes a seaweed aroma from the sea breezes and also
contains sea vegetation. This 'briny' characteristic is passed on
to the water which flows through it and is subsequently used to
steep the barley in the island's three malting plants, at Bowmore
and Laphroaig distilleries and at the maltings in Port Ellen. The
peat water is also used in each distillery during the *mashing* process. Peat is utilised in varying degrees to dry the grain, with each
distillery having its own formula for peated barley malt, and it
stamps its trademark on the eventual whisky during this malting
stage.

During *maturation* in coastal warehouses the sea air penetrates
the whisky barrels, and few modern commentators would agree
with Barnard's contention that 'the Distillers maintain that the
sea air has no effect whatever on the Whisky, and that the pecul-
iarity of the Islay make arises principally from the flavour of the
peat, dug in the island, and which is more strongly impregnated
with moss than some other districts' (p.116).

Though Islay malts share stylistic characteristics, it is interesting to consider the differences between the products of the various distilleries. Having tasted five of the Islay malts, Cooper was amazed by the 'subtle differences between them. The medical flavour of Laphroaig, the less powerful Lagavulin, the rich Bruichladdich, the fruity Bowmore and the peaty Ardbeg are all evidence that even in a micro-climate like Islay, the product of a pot still can be perpetually unpredictable' (*Century Companion*, 39). The three whiskies produced on the southern shores of Islay are generally considered to be the most 'briny' and archetypally Islay in style, with Lagavulin and Laphroaig vying for the title of regional 'classic'. Laphroaig is probably the best known of all the Islays, with HRH The Prince of Wales being known to take a *dram* of the fifteen-year-old version. Daiches calls it 'perhaps the most distinctive of all Islay whiskies', and its distinctiveness can partly be explained by the fact that the peat used during *malting* contains an even higher concentration of moss than most Islay peat. There is a greater tendency to gentleness in the whiskies from further north, though Caol Ila (Gaelic for Sound of Islay) is rather drier and more peaty than one might expect. The traditional Islay characteristics are sufficiently muted in Bunnahabhain for Hills to consider it 'An Islay for those who don't like Island whiskies' (p.106).

Not surprisingly, malt whisky from the now *silent* Port Ellen distillery is the rarest of all the Islay whiskies, and is obviously destined to become even more scarce, with little or no prospect of a resumption of distilling. In terms of flavour it is medium-bodied and comparatively lightly peated for a southern Islay malt. Dwarfing the distillery is a large malting plant, erected in 1973 and producing malt which is used to some extent by all seven working Islay distilleries.

The last word on Islay whiskies goes to Michael Jackson, who considers them to be 'the most Scottish of whiskies', and maintains that 'Theirs is the character that makes a blended Scotch unmistakably Scottish, and thank heaven for that' (*World Guide*, 36).

J igger The name given to a measure of spirits, specifically for use in *cocktails*, and also to the measuring vessel itself. According to Jackson, 'Since most classic cocktails originate from the Americas, the "jigger" used in bars in the United States is a common basic measurement in recipes. A jigger contains 1½ US ounces...' (*Pocket Bar Book*, 19). Chapman *(American Slang)* considers the *jigger* equivalent to a *shot glass*.

The word 'jigger' is first recorded in 1824 as a slang term for an illicit distillery – 'He said Probert and two others were in the jigger at Gill's Hill' – and the term *jigger stuff* as a slang allusion to the product of an illicit distillery occurs in 1851: 'They carry about their persons pint bladders of "stuff" or "jigger stuff".' Partridge *(Historical Slang)* lists no fewer than twelve different slang senses of 'jigger', and he considers that with regard to what he terms 'a private or secret still' jigger was current from the 1820s until *c.*1910, while 'jigger stuff' dates from *c.*1840 to 1900, probably having underworld origins.

Partridge notes, too, the term *jigger worker* (*c.*1840-1905), 'A vendor of illicitly distilled spirits', and also 'a drinker of whisky especially if illicitly distilled'. The past participle *jiggered*, with the sense of having been made from an illicit still, is said by Partridge to date from *c.*1880, first being recorded in 1886: 'jiggered gin'.

The modern cocktail-related use of jigger probably evolves from the occurrence of the word as an American synonym for *dram* in 1889, 'After giving him two small "jiggers", the civilities were brought to an end.' Three years later A.E. Lee *(History of Colombus)* is more specific about the size of such a jigger, writing that 'The "jigger" was a dram of less than a gill, taken (5 times a day)'.

juice of the barley See *barley, juice of the*.

julep, mint A *cocktail* which Jackson considers to be 'Redolent of the South, with pulchritudinous young women lolling provocatively on the porch, or in a swing, waiting for a long drink to cool, or inflame, passions' (*Pocket Bar Book*, 120).

There are a number of variations of the *mint julep*, with some barmen adding Angostura and some a touch of rum, but a basic recipe would be along the lines of muddling four fresh mint sprigs

107

with a teaspoon of sugar and either a little soda or water in a tall glass, then adding crushed ice and at least 2oz of whiskey. *Bourbon* is usually specified, but a blended Scotch could be substituted, and Fleming suggests that a julep could be made with Southern Comfort liqueur rather than Bourbon. Some recipes substitute brandy for whiskey, an Old Georgian Julep being made with brandy and peach brandy, while a Southern Mint Julep is made with liqueur brandy and peach brandy. Whatever the spirit employed, the drink is finished off with a garnish of mint, and opinion is sharply divided on whether or not it should be stirred before serving.

The word 'julep' is an adaptation of the Arabic *Julāb*, itself adopted from the Persian *gul-āb* rose-water, and in its original sense was simply a sweet drink, often just a liquid sweetened with sugar or syrup and taken with medicine. It is first recorded in *c.* 1400: 'To ȝene him in þe begynnynge Iulep – þat is a sirrup maad oonly of water and of sugre'. The figurative sense of something to cool or assuage the heat of passion first occurs in 1624: 'She is no fit electuary for a doctor: A coarse julap may well cool his worship'.

The first recorded reference to alcohol and the julep is made in an 1804 issued of the *European Magazine*, 'The first thing he did on getting out of bed was to call for a Julep; and I... date my own love of whiskey from mixing and tasting my young master's juleps.'

K **ieve** The Irish term for a *mash tun*. Magee writes, 'the distillery men continue to use the ancient terms which baffle the layman, strange words like grists, worts, worms, washes, tuns, kieves and backs' (p.10). *Kieve* is also used as a synonym for mash tun in the Irish brewing industry.

'Kieve' has its origins in the Old English *cyf*, which was later regularly spelled *keeve*, specifically a tub or vat for holding liquid during brewing or bleaching, though the *keeve* or *kive* was also used in the mining industry as a vessel in which copper or tin ore was washed. In *c.*1000 Ælfric wrote in *Homilies*, 'Se het afyllan ane cyfe mid weallendum ele' – 'he commanded a keeve to be filled with welling ale', and with a number of spelling variations kieve occurs in England, Ireland and Scotland. *Keeve* is recorded in Ireland in 1776 with reference to cider-making, and the current Irish distillation-related spelling is first recorded in an English publication in 1875.

The variant *kiver* also occurs, having the sense of a shallow wooden vessel or tub, not so specifically related to brewing. With the spelling *kevere* this is first attested in 1407, but the earliest written reference to alcohol production and kiver occurs in the *West Sussex Gazette* in 1884: 'Brew vat and stand, oval kiver, two 50-gallon casks'.

kiln During *malting* the *green malt* is dried in a *kiln*, and 'gives the typical malt distillery its best known feature: the pagoda-style roof, which will immediately identify an otherwise unremarkable collection of commercial buildings' (Morrice, 22). In Scotland the pagoda-roofed kiln dates from the 1750s, when the techniques of English maltsters were first copied. 'The kilns had tapering roofs to draw the heat from the furnace through the drying floor on which the malt was laid out', Moss explains (*Chambers*, 75); 'The kilns were capped with horizontal ventilators, often designed to look like the roofs of Chinese pagodas'. He says that earlier kilns were 'normally made of stone and shaped like a bowl in the ground, with an arched furnace beneath. The kiln would have been covered with a simple thatch and used for drying the barley and oats grown in the township as well as malt.'

The word 'kiln' comes from the Old English *cylene*, adopted from the Latin *culina* kitchen, cooking-stove, burning-place. The

109

first record of kiln occurs in *c.*725, and with specific reference to drying malt in *c.*1440 in *Promptorium Parvolorum*, 'kylne for malt drying'. The first use of kiln as a verb is recorded in 1715, 'It must be employed as soon as kiln'd', and ten years later, in his *Family Dictionary*, Bradley writes under the Malt heading: 'There is also another Error in drying and *kilning* of Malt'.

The purpose of kilning the green malt is to kill the germ of the growing grain, once germination to the required degree has been achieved. This is done by the application of heat, and in modern, purpose-built *maltings* fans spread hot, peat-flavoured air, and the processes of germination and kilning may take place in the same vessel. McDowall makes the point that 'Many of the new or reconditioned distilleries have no typical kiln house, or, if they have, they use it for other purposes' (p.102), but where the more traditional distillery-based maltings survive, green malt is spread on a perforated floor above a peat fire and is turned regularly during kilning. Hot air from the fire passes up through the malt, with ventilation being provided by the open pagoda head.

Once nothing but *peat* was burnt in distillery kilns in Scotland, but its principal role now is to provide flavour rather than heat, with more efficient fuels such as coal, coke and oil being employed after an initial period of peat-drying lasting some twenty-four hours. Anthracite and coke have been used in kilns for drying purposes since the late eighteenth century. Kiln temperatures are kept below 70°F so that the enzymes which are converting starch to sugar will not be destroyed, and the malt is dried until it has a final moisture content of only 3 or 4 per cent. The kilning time varies from around forty-eight hours in a traditional floor malt-ings, such as that at *Islay*'s Laphroaig distillery, to forty-two hours at Bowmore, where fans blow re-cycled heat through the green malt, and other fans above the floor draw the air up and thereby accelerate the drying process. Kilning takes as little as thirty-six hours in a modern plant such as Port Ellen on Islay. Once dried, the malt is ready to be turned into *grist* for *mashing*.

Lightning Now used almost exclusively in the United States and with the qualifying adjective 'white'. *White Lightning* is a synonym for *moonshine*, white implying new, unmatured and therefore usually illegal whiskey. The expression is first recorded in 1921, and was adopted for the vocabulary of the drugs culture in the early 1970s to refer to a kind of LSD.

Lightning is first attested in 1781 as a slang term for gin, 'Noggin of lightning, a quartern of gin', though it later came to mean 'any strong, often low-quality alcoholic spirit' *(Modern Slang)*. In 1851 'The stimulant of a flash of lightning' is recorded, and it is clearly that sense of lightning which is valid in this context; a swift, sharp and even dramatic drink of spirits, which makes the expression particularly apt for application to the often 'rough and ready' product of moonshine stills. White lightning is celebrated in the eponymous song, recorded by American country singer George Jones.

liqueur The French word for *liquor*, but now with a substantive meaning, given by Henry McNulty as 'a flavoured spirit, usually sweet, which can be based on any grain alcohol, brandy, whisky, rum, vodka, or any other pure alcohol' (p.68). The flavouring agent, which can be herbs, flowers, fruit, seeds or roots, is introduced to the spirit base by re-distillation, infusion or maceration. While the term *liqueur* is used in the United States, American drinkers also often use *cordial* as a synonym, and the *Encyclopaedia Britannica* records the use of 'liquor' as a synonym for 'liqueur' in 1797: 'Liquors of various sorts are compounded and distilled on Montpelier'. Almost a century later the *Encyclopaedia* noted that 'bitters form a class of liqueurs by themselves'. The first attestation of liqueur occurs in 1742: 'He... Try'd all *hors d'oeuvres*, all liqueurs defin'd, Judicious drank, and greatly-daring din'd'.

Some whisky blenders have been known to describe their product as 'liqueur whisky', but as Jackson points out, '"Liqueur whisky" has no real meaning, and such terms are falling out of use. A whisky liqueur is another thing altogether' *(World Guide, 26)*. Presumably the term 'liqueur' applied in the context of blended whisky was intended to convey a sense of sophistication – perhaps the French sound of the word was itself enough – and an 'after dinner' quality to the product. Dunkling makes the point that 'By

111

implication, a liqueur is of high quality, to be savoured rather than hastily gulped' (p.196). (See also *de luxe*). Ireland, Scotland and the United States all produce whisky-based liqueurs, a number being internationally known by their trade names and the romantic stories attached to their creation.

Irish Mist was the first Irish liqueur to be commercially marketed, being developed by the Williams family in the County Offally town of Tullamore, with the aid of a German refugee and liqueurist towards the end of the Second World War. The recipe which this liqueurist brought to Ireland is sometimes claimed to be the long-lost original Irish liqueur recipe which was taken to Europe by Irish refugees fleeing from the Tudor armies of England. Irish Mist is made from a blend of four *pot still* and *grain* Irish whiskeys, which are subjected to maceration with clover, heather, herbs and honey.

During the last two decades a new type of cream-based Irish liqueur has gained substantial sales around the world, and most drinks cupboards house a bottle of Bailey's Original Cream Liqueur around Christmas time, and frequently for many months afterwards. Though there have been a flattering number of imitators, Baileys was the first Irish cream liqueur, launched in 1974, and it is made with whiskey, cream, chocolate and additional flavourings. Grindal is less than flattering in his judgement on this particular drink, describing Bailey's as 'that Anglo-Irish low alcohol milk shake' (p.197).

The Scottish whisky-based liqueur Drambuie – considered by Jackson to be 'the oldest and most famous whisky liqueur' – can claim an even more romantic provenance than Irish Mist. It is reputedly made to a recipe given to the Mackinnons of Skye by Prince Charles Edward Stuart as a reward for their service during the failed Jacobite rebellion of 1745-6, when a Captain Mackinnon of Strathaird helped the prince escape from Skye to sanctuary in France. The prince's recipe had been devised for him when he was living in the French court. The distinctive, squat Drambuie bottle carries the slogan 'Prince Charles Edward's Liqueur. A link with the '45', and though the Drambuie Liqueur Company is now based in Edinburgh, it is still in the hands of the Mackinnon family, who are Britain's largest producers of liqueurs. The name *Drambuie* is usually said to be an Anglicisation of the Gaelic 'an *dram* buidheach', which translates as 'the drink that satisfies', but *dram buidhe* in Gaelic means 'golden drink', and the name could have originated with either phrase. Milsted suggests that the phrase 'the drink that satisfies' is merely a marketing man's invention which sounds more acceptable than the 'true' and slightly off-putting definition of 'yellow drink' (p.11). Drambuie shares stylistic characteristics with Irish Mist, being made principally from malt Scotch whisky and heather honey, flavoured with herbs.

Southern Comfort is the classic American liqueur, produced in St Louis, Missouri. 'One of the few indigenous American liqueurs, and surely the oldest', according to Jackson (*Pocket Bar Book*, 83), Southern Comfort is thought to have originated in a *cocktail* of *Bourbon* and peaches in either New Orleans or St Louis. The modern drink is certainly Bourbon-based, being flavoured with peaches, oranges and herbs, and Jackson considers it to be more of a flavoured whiskey than a true liqueur, due to its strength (50 per cent in the United States, though sold at 40 per cent in Britain) and its comparative dryness. The manufacturers of Southern Comfort recommend it for a number of cocktails, such as the *Manhattan*, *Old-fashioned* and *Whiskey Sour*.

liquid fire See *firewater*.

liquor In old French *licur*, *licour*, *likeur*, and modern French *liqueur*, adopted from the Latin *liquor* – liquidity. Used in the primary Latin sense of simply a liquid, matter in a liquid state, *liquor* is obsolete, though it is interesting to note that in *brewing* 'liquor' is still used to mean water. The first record of this usage occurs in 1741, 'The Day before you intend to brew, you should boil a Copper of Liquor, (Water being an improper Term in a Brew-house)'. In the current sense of liquid for drinking, and specifically a drink produced by fermentation and/or *distillation*, liquor is first attested prior to 1300, 'Dranc he neuer ar sli licur', and the first use of liquor with reference to its intoxicating effect dates from 1529, 'Thou hast wylde lycoure, the whiche maketh all thy stomacke to be on a flambe'. The phrase *in liquor* to connote *drunk* is first attested in *The Scots Magazine* in 1753. The term *liquor-back* – a synonym for the *washback* – is recorded in 1691.

Liquor gained currency as a slang term for an alcoholic drink from the 1860s in the United States, with *liquor-up* – an American equivalent of a *booze* or *piss*-up – being first attested in 1872, and though compounds such as *liquor store* are first recorded in Britain (1815), their use is now largely confined to America: 'on Sundays the bars did not open till two in the afternoon and the liquor stores did not open at all' (Charles Jackson, *The Lost Weekend*, 1944).

Some interesting extensions of 'liquor' occur in English usage, with Thomas Hardy coining the phrase 'Her liquor-fired face' in *Wessex Poems* (1898), whilst 'Some getting liquor-seasoned as they grow older' occurs in 1894, and from 1894 we find the transferred sense of liquor as a verb, meaning to adulterate spirits with water: 'They will be obliged to "liquor" their spirits – that is to say, they will dilute them with water.' The sense of supplying or plying with liquor is also recorded, first occurring in c.1560 as 'I thinke, he is at Alhouse, a lickeringe ones brayne', and the intransitive use of liquor as in 'It's a bargain then...come let's liquor on it' is recorded in 1839. The adjectives *liquorsome* – 'Men of shallow minds and liquorsome bodies' (1656) – and *liquorish* – 'A rare seaman but liquorish' (1894) – also occur. Ogden Nash observed in 'Reflection on Ice-breaking' in 1931 that 'Candy is dandy/But liquor is quicker'.

loch, whisky A phrase first coined in the mid-1980s to signify the Scotch whisky industry's equivalent to the European Community's notorious wine lake. The *loch* was created by over-production of both *malt* and *grain* whisky as demand for brown spirits fell due to changing consumer preferences during the late 1970s and early 1980s. The term 'whisky lake' has also been used, but generally by English commentators who failed to grasp the aptness of the Caledonian alternative.

Skipworth writes that 'In April 1985, the size of the "whisky lake" was believed to be the equivalent of two years' supply to the UK market alone!' (p.37). Relatively drastic rationalisation took place within the industry, The Distillers Company alone closing eleven of its forty-five operational malt distilleries in May 1983 and a further ten in March 1985, in an attempt, as they put it, to 'attain the requisite balance between maturing stocks of whisky and the anticipated level of future sales'. Neil Wilson noted that 'The malt sector had shrunk from 83.7% of its potential output in 1978 to 38.6% in 1982...' (p.85), and victims of the two rounds of DCL closures included such famous names as Dallas Dhu on Speyside and Port Ellen on Islay, while the Highland capital of Inverness lost its entire distilling capacity with the closure and subsequent demolition of Glen Albyn and Glen Mhor in 1983 and Millburn in 1985.

In a *Daily Telegraph* feature of February 1985, John Williams profiled the Highland village of Carron where 'Imperial is one of 10 SMD plants scheduled to close with the loss of 180 jobs from Montrose to Alness because of a "whisky loch".' Happily, Imperial is now back in production in the ownership of Allied Distillers, as fortunes in the distilling industry have improved, with malt production having risen from a mid-1980s low of less than 100 million litres of pure alcohol per annum to almost 200 mlpa in 1990.

Lomond still A short-necked type of *still* developed by Hiram

Walker & Sons Ltd, producing a comparatively heavy and oily malt whisky. The short neck gives a low degree of reflux – condensing of vapours in and on the neck of the still. The name *Lomond* was given to this design of still, which was installed in 1938 within what is now Allied Distillers' Ballantines complex at Dumbarton, as the plant draws its water from nearby Loch Lomond. The whisky it produces has never been released as a single malt, going exclusively for *blending*.

Jackson describes the still as having 'a passing resemblance to a brandy alembic' (*World Guide*, 30), and Morton describes it as resembling 'an oversized, upside-down dustbin made of copper, or the expanded head of Dorothy's tin man. Instead of being boiled with heat applied from below, the *Lomond still* has steam pipes inside its jacket, thus giving, so it is said, a heavier, oilier result' (p.40).

low flyer A colloquial name for the popular blended Scotch whisky 'The Famous Grouse', principally used by Scots ghillies or gamekeepers, and emanating from the game bird's characteristic low flight, though no written attestation can be traced. The grouse is the national game bird of Scotland, so it is fitting that it should have been adopted for the country's national drink, first being used in 1897 by Perth whisky company, Matthew Gloag and Son Limited, who marketed their whisky as The Grouse Brand. According to Morrice, 'As its popularity increased in and around Perth it was increasingly referred to as "The Famous Grouse" until that was eventually adopted as the registered brand name' (p.235).

The International Ornithological Congress has announced the aim of standardising the international English names of bird species, with the red grouse to be officially designated the willow ptarmigan. It seems unlikely, however, that Highland Distilleries Co. – of which Matthew Gloag is now a subsidiary – will take to marketing their product as 'The Famous Willow Ptarmigan'.

low wines In the *pot still* whisky-making process, *low wines* are the product of the first distillation in the *wash still*. They are impure and weak, consisting of alcohol, secondary constituents and water, and a second distillation in the *spirit* or low wines *still* is subsequently necessary. McDowall notes that 'Every 2,500 gallons of wash will produce from 500 to 600 proof gallons of low wines...' (p.106). The low wines are stored between distillations in a low wines *charger*. The term 'low wines' is not exclusive to the whisky industry, being current, for example, in Jamaican rum-making circles.

'Low' here clearly has the sense of wanting in strength, weak;

a sense first attested in 1398, 'Dryness makyth the body lene and lowe', and the term 'low wines' first occurs in 1641: 'There will come forth a weak Spirit, which is called low Wine'. The plural use, which is now always employed, is first recorded in 1657, 'wines' being used because rectified spirit alcohol is also known as spirit(s) of wine. The first specific reference to low wines in the context of whisky distillation occurs in 1790, with the Scots spelling variant *lowins*, 'Whauks o'gude ait – far'le cowins, Synt down wi' whey, or whisky lowins'. (See also *congenerics*, *singlings*).

Lowland   As with the other three generally recognised Scotch whisky-producing regions, *Lowland* is a strictly interpreted geographical area and also has a style of its own. 'Lowland' was first applied in relation to Scotland in 1631, 'The necessitie of his advis doeth ofttymes invite him to the Lowlandis'.

The Lowland appellation is applied to whiskies produced in that mainland area south of the theoretical *Highland* line, and it is fair to say that Lowland whiskies can be characterised as the lightest of the Scottish malts, Jackson writing that 'The Lowlands tend to produce whiskies in which the softness of the malt itself is more evident, untempered by Highland peatiness or coastal brine and seaweed' (*Malt Whisky Companion*, 12). Grindal is inclined to view rigid categorisation of malts with some suspicion, making the perfectly valid point that 'The division of distilleries into Highland and Lowland was originally made for licensing purposes and not because of any differences in the whisky' (p.33). He also remarks that 'Glengoyne is only fractionally north of the Highland Line, just as Auchentoshan is fractionally to the south of it, and to pretend that this purely geographical division should have any material effect on the whisky that the two produce seems absurd' (p.65).

Historically speaking, Lowland malts have received a far from generous press, Robert Burns famously describing in a letter of 1788 the products of such southern stills as 'a most rascally liquor'. The no-doubt real inferiority of much Lowland whisky was in many ways attributable to the iniquities of the *excise* laws which served to discriminate against it until 1816, when Highland and Lowland duties became equable. There was, however, a phenomenal level of growth in Lowland distilling in the wake of the *Wash Act* of 1784, many new distilleries being constructed and ambitious programmes of expansion taking place at existing plants. It is interesting to note that not all of the *make* was whisky, James Stein's Kilbagie distillery in Clackmannanshire being equipped to produce nearly five thousand gallons of gin per day for sale to London.

More than half a century after the levelling of duty across the
Highland Line, Alfred Barnard was little more impressed with
Lowland whisky than Burns had been. Writing about blending,
he was of the opinion that 'Lowland malts alone, without Highland whiskies, would be of little use; the best makes are useful
as padding when they have considerable age and not too much
flavour, for they not only help to keep down the price of a blend,
but are decidedly preferable to using a large quantity of grain
spirit' (quoted in Cooper, *Century Companion*, 38). This negative
view of Lowland malts has persisted until more recent times.
When McDowall wrote *The Whiskies of Scotland* in 1967, he
remarked that of the Lowlands only Bladnoch and Rosebank were
available as *single* malts, commenting that 'It is of some interest
that the Lowland malts were the first whiskies to be drunk in
quantity in England, and about 1850 most larger towns in the
south of Scotland had a distillery'. Doubtless the Lowland malts
found favour in England because of their lightness when compared with the more intimidating Highland malts of the earlier
nineteenth century. Cooper is of the opinion that the Lowland
malts may have suffered because the distilleries where they are
made tend to be less visually pleasing and dramatically situated
than their counterparts north of the 'Line', a view echoed by
Daiches, who admits that Highland malts are whiskies 'of greater
character and grander flavour' (*Scotch Whisky*, 162), but considers
that 'a well-matured Lowland malt is – especially for those who
do not prefer a heavily peated whisky – a pleasant and civilized
drink of distinctive quality and makes a good all-purpose whisky.'

As interest in malt whiskies has increased during the past few
years, a modest though welcome renaissance in Lowland fortunes
has been in evidence, with United Distillers choosing the previously very elusive Glenkinchie from Pencaitland near Edinburgh
for its heavily promoted line up of 'Classic Malts'. Five Lowland
malts are now generally available, with triple-distilled Rosebank
from Falkirk usually being considered the regional 'classic'.
McDowall thought Rosebank to be not dissimilar to the relatively
light and delicate Highland malt Glenmorangie. The second surviving Lowland distillery to use a triple-distillation process is
Auchentoshan, which lies almost in the shadow of the Erskine
Bridge, to the north of Glasgow. Littlemill distillery is situated
at Bowling, between Glasgow and Dumbarton, and until the
1930s the make was triple-distilled. Littlemill is one of the oldest
distilleries in Scotland, reputedly founded in 1772, and it produces a whisky described by Milroy as 'mellow-flavoured, light,
slightly cloying yet pleasant and warming' (p.10).

If Littlemill is probably Scotland's oldest distillery, Bladnoch is indisputably Scotland's most southerly distillery, situated in the village of Bladnoch in Galloway. Sadly that distinction did not prevent it from becoming a victim of United Distillers' decision to close four malt whisky plants in early 1993. Bladnoch single malt is described by Jackson as having 'a very delicate aroma, with a distinctively lemony character, but (it) becomes bigger in its sweet palate' (*World Guide*, 31).

lush   The principal current drink-related sense of *lush* is, as *The Dictionary of Drink* states, as American slang for 'A heavy drinker, especially a female one (an alcoholic)', which perhaps reflects its more usual sense of juicy, luxuriant. The OED also considers it to mean alcoholic liquor, or, as a verb, to ply with alcoholic liquor, though these uses are now almost obsolete. *The Oxford Dictionary of Modern Slang* when referring to lush as an alcoholic or drunkard notes 'From earlier sense, alcoholic drink; perhaps a jocular use of lush (adjective), luxuriant'.

Lush is first attested in 1790 as a slang synonym for alcoholic drink itself, and the OED suggests this usage may have its origins in the earlier sense of lush as a stroke or blow, first recorded in the fourteenth century *Morte D'Arthur*, 'With the lussche of the launce he lyghte one hys schuldyrs' (cf. *shot, slug*). By 1841 'lush' had also taken on the meaning of a drinking bout – Colonel Hawker recording in his diary, 'We ended the day with a lush at Vérys' – and it had also developed a transitive sense of plying with lush or drink, just as *liquor* took on a verb sense. 'We had lushed the coachman so neatly, that Barney was obliged to drive' (1821). Intransitively it had the sense of to drink, or indulge in drink (1811), 'Smoke, take snuff, lush', and in 1829 Sir Walter Scott wrote in his journal of 'Cigars in loads, whisky in lushings'. *Lushy* or *lushey* as slang for drunk is attested in 1811, and in 1861 the adjectival sense of lushing is applied to a London prostitute known as 'Lushing Loo'.

Partridge notes the use of *lush*-ken or *lushing*-ken (suggesting that *ken* may be 'a corruption of Romany *tan*, a place, or a corruption of the original whence *tan* itself springs') to connote a low public-house or bar in the late eighteenth century. The term is synonymous with *lush-crib* (Partridge here suggests *crib* as lodgings, public house, from crib as a low synonym for bed from c.1810), *lushery* and *lush-house* (pre 1896).

The principal modern sense of 'lush' as a synonym for a drunkard is almost certainly a contraction of 'lushington', which comes from a punning use of the surname Lushington, itself alluding back to 'lush'. In 1840 'The Lushington of each young Doctor's

Commons' is recorded, though in 1823 'dealing with Lushington' had been noted as meaning taking too much drink. Partridge considers 'Lushington the brewer' to be one possible origin, and the OED records that 'The City of Lushington' was the name of a convivial society (consisting chiefly of actors) which met at the Harp Tavern, Russell Street until about 1895. It had a 'Lord Mayor' and four 'aldermen', presiding over 'wards' called Juniper, Poverty, Lunacy, and Suicide. On the admission of a new member, the 'Lord Mayor' (of late years at least) harangued him on the evils of excess in drink. As the 'City' claimed to have existed for 150 years, it may be that lush in any of its drink-related forms actually dates from a period considerably prior to the first attestation.

lyne arm The wide-diameter pipe which attaches the head of the *still* to the *worm* or condenser. Explaining the process of whiskey distillation, Magee likens the still to a large copper kettle: 'When the *wash* comes to the boil the vapours are conveyed along the lyne arm or "spout" of the kettle into the worm...' (p.11). The *lyne arm* is far more than just a connecting pipe, however, as the angle at which it is raked is considered to be a significant factor in the style of whisky produced. Cooper recalls being told by one distiller of a plant where the lyne arm was on a pulley, with the angle being altered depending on whether heavy or light spirit was required (*Century Companion*, 156). He was unable to decide whether this anecdote was a significant addition to his knowledge of distilling or simply a skilful joke. Grindal lends the story credibility by recalling a visit he made to an unnamed distillery where the officials claimed 'that by adjusting the heads of the stills they were able to produce different whiskies' (p.209).

> Some lynne arms [*sic*] curve like the tops of coat hangers. Others wiggle away in right angles. Some are narrow, some wide. The lynne arms at Talisker go straight out horizontally, as if to suggest there will be no nonsense at Talisker. The lynne arms at Macallan are extraordinarily thick – about fourteen inches in diameter – and slope downward on a gentle grade. (McPhee, 113)

At several distilleries, including the well known Glen Grant, a condenser known as a purifier has been fitted into the lyne arm to increase the reflux of condensing of vapours in and on the neck.

The lyne arm is also sometimes known as a 'lying arm', 'lying' having the sense of reclining, resting, being in a horizontal position, which is approximately physically appropriate in the distilling sense. Obsolete now except in distilling circles, 'lyne' is a form of *lean*, from the Old English *lēan*, and arm in the sense of what the OED terms 'a narrower portion or part of anything projecting from the main body', first recorded in c.885 relating to an arm of the sea. In the context of machinery, or any references not applied to sea or land, *arm* is first attested in 1833, 'On a projecting arm...'.

M **ac, whisky** A simple whisky *cocktail* usually consisting of two measures of Scotch whisky and two of green ginger wine – of which the Edinburgh firm of Crabbie produces the best known version – served in an *Old-fashioned glass*. Some recipes suggest rather less wine than whisky, perhaps proportions of two-thirds to one-third.

Grindal describes the *whisky mac* as being 'old enough to be an institution in Scotland' (p.198), and unlike most cocktails its origins are clearly Scottish rather than American. It is very much a 'winter warmer' of a drink, ideal, as Grindal suggests, as an accompaniment to the sport of curling or after a cold round of golf. The genesis of the name is unclear, though 'mac' serves to root the drink firmly in the Celtic tradition. *Mac* is the Gaelic word for 'son', which of course occurs in many Scots and Irish names of Celtic origin, so something along the lines of 'son of whisky', 'a drink from whisky' is a plausible possibility. It may also have the sense of a diminutive, a 'diluted' form of the original.

McCoy, the Real Most whisky writers confidently assert that this expression, which is parallel in meaning and application to *the Real Mackay*, has its origins in the *Prohibition* period in America, though one alternative view dates it to the last decade of the nineteenth century. Whichever version is preferred, it seems likely that it was taken up in the States as a mild pun on the extant Scottish expression 'the Real Mackay', and its first attestation occurs in 1922.

The popular story goes that when supplies of spirits were carried by ship from various locations – most notably the Bahamas – for illegal sale and consumption in America, the ships would lie at anchor while small boats operated by *bootleggers* would sail out to buy supplies of spirits, the stretch of coast between Atlantic City and Boston becoming known as 'Rum Row' because of this trade. ('Rum' was often used during prohibition to denote any alcoholic drink.) One man who regularly sailed between Nassau and Rum Row was Captain William McCoy, of Scots origin and living in Florida, who began running liquor in 1921 using a schooner named *Arethusa*. By this time suppliers and distillers were often meeting the immense consumer demand with very poor quality liquor, and McCoy decided to make his reputation by supplying high quality

121

products, chiefly Scotch whisky. This strategy worked well, to
the considerable financial benefit of McCoy, whose name entered
the English language as a result of the reputation he acquired. In
particular, McCoy ran large quantities of the popular blended
whisky Cutty Sark for the London firm of Berry Bros and Rudd
Ltd, and as Neil Wilson puts it, 'under his pilotage "Cutty Sark"
remained "the real McCoy" for thousands of thirsty Americans'
(p.84).

The second version of the origin of 'The Real McCoy' – and
the one favoured by *The Oxford Dictionary of Modern Slang* –
concerns the boxer Charles 'Kid' McCoy (real name Norman
Selby), who was born in Indiana of Irish parents and was world
middleweight champion in 1897. He was a notably inconsistent
boxer who would sometimes 'throw' fights but when 'the real
McCoy' fought he was outstandingly good. He fooled the reigning
champion Tommy Ryan into believing he was dying of consumption and then knocked him out to take the middleweight title,
appropriately going on to become a film actor before committing
suicide in 1940.

It may that there is an even earlier claimant to be the source
of the expression, namely Joseph McCoy, who made his fortune
in the 1860s by transporting cattle from the railhead at Abilene,
Kansas, to the stockyards of Chicago. According to Andrew
Fraser of Inverness, 'McCoy had boasted he could deliver 200,000
cattle in a decade but sent over two million within four years,
hence the expression, "The real McCoy"' (*Scotland on Sunday*,
17 November 1991).

Mackay, the Real   A colloquial synonym for 'the real thing', 'the
genuine article', first recorded in 1883 and originally applied
specifically only to good Scotch whisky, but now much more
widely used. Often thought to be no more than a Scottish variant
of the more usual *Real McCoy*, the *Real Mackay* probably pre-
dates that expression, being in regular use well before 1900,
according to Partridge *(Historical Slang)*. The origins of the
expression are obscure, though *The Oxford Dictionary of Modern
Slang* notes the suggested derivation that 'it refers to the true
chieftain of the clan Mackay, a much disputed position...'. Hugh
McDiarmid *(A Drunk Man Looks at the Thistle)* uses it in its
original context:

> 'Forbye, the stuffie's no' the real Mackay,
> The sun's sel' aince, as sune as ye began it,
> Riz in your vera soul; but what keeks in
> Noo is in truth the vilest 'saxpenny planet'.

maize   An American graminaceous plant or the grain produced by it, otherwise Indian *corn*. From the Spanish *maiz*, a word of the Cuban dialect, also the Arawak *marisi* and the Caribbean *márichi*. In French *maïs*, *mahiz* in the sixteenth century. The first attestation of *maize* occurs in 1555, 'This kynde of grayne they call maizium', and specifically regarding whisky at what seems the late date of 1893, 'Maize-whiskey could be bought at fifteen cents a gallon'.

Along with malted *barley*, maize is a staple ingredient of *grain* whisky in Scotland and Ireland and is used extensively in American distilling, where it is known as corn.

make The product of a distillery, whisky. Writing in the 1880s of Scotland's northernmost mainland distillery of Pulteney in Wick, Caithness, Barnard observes that 'Previous to its erection, Mr Henderson was the proprietor of a small Distillery further inland for a period of nearly thirty years, but on finding the demand for his "make" increasing, he determined to start a Distillery nearer the sea coast, which in those days was the only mode of transit to the south...' (p.137).

The OED lists no sense of *make* which is totally appropriate to the term's whisky-related usage, the closest being 'the amount made or quantity produced', first attested in 1865: 'The make of puddled iron has been materially reduced at many of the works.' 'Make' is still current in distilling circles, Lamond writing of experiments on the *spirit safe* carried out in the 1820s at Port Ellen distillery on Islay, 'Test had to be made to ensure that it had no harmful effects on the make' (*Malt File*, 116).

The term *new make* as a synonym for *spirit* which has not undergone a period of *maturation* also occurs.

When all the *foreshots* have been distilled, whisky starts to be produced. Known as 'new make', this is piped away to the spirit receiver. It is colourless and contains about 60 per cent alcohol by volume. Until the First World War when legislation was introduced prohibiting the sale of whisky matured in the wood for less than three years, new make was a popular drink. It was stocked by many public houses, particularly in industrial districts, and drunk as a chaser with beer. Pot still malt new make has a tang of iodine, but a distinctive whisky flavour. (Moss, *Scottish Drink Book*, 81).

malt OE *mealt*. As a noun, *malt* is *barley* or other grain prepared for brewing or distilling by steeping, germinating and *kiln*-drying. The first attestation occurs prior to 700. As a verb, with the sense of *to malt*, to convert *grist* into malt, the first recorded use is in c.1440, 'Maltyn or make malt...'.

The word *maltings* for the place where malt is prepared and stored is first recorded in 1846, 'A spacious malting', and the term came to supercede *malt-house* which is first attested in *c.*1050 as *mealthus*. The phrase *malting floor* is first recorded in 1840, and *maltman* – one who malts – is first attested in 1408, 'Iohn plot, Citaysyn and Maltman of london'. The Scots variant *mautman* dates from the seventeenth century, and is now largely confined in usage to Caithness and north-east Lothian. Neil Gunn – a native of Dunbeath in Caithness – is one of the few writers on whisky to use 'maltman' rather than the more usual *maltster* (first recorded between *c.*1370 and 1380): 'As one old maltman put it . . .' (p.132).

Inevitably, 'malt' came to have colloquial associations with drinking and being drunk, for example *malt-worm* – a weevil which infested malt – gained the transferred sense of a lover of malt liquor, attested in *c.*1550: 'Then dothe she troule To me the bolle As a good malte worme sholde'. The verb 'to malt' also gained a slang usage to connote getting drunk, first noted in 1813, 'Well, for my part I malt'. The transferred colloquial use of malt to mean malt liquor also occurs, and is first attested in 1718, using the Scots spelling *maut*: 'The bauld billy took his maut, And scour'd aff healths anew'. The expression 'a glass of malt' is some-times used to indicate malt whisky as opposed to blended, and in Ireland the expression a *ball of malt* is current, though rather perversely it is very unlikely that the Irish drinker means malt whisky by this request; he uses the phrase to mean Irish whiskey, since very little Irish is actually malt whiskey within the usual terms of definition. The Scots phrase 'The maaut is abune [above] the meal' – current from the eighteenth to the early twentieth century – meant under the influence of drink. A good example of usage occurs in Scott's *Old Mortality*, 'when the malt begins to get aboone the meal . . . thay are like to quarrel'.

The first attestation of *malt whisky* occurs as late as 1839, 'The distiller of malt whiskey calculates on obtaining two gallons of *proof* spirits from one bushel of malt.' In Scotland and Ireland malt whisky must by legal definition be distilled in a *pot still* and made only from malted barley, though the American definition of malt whisky is very different, namely a whiskey made from not less than 51 per cent malted barley in either a pot or *continuous* still. For Gunn, malt whiskies were 'the real uisgebeatha', and after almost a century during which their identities were nearly always submerged in blends, *single* malts have again found a grow-ing market. As well as being the staple ingredient in malt whisky production, a quantity of malt is also essential when making *grain* whisky.

In whisky distilling, as in beer-making, malt is barley which has been prepared for successive stages of the production process by converting the starch stored in it into a soluble sugar called maltose. This is then utilised in the *fermentation* process to produce alcohol. Essentially malting merely serves to speed up a natural sequence of events. The barley is soaked in a tank of water called a *steep*, where it absorbs enough water to enable germination to occur. It is then placed in a *couch* to drain before being spread out on the malting floor to a depth of two to three feet and allowed to germinate. Once spread on the malting floor a batch of barley is known as a *piece*. Whilst on the floor the barley sprouts, and its temperature is controlled by regular turning of the piece with *shiels*, an action which also has the effect of preventing the roots from becoming entangled. The bed of malt is gradually thinned out over eight to twelve days, until it is only three or four inches deep. The barley is kept at a constant temperature of around 16°C, and once it has sprouted to an optimum degree it is known as *green malt*, although it is actually still pale yellow in colour. As Gunn explains, 'By this time the acrospire or growing stem has almost reached the point of coming through the husk and the starch has become soft and chalky. As one old maltman put it: "When you can write your name on the wall with it [the ear], it's ready"' (p.131). Further growth is then prevented in order to conserve the sugars for fermentation by *kiln* drying, during which *peating* also takes place.

Only eight distilleries in Scotland currently operate their own traditional floor maltings, as they are labour intensive, occupy a comparatively large area of space and take a relatively long time to produce malt. As early as 1910 the cramped Glengoyne distillery in the Campsie Hills of Stirlingshire decided to buy in malt and abandoned its own maltings in order to devote the space to other distilling activities. It follows that in most distilleries now the first stage in the whisky-making process is the production of grist from malt.

Several of those distilleries which still malt their own barley do so principally as a visitor attraction. Units whose maltings are still in use include Bowmore and Laphroaig on *Islay* and Highland Park near Kirkwall on Orkney. The *Cambeltown* distillery of Springbank recently restored and extended its floor maltings and now no longer needs to buy in any malt at all, though in this instance the adherence to floor maltings has everything to do with a belief in their importance when distilling on a small scale and nothing to do with pleasing casual sightseers, who are not encouraged at the little plant off Longrow.

Most malt is now produced in highly mechanised centralised

maltings such as those at Burghead on the Moray Forth in north-east Scotland. Two principal processes of mechanical malting are used, namely drum malting and *Saladin* malting, though in the most sophisticated modern plants germination and kilning can take place in the same vessel, and Morrice notes that the Static Box is 'a more sophisticated piece of equipment capable of doing the steeping, germinating and kilning processes in sequence'. In drum maltings the barley is placed in large revolving drums in which the temperature is controlled by blasts of air. A form of drum malting was introduced at Glen Grant distillery on Speyside in the 1890s, and was also in use at the North British distillery in Edinburgh and at the now demolished St Magdalene *Lowland* malt distillery from the 1920s until the 1950s. The concept was developed on a large scale during the late 1960s and early 1970s, notably by Scottish Malt Distillers (a DCL subsidiary) who instal-led drum maltings in their new malting plants at Burghead, Glenesk, Ord and Port Ellen as increasing labour costs and the greater relevance of economies of scale dictated the closure of many distiller-based maltings in favour of centralisation.

McDowall describes the dry malt as 'crisp and friable like toast, pleasant to the taste'; it 'may be kept in malt bins for several weeks till required' (p.102). Gunn writes, 'In all this malting process, skilled judgment is needed, for the goodness of the malt determines not only the quantity of alcohol that may result from its fermentation but the quality of the ultimate distillate itself' (p.133).

Manhattan A classic whisky *cocktail*, usually made with *rye*, though *Bourbon* is substituted in many recipes. As its name implies, the Manhattan is a product of New York, and was first included in Harry Johnson's 1882 *Bartenders' Manual*. It was therefore well established before what Alan Reeve Jones describes as 'the so-called Cocktail Age of the 1920-37 period' (p.99). Its exact ingredients and proportions are disputed, but Reeve Jones gives 'the authentic recipe' as one measure of Bourbon whiskey, half a measure of dry vermouth, half a measure of sweet vermouth and a dash of angostura bitters, stirred, strained into a cocktail glass and served with a cocktail cherry.

marriage In the whisky trade *marriage* is the harmonising of spirits prior to bottling. 'After thorough mixing the blended whisky is stored in casks for a further period, usually of no more than eight months to "marry" before bottling' (Morrice, 39). The term is not confined to blending, however, as Cooper uses it when writing of *single* malts, 'Before bottling, a selection of casks distil-led in different months and years will be married together' (*Little*

Book, 24). Similarly, regarding *vatted* malts, he writes that they are 'malt whiskies from various distillers which have been married or "vatted" together to produce a harmonious whole'.

From a semantic point of view the transferred sense of marriage from 'wedlock' to a more general term to imply an intimate union is first attested in *c.*1420, 'Into the lond let synke A reed right by, and bynde in marriage Hem to, lest wynde offende her tender age'. The first attestation to be concerned with the marriage of liquids occurs in 1855: 'I . . . crost By that old bridge . . . where the waters marry'.

mash Used as a noun in brewing and distilling, *mash* is *malt* mixed with hot water to form *wort*. From the OE *másc, máx*, possibly related to OE *miscian*, to mix. Mash is first attested in *c.*1000 in the combination 'mash-wort', 'Drince wermed on max-wyrte awyllede'. The use of 'mash' as a verb, to mix malt with hot water to form wort, is recorded during the fourteenth century, where it is implied in *mahssingfate*, mashing fat or vat.

Mashing – also known as extraction because it is a process which brings about the extraction of fermentable sugars – takes place in the *mash house*, following *malting* and preceding *fermentation* and *distillation* in the whisky-making process. Together with fermentation, mashing is usually considered to be part of the *brewing* stage, and certainly much of the vocabulary is common to the production of both beer and whisky. In malt whisky the mash consists entirely of malt, but in *grain* whisky production the mash usually consists of some 20 per cent malted barley and 80 per cent unmalted grains.

The mash of *grist* and hot water is mixed in a large circular vessel, known as a *mash tun* – a term first attested in 1889, 'leaving the mashing stage we descended to the underback room below the tuns'. Modern mash tuns are covered to conserve heat and are usually constructed of stainless steel, though iron and even copper tuns are still in use. Their capacity can vary from 2,000 to 8,000 gallons, and they have perforated floors, through which the wort can be removed, along with an arrangement of stirrers attached to a central axle which ensure maximum sugar extraction from the grist. Moss and Hume make the observation that 'More complete extraction of the grist has been made possible by the use of the German Lauter tun, adopted from brewing practice, and pioneered at Tomatin distillery. Many distilleries have installed tuns of this type, or "modified Lauter" tuns as developed by Newmill of Elgin and other distillery engineers' (*The Making of Scotch Whisky*, 179). Once in the tun the mash looks like thin porridge. 'While the water and the grist marry together, stirred and kept at a critical temperature, the starch is converted into maltose and dextrin and the sugary mixture that results is known as wort' (Cooper, *Century Companion*, 22).

The wort is drained out of the mash tun to a worts *receiver* or *underback*, prior to fermentation, and more hot water is pumped into the tun and mixed with the residue from the first mashing. Further mashings are made on the grist with increasingly hot water until all the fermentable sugar has been removed. Daiches notes that 'the characteristic smell that hangs around a distillery is compounded of many factors, but the pungent smell of the mashing is central' (*Scotch Whisky*, 11). See also *sparge*, *draff*.

Along with *Bourbon* and *rye*, *Tennessee sour mash* is one of the distinctive styles of American whiskey, though the sour mash process is by no means unique to Jack Daniel's and other Tennessee whiskeys (Old Crow advertises itself as 'The Original Sour Mash'), being used to some extent by all distillers of *straight* American whiskeys. It is during the filtration process that Tennessee whiskeys gain the distinctive character that warrants their comprising a whiskey category of their own.

The sour-mash technique was first used by Jack Daniel's in the early years of the nineteenth century, when it was known as 'yeasting back'. As Jack Daniel distillers point out 'there is nothing really "sour" about Sour Mash Whiskey. We call it sour mash, because our distiller uses part of the previous day's mash to start the fermentation in each new batch. Therefore, all the mash is "related".' This process is thought to reinforce the flavour and bouquet. Jackson writes that the residue 'is known as "backset" or "setback", and is taken from the base of the still. It may be added to the grain mash in the cooker, the yeast mash, the fermenting vessels or all three' (*World Guide*, 140).

maturation   Adopted from the French *maturation*, itself adapted from Latin *mātūrātiōn-em*, a noun of action from *mātūrāre*. The earliest use of *maturation* was with regard to the formation of purulent matter (first recorded in 1541), from which came the sense of ripening and of development, initially relating to fruits and plants, but also to man and his faculties, the progress to full growth and development. The earliest use of the word *mature* – adapted from the Latin *mātūrus*, ripe, timely, early – was with regard to prolonged and careful deliberation; plans formed, conclusions reached after adequate consideration. The first attestation occurs in 1454, 'The Justicez, after sadde communication and mature deliberation...'

With regard to liquors undergoing preparation for use, the sense of 'maturation' is of having their natural development

completed, and the first attestation occurs in 1605, 'So wee see
that wine in whose maturation or ripening the heate of the sunne
Failed are made more crude and sharpe'. The precise sense usually applied to whisky, what happens to it in the *cask*, is said by
the OED to be first recorded in 1902, 'A lengthy process of maturation in sherry casks is required to make it [whisky] a wholesome
beverage'. However Barnard refers to a bonded warehouse 'celebrated for maturing the Whisky in two or three years...' in his
1887 publication *The Whisky Distilleries of the United Kingdom*.

Neil Gunn elegantly captures the essence of the process of
maturation and its virtues when he writes 'the maturing of whisky
is a natural slow process, during which an ethereal aroma is
developed and the pungent taste of the new spirit gradually dis-
appears giving place to a mellowness and flavour that suggest
body without loss of cleanness to the taste' (p.158). For Grindal,
the transformation from 'fiery, crude and unpalatable' new *make*
to '... smooth, mellow spirit' is 'one of nature's miracles' (p.98).
New make whisky is colourless, and as Moss writes, 'As it matures
the whisky changes in character drawing colour and flavour from
the wood. Some of the higher alcohols gradually change into esters
and other compounds with delicate subtle aromas, strengthening
the individuality of each whisky' (*Scottish Drink Book*, 83).

Gunn observes that no one seems to know who first discovered
that whisky improved by being kept in *wood*. He conjectures that
a smuggler's keg was perhaps once hidden or misplaced and redis-
covered after some years. The spirit was then found to be so much
improved that the practice was deliberately adopted and in time
spread further afield (p.149). In the early days of illicit distillation,
the difficulties of concealing the whisky casks would have discour-
aged maturation. As Jackson writes, 'Although the benefits of
maturation are said to have been known to wealthy cellar-owners
since the early days of distilled spirits in Britain, whisky was not
systematically aged until the late 1800s' (*Almanac*, 17). The first
reference to whisky maturation occurs in Elizabeth Grant's
Memoirs of a Highland Lady when she is writing of King George
IV's visit; the king drank only *Glenlivet* and she was instructed
by her father to provide some from the family cellar. She describes
this whisky as 'long in wood, long in uncorked bottles, mild as
milk, and the true contraband goût in it'. Maturation remained
no more than a matter of good sense amongst distillers and blenders concerned with the reputation of their product until 1915,
when Lloyd George introduced the Immature Spirits Act which
stipulated a minimum maturation period of two years, soon
extended to three years. Lloyd George's action had more to do

with his concerns over drunkenness, particularly amongst mun-
ition workers, and a desire to cut general consumption of whisky
than with any interest in the quality of the product, but the outcome was actually to the great advantage of the whisky trade.
One regret among reputable *pot still* distillers had been that the
Royal Commission of 1910 failed to recommend a minimum
period of maturation when it supplied its definition of whisky,
and large quantities of almost new *patent still* spirit had for some
years been finding its way on to the market.

No spirit, either malt or grain, is legally entitled to be termed
Scotch whisky unless it has been both distilled and matured in
Scotland for a minimum of three years, and in practice very few
distillers would consider anything less than five years an acceptable maturation period, though grain whisky is rarely considered
to improve with age. Irish whiskey also has to be matured for
three years, whilst in the United States 'the American classics are
usually aged for not less than four years', according to Jackson
(*World Guide*, 13). *Corn* whiskies, however, are marketed without
maturation, the Georgia Moon brand being guaranteed 'less than
thirty days old'!

'At seven to eight years a pot-still whisky may be fully matured
in a small cask', writes Gunn (p.152). He also makes the point
that 'After fifteen years in wood, whisky as a rule begins to
deteriorate'. Grindal points out that malt whiskies with a fuller
flavour, such as those from Islay and Speyside, tend to take longer
to mature than milder *Highland* and *Lowland* whiskies, 'As a
general rule between ten and fifteen years is a good age for a single
malt Scotch, ten for the Lowland and the less full-flavoured Highland malts, twelve or fifteen for the island and the best of the
Speyside malts' (p.8). Grindal considers that in most cases a malt
whisky marketed at more than eighteen years of age is likely to
be only marginally better than it was at fifteen, and may well be
no better at all. In time even the best whiskies will deteriorate by
taking on a woodiness from the cask in which they are stored.
The process of maturation is generally considered to cease once
whisky is in the *bottle*, though dissenting voices have been raised
on this subject. Maturation is an expensive business, partly
because of the cost of keeping non-earning stocks of spirit tied
up in warehouses and partly because as it matures whisky loses
both bulk – the *angels' share* – and strength.

Gunn contends that during the first couple of years in the cask
the spirit is even less palatable than when it leaves the still. 'In
these early years of maturing it becomes gawky and angular, an
early green adolescence capable of being very self-conscious and

horrid between the first marvel of birth and the final round fulness of maturity' (p.150). Moss also takes the personificatory approach: 'Each malt reaches perfection at a different age and some will peak twice in their life – early and late with a dull middle age' (*Scottish Drink Book*, 83).

The rate at which optimum maturity is reached varies from whisky to whisky and also depends on other factors, such as the type and size of cask in which maturation takes place. As Gunn explains, 'The smaller the cask the greater is the percentage of loss through absorption, transfusion, exposure to damp or cold or heat, and therefore the quicker does the whisky in it mature – and deteriorate' (p.153).

The environment in which maturation takes place is a significant factor, and it is a general rule that a damp warehouse causes a whisky to lose strength but maintain bulk, and is considered better for maturation than a dry one where strength is less affected but bulk falls. Whisky matured on moist islands such as Islay would tend to lose strength, whilst bulk would be lost on Speyside where the atmosphere is drier. In the United States, where warmer and drier conditions prevail, the strength of the spirit may actually increase during storage.

The 'breathing' of the casks – slight contraction in winter and expansion in summer – can also cause quite distinctive changes to the character of the finished whisky in respect of local atmosphere. Writing of *Campbeltown* whiskies, Jackson notes their 'fresh, salty aroma and palate'; pointing out that it is situated on a narrow peninsula, he writes, 'There is no denying the sea mists in Kintyre, and every reason why they should be taken up by the breathing of the barrels in maturation' (*World Guide*, 34). The salty atmosphere may also penetrate the earth floors of the old-fashioned warehouses, floors that serve to regulate humidity by giving moisture to the internal atmosphere during hot, dry weather and absorbing moisture during wet periods.

At the opposite end of the sophistication scale, the Macallan distillery on Speyside has recently constructed a new warehousing complex capable of holding 50,000 *butts* of whisky, which boasts air conditioning and insulation designed to maintain constant optimum temperature and humidity levels during maturation.

It is difficult to over-stress the importance of maturation to the finished whisky, and Gunn considers it probable that 'the most desirable flavours in whisky are produced on the malt-kiln and in the cask' (p.153). Russell Sharp concludes his writing on the subject of maturation with a comment that would have brought a smile to the face of Neil Gunn and many others who prefer to think of maturation as 'one of nature's miracles' rather than an entirely quantifiable scientific process.

'Since the lengthy maturation process imposes considerable costs on the distiller, much effort has gone into trying to accelerate the process and control the chemical changes that take place within the cask. But so complex are those changes that, for the forseeable future, it seems likely that the most economical and convenient way of ensuring that whisky matures to perfection will be the simple one which our forebears discovered. You make a good malt spirit, you fill it into a good oak cask, and you wait 10 or 20 years' (in Hills, p.177).

mellow   Affected with liquor, but not generally truly drunk. Certainly the adjective usually implies a good-humoured, non-aggressive state. The drink-related usage is adopted from the figurative sense of *mellow* as soft, softened or sweetened with age and/or experience, lacking harshness. With reference to drink, mellow is first attested in 1611, 'to be drunke, or in drinke; to be mellow, tipled, flusht, ouerseene'. The verb sense of mellow also occurs, first being attested after 1761, 'When mellow'd with a cup of nectar'. As an adjective, it is also part of the whisky-taster's vocabulary and obviously a positive term, as in Milroy's verdict on the *Highland* whisky, Imperial: 'Rich and mellow with an absolutely delicious finish' (p.87).

In the United States, 'mellow' has the sense of 'satisfying, attractive, skilful, pleasant' according to the *Oxford Dictionary of Modern Slang*, which also notes the drugs-related sense and the expression *mellow out*, to become relaxed under the influence of drugs, first attested in 1974.

middle cut   See *cutting*.

mizuwari   Writing of Japanese whisky-drinking habits, Jackson explains that 'The word *mizuwari* (pronounced rather like Missouri, and meaning "diluted with *water*") almost always refers to an after-work whisky' (*World Guide*, 197).

moonlight   Now almost obsolete, and synonymous with the more commonly used term *moonshine*, *moonlight* is smuggled or illicitly produced spirit. In its literal sense as 'the light of the moon' the term moonlight is first used by Chaucer prior to 1366, and as illicit spirit in 1809, 'Yon *cask* holds moonlight, run when moon was none'. Barnard (1887) uses the phrase when writing of Lagavulin distillery on Islay, recording that at the time of its founding in the 1740s 'it consisted of ten small and separate smuggling bothys for the manufacture of "moonlight"'.

The basic derivation 'moonlight' as a colloquialism for illicit spirit is from the fact that its production was carried out by the light of the moon, and there is a strong implication of illegality in most examples of usage. Use of *moonlighting* to denote the manufacture and smuggling of moonlight extended to include other illegal nocturnal occupations, such as the late nineteenth century attacks on landlords and their property by the Land League in Ireland, as celebrated in the well-known Irish folk song 'The Rising of the Moon'. It also had colloquial currency as a term for prostitution during the second half of the nineteenth century. It has developed a widely used modern colloquial sense, defined by the *Oxford Modern English Dictionary* as to 'have two paid occupations, esp. one by day and one by night'. Again, a sense of wrong-doing is often implied in the term, which is American in origin, first being attested in 1957.

moonshine   In a literal sense *moonshine* was first used as a synonym for moonlight in *c.*1500; and with the transferred sense of illicit spirit it is first attested in 1785, 'The white brandy smuggled on the coasts of Kent and Sussex is called moonshine'. According to Partridge *(Historical Slang)* the term had become standard English by *c.*1890, and was used 'Often with a specific sense: white brandy, in Kent, Sussex; gin, Yorkshire'. The first direct reference to moonshine whisky occurs in 1829, 'Moonlight, moon-shine...smuggled whiskey'.

Writing of eighteenth century Irish and Scots Protestant colonists in the United States, McGuffin declares that 'The name "Moonshine", which soon came to be applied to all illicit corn liquor derives from "moonlighter" and was originally used in England to describe the brandy smugglers who landed at night bringing their contraband from Holland and the low countries to thirsty English customers. In some parts of the States, notably North Carolina, Southwest Virginia and Georgia itself illicit distillers were often called "blockaders"...' (p.47).

The principal usage of 'moonshine' to denote illicit and often harsh, new whiskey is now restricted to the United States, though Irish and Scottish examples do occur. The first implied use of the term moonshine in the United States occurs in 1860, 'The moonshiners had no cargo to defend', and with specific reference to distilling rather than smuggling liquor, moonshine is attested in 1901, 'Georgia and Arkansas have the greatest number of moonshine stills'. The southern states were what McGuffin calls 'the moonshiners' heartland' (p.55), Georgia, Kentucky, North and South Carolina and Tennessee being particularly noted for moonshine manufacture, just as in Ireland the parallel product of *poitín* was traditionally made in greatest quantities in the north and north-west of the country. Moonshining continues to thrive in some areas of America just as poitín-making does in Ireland, with the contraction *shine* often being used to describe the spirit in colloquial usage. The distribution of the illicit liquor is frequently known as *running shine*. Moonshine is also known as white liquor or *white lightning*, and the specification of colour is highly significant, as white or clear liquor has not had the benefit of a period of *maturation*. The usual implication of trading in and drinking new spirit is that it has been illegally produced.

Moonshining in America began as a result of the imposition of the 1791 Excise Tax, the first American tax on distillation, which led to the Whiskey Rebellion of September 1794 and the growth of *corn* whiskey manufacture. Like his Irish counterpart, the American moonshiner traditionally took a great pride in his craft, grain meal always being the principal ingredient, but the advent of prohibition in the United States led to a great increase in moonshining throughout the country, an astonishing 172,537 stills being captured in 1925 alone. With the increase in quantity went a serious decline in quality and the replacement of grain meal with cheap corn sugar even in many of the 'reputable' operations, a development much deprecated by the moonshining traditionalists. As McGuffin puts it, 'Much of the stuff made was vile tasting and in many cases highly dangerous. The unscrupulous were out for a quick buck and didn't care who they maimed or killed with their poisonous "Smoke", "Jake", "Nigger Gin", "Yack yack bourbon", "Stingo", "Soda Pop Moon" or "Straightsville Stuff"' (p.54). McGuffin records that 'Jake' was 'almost 90% alcohol fluid extract Jamaica ginger with wood alcohol added [which] permanently paralyzed at least 15,000 people'.

With reference to both 'moonlight' and 'moonshine', in addition to the most obvious derivation of 'made by the light of the moon' there is another relevant dimension: folklore invests the moon with magic powers over earthly things; for example, plants would have greater healing properties if they were collected when there was a full moon, and liquor made under the same circumstances could be thought to possess a magic power, that of intoxication. Also a natural analogy exists in that the light of the moon was traditionally believed to fuddle the wits, hence the fact that 'moonshine' can also mean nonsense, and 'moonstruck' signifies one who is mentally deranged. The now obsolete adjective 'moony' was standard English for silly, but was also used as a slang expression for slightly drunk, first being recorded with this meaning in 1854. The extant American expression 'moon-eyed' for drunk is first recorded in 1737.

MacDiarmid uses the analogy in *A Drunk Man Looks at the*

Thistle, punning on the Scots word *'fou* with its colloquial meaning of drunk and its literal meaning of full.

It's no' that I'm sae fou' as juist deid dune,
And dinna ken as muckle's [much as] whaur I am
Or hoo I've come to sprawl here 'neth the mune.
That's it! It isna me that's fou' at a',
But the fu' mune, the doited [mad] jade, that's led
Me fer agley [off course], or 'mogrified the warld'.

mountain dew   A fanciful yet apt term usually taken to mean illicitly produced whisky or *moonshine*, though it is also sometimes used as a rather pompous synonym for any whisky. The first attestation of *mountain dew* occurs in 1816, 'A pleasing... liquor, which was vended under the name of mountain dew', and the existence in 1837 of a *Campbeltown* distillery called the Mountain Dew suggests the term may have been in general Scottish use for some considerable time prior to the first attestation.

The term *mountain wine* occurs from 1710, and the transferred sense of *dew* applied to other fermented or distilled spirits dates back to 1559 and a reference to wine, 'Sowst in Bacchus dewe'. In 1884 the phrase 'dew of Glenlivat' is recorded, and a blend of Irish whiskey and ginger wine is currently marketed under the brand name Clan Dew.

Dr John Mackenzie, quoted by his nephew Osgood Mackenzie, illustrates colloquial use of the expression 'mountain dew' in Scotland during the first half of the nineteenth century when he writes 'Then I began to see that the "receiver" – myself, for instance, as I drank only "mountain dew" then – was worse than the smuggler'. Illicit whisky was often made in mountainous areas for the obvious practical reasons that stills and physical signs of distillation could easily be concealed, and detection in remote, sparsely populated places was relatively unlikely. The mountain distillers would also usually have far more detailed local geographical knowledge than any inquisitive *gauger*. In the United States the Appalachian and the Smoky Mountains were legendary centres of moonshining, as were the mountains of Connemara in the west of Ireland, where the product was also known as *mountain tay*, *tay* being an Irishism for tea.

'Dew' is a particularly appropriate noun to use for the product of distillation, as the OED's literal definition is 'The moisture deposited in minute drops upon any cool surface by the condensation of the vapour in the atmosphere'. Partridge *(Historical Slang)* considers 'mountain dew' to have been a standard English expression since *c.*1860, and he specifies that it is Scotch whisky, though American and Irish usages also regularly occur. The Irish folk song 'The Rare Ould Mountain Dew' contains the exhortation to 'Take off your coat and grease your throat/with a bucketful of mountain dew'.

N **eat** An adjective used to describe a drink – usually of *spirits* – which is consumed undiluted or *straight*. The first sense of *neat* is of clean, free from dirt or impurities, and with the meaning of *liquors* pure and undiluted, specifically not mixed with water, the first attestation occurs in 1579, 'The Wine that runneth on the lees, is not therefore to be accompted neate...' *Neat* is adapted from the Anglo-French *neit, net*, in Latin *nitid-um*, from *nitēre*, to shine.

new make See *make*.

nip A small or *single* measure, now usually whisky. Begg writes that 'The word "nip" used alone refers to whisky; if other spirits are required they are named – e.g. "a nip of rum"' (p.20). In bar terms the nip is usually one-sixth *gill* in England, one-fifth in Scotland and one-quarter in Ireland. A nip *glass* is the same as a *shot* glass, designed to hold a single measure of spirits.

Nip is an abbreviation of *nipperkin*, now obsolete as a term for a half pint of ale, and by extension for any small quantity of liquor. Nipperkin is of obscure etymology, though the form suggests Dutch or Low German origins. In Middle Dutch, *nypelkin* occurs as the name of a game. As a quantity of liquor, nipperkin is first attested in 1671, ''Tis something cold, I'le go take a Nipperkin of wine', and as a measure or vessel of small capacity, containing half a pint or less the first attestation occurs in 1694, 'Barrels, Nipperkins, pint-pots, quart-pots'. The first reference which – by implication – features whisky occurs in 1792, when Robert Burns writes 'I have a nipperkin of toddy by me'. The OED notes that in later use nipperkin was chiefly confined to Scotland. The modern abbreviation, nip, is first recorded in 1796, 'Nyp or nip, a half pint, a nip of ale; whence the nipperkin, a small vessel'. References are all to ale until 1869 when the following occurs, 'A so-called nip of brandy will create hilarity, or, at least, alacrity.'

It is interesting to note that nip also has the sense of a small portion, a fragment or a pinch from 1606, 'If thou hast not laboured... looke that thou put not a nip in thy mouth', which raises the possibility of a derivation unrelated to nipperkin.

A peculiarly Scottish use of nip also occurs to signify something pungent or sharp, or of hot or pungent flavour, being first attested

137

in 1825: 'Bread, and especially cheese, is said to have a nip, when it tastes sharp or pungent.' It is possible that this usage derives from a nip of drink, particularly of spirits, which when taken neat is hot, sharp, pungent. In 1894 'I dinna like whiskey wi' a nip' is recorded.

noggin   Now used colloquially and without implication of quantity to indicate any alcoholic drink, though usually beer, a *noggin* is also described in the *Dictionary of Drink* as 'A liquid measure equal to a gill'. It was originally a small drinking vessel with a capacity of a *gill*, first attested in 1630, 'Of her ale, her custome was to set before me two little noggins full', and with specific reference to whisky in 1859, 'The pewter counters and the brasswork of the beer-engines, the funnels and the whisky noggins'. From being the name of the vessel itself, noggin came to connote the contents of the vessel, a small quantity of liquor, variously specified as being a quarter or a third of a pint. With this sense it is first attested in 1693, 'the Humble servant of ev'ry one that Treats him with a Noggin of cool Nants', and with reference to whisky in 1853, 'While we were joking about his adventure over a quiet little noggin of whisky punch'.

Marshall Robb notes that a serving of spirit was in use in Scotland at the end of the First World War which 'measured one-third of a gill, cost 6d., and was called a "noggin"' (p.70). The word is of obscure origin, and though *noigean* occurs in Scots Gaelic and *noigin* in Irish, it is thought that both forms have their roots in English.

North Country   Cooper states that 'In the nineteenth century malt whiskies were somewhat arbitrarily divided into five classes: Islay, Glenlivet, North Country, Campbeltown and Lowland' (*Century Companion*, 37). The *North Country* classification embraced all those Highland whiskies not included in the *Glenlivet* appellation, and has long since been absorbed into the *Highland* category of malts.

The term North Country is first recorded in 1297, 'Hii... barnde & destrude þe norþ contreie vaste', and the usual implication is of England north of the river Humber, though a less specific usage to imply the north also occurs.

nose   The *nose* is the aroma or bouquet of a wine or spirit. Along with colour, *body*, *finish* and *palate*, the nose of a whisky is an essential element which is isolated and analysed in order to help distinguish it from other whiskies. It is sometimes thought that the nose of a malt whisky is an accurate reflection of the palate; that, as Jackson puts it 'single malts are unusual in the honesty of their aroma' (*Companion*, 22). Jackson, for one, disagrees, writing that 'in my perception, characters in the nose can move into the background of the palate, then re-emerge in the finish'.

With the transitive verb sense – to perceive the smell of something – nose is first attested in 1577/87, 'He neuer ceasseth to range till he haue nosed his footing', and used intransitively – to apply the nose in examining or smelling – in 1783, 'Closely nosing o'er the Picture dwell, As if to try the goodness by the smell'. In 1894 'The room was like a barn after a bad cold harvest, with a musty nose to it' is recorded.

A vocabulary has evolved to describe the nose of a whisky, and, as with wines, the images used for the purposes of evocation range from the eminently sensible and helpful to the wilfully pretentious and almost surreal. Jackson usually operates at the more useful end of the spectrum, with comments such as 'Fresh, dry, with a hint of sea air', for Pulteney, and 'pungent, with smoke, seaweed, brine and sweet maltiness' for Talisker. Oz Clarke, in a *Daily Telegraph* article (20 January 1992) on malt whiskies, tends to the opposite extreme when he describes a *tasting* session with his brother during which the nose of the *Lowland* St Magdalene was likened to Snowcem paint and half-used drums of Burmah oil, and the *Campbeltown* Longrow to Whitstable harbour. Writing of Irish whiskey in his *Sporting Life* column, Sir Clement Freud makes the observation that it 'eschews social niceties, deflates pretension and unlike learned assessments made in respect of single malts: "This is a complicated, gustatory dialectic in which the antithesis of taste meets the thesis of the nose to provide a synthesis of sensation"'. Freud declares of Irish whiskeys that 'The smell is redolent of shredded tote tickets mouldering in privet' (28 April 1992). Jackson notes that 'people sometimes talk wistfully about the aroma of saddlery, or new leather, when they seek to define the nose of Irish whiskey' (*World Guide*, 102).

Not only is the art of *nosing* – analysing by sense of smell – of general use when considering the merits of different whiskies but in its most sophisticated form it is a crucial tool of the professional blender. As Lamond remarks, 'The master blender has an "educated" nose and can detect more than 150 separate flavours or effects in a product such as whisky' (*Malt File*, 10). According to Lamond, nosing rather than tasting is preferred partly because the tasting mechanisms are adversely affected by the first sample of any distilled spirit and also because nosing is more direct. 'Our sense of aromatics (or "volatiles" as they are sometimes called), is derived from an area known as the olefactory epithelium, which has a direct link to the brain. It is located at the back of the nasal passage...Using the nose to detect the aromatic ingredients provides a more immediate route to this area than through the back of the throat.'

The whisky blender is not unique in his role, as Hugh Williams, a gin distillery manager for Gordon's in Essex makes clear in an advertising feature. 'There are people working on scientific alternatives', he is quoted as saying, 'but they are light years away from producing anything as good as the human nose'. According to Williams, the master distiller or *noser* as he is usually known will develop his own shorthand which he uses to describe odours. 'We had a man who compared smells to Kentish cobnuts, another who would say an odour had a green spike through it!' (*Scotland on Sunday*, 16 August 1992).

Describing the work of the Scotch Malt Whisky Society tasting committee – on which places are understandably at something of a premium – Hills suggests the following nosing procedure: 'Put a little of the stuff in the glass, swirl it around, stick your snout in the hole and sniff. Do that a few times and then put water to it. Usually about as much water as whisky. Snout and sniff again. It is astonishing how the nose changes with the water, and often how it alters over time' (p.184).

Octave   The smallest *cask* used for the bulk storage and *maturation* of whisky, the *octave* is generally less popular than the *butt* or *hogshead*. It has a capacity of 45-68 litres, one-eighth that of the butt and half that of the hogshead. With the sense of a small cask, octave is first attested in 1891, 'Importing and delivering sherries in Octaves'. Octave is adopted from the French *octave* itself an adaptation of the Latin *octāva*, feminine of *octāv-us*, eighth.

Old-fashioned   Dunkling notes that 'One of the earliest definitions of "cocktail" ever found in print (1806) gives the formula "spirits of any kind, sugar, water and bitters", which is almost an Old-Fashioned' (p.213). This classic *cocktail* is commonly made with a whisky base, and usually consists of ice, sugar, Angostura bitters and water, to which the whisky is added and the mixture stirred. Lemon peel, a cherry and a slice of orange and lemon are optional extras. Some drinkers insist that a true *Old-fashioned* can only be made with American whiskey, and even specifically with *rye*, but many commentators consider Scotch whisky to be a perfectly acceptable alternative. The Old-fashioned has given its name to the squat tumbler in which it is usually served, and this is also known as an *on the rocks glass*.

With the sense of antiquated in form or character, 'old-fashioned' is first attested by Walton in *The Compleat Angler* (1653): 'they were old-fashioned Poetry, but choicely good'.

on the rocks   A drink served *on the rocks* consists of undiluted spirit poured on to ice cubes, and the phrase is first recorded in 1946. The expression and the practice originated in the United States, where temperatures were more likely to lead to a desire for a cold glass of spirits than, for example, in Scotland. The serving of neat whisky with ice developed in Britain with the increasing popularity of blended spirit in what may be termed polite society towards the end of the nineteenth century. As Hills remarks, 'The whisky which was elevated to the status of a drink for the upper classes at the end of the century was blended whisky and it was taken with ice and soda' (p.181). Most connoisseurs are united in their disapproval of drinking whisky on the rocks or in adding anything to it other than pure *water*. Writing of American drinking preferences, McDowall notes that 'They prefer all drinks cold, forgetful of the fact that the bouquet of whisky or wine does not come off cold fluids' (p.127).

The origin of the expression 'on the rocks' may perhaps be traced back to the American sense of rocks as money or diamonds, a usage first attested in 1847. Ice cubes in a glass bear a physical resemblance to diamonds, and could also be seen to look like rocks submerged in the ocean when spirit is poured over them. Partridge *(Historical Slang)* lists the colloquial use of 'on the rocks' as denoting destitution, from the sense of a ship being wrecked on rocks, from before 1889, and also considers *rocky* to have colloquial currency as unsteady, unstable – as in 'rocky marriage' – or tipsy.

The expression 'Scotch on the rocks' was taken by Douglas Hurd and Andrew Osmond and used in a punning sense for their eponymous 1971 political thriller, in which Scotland's fight for independence brings Britain to the brink of civil war.

one for the road   See *road*.

optic   Properly used with a capital initial, *optic* is the proprietary name of a device attached to the neck of a bottle for measuring spirits, usually found in bars. The name derives from the fact that it is a visual, automatic measure which serves a pre-set amount of drink in the relevant fraction of a *gill*, so that customers know they are not being given short measure.

The first attestation of optic occurs in 1926, '*Optic*, an apparatus included in Class 8 for delivering a measured quantity of Spirits or other Liquids', and a patent for the 'Optic Pearl' was registered in 1932. According to *Licensed Houses and Their Management* (1949), the Optic Pearl measuring tap is 'inserted into the bottle and the bottle is held in an inverted position by means of a bracket or standard...'. The same publication notes that 'A new type of measuring tap called the "Pushoptic" is becoming very popular. To operate this measure the glass is pushed up against a rubber covered bar. This action instantly releases an accurate measure.' Writing of English licensed premises, Grindal notes that 'Most pubs will have at the most two "pouring" Scotches on the optics...' (p.203). From January 1992 legislation made compulsory the replacement of the old-style metal optics common in most bars with new plastic versions, with improved tamper-proof mechanisms.

overshot   Very drunk. See *shot*.

P **alate** With the literal meaning of the roof of the mouth, the structures which separate the cavity of the mouth from that of the nose, *palate* is first attested in 1382, and with the transferred sense of taste – because the palate was popularly considered to be the seat of taste – in 1526, 'Breed to a sore mouth is sharpe & harde, whiche to a hole palate is swete & pleasaunt'. The word is adopted from the Latin *palātum*.

Palate is widely used to define taste elements in wine and whisky, and according to *The Dictionary of Drink*, it is 'The area of the mouth where the wine tastes are pronounced and experienced. Used to describe the taste of a beverage.' In his *Malt Whisky Companion*, Jackson details the *body*, colour, *finish*, *nose* and palate of each sample, noting that some malts 'present a very extensive development of palate'. Examples of palate descriptions include 'Caressing, lightly malty, with the faintest hints of sherry, raisins, licorice. Very complex. Opens up with a dash of water (Glen Rothes), and 'Smoky, malty-sweet, with sourness and a very big pepperiness developing' (Talisker).

patent still Used for the production of *grain* whisky, and also known as the *Coffey*, *column* or *continuous* still. McDowall writes, 'The idea that the alcohol in fermented wash could be driven off by steam was first developed by Robert Stein, a distiller in Kilbagie in Clackmanan, who patented a still on this principle in 1826' (p.109). Four years later, Aeneas Coffey produced a vastly superior version of the *patent still* which was soon in widespread use. The patent still consists of two large connected and parallel columns, known as the analyser and the rectifier. As McDowall explains, 'The cold fermented wort i.e. the wash, goes in at one end and trickles over a series of perforated trays, through which steam is driven from below. The steam drives off the alcohol while the cold entering wash, cools the alcohol which is condensed by a cold water coil at the top of the second or rectifying column' (p.109).

The word 'patent' is adopted from the French *patent, patente*, and adaptation of the Latin *patēnt-em*, open, lying open. With the sense of letters patent, an open letter or document which confers rights or protection, patent is first attested in 1292. With specific reference to patented inventions, where a person or

143

number of people are granted sole rights to make, use or sell some invention, the first attestation occurs in 1707, 'Madder . . . In King Charles The First's time . . . was made a Patent Commodity'. In our context, 'patent' is used as in patent leather, to signify something originally but now no longer protected by patent.

peat Vegetable matter decomposed by water and partially carbonised by chemical change, often forming bogs or mosses, from where it is cut and 'made' into *peats*. These are still a significant fuel source in parts of the Scottish Highlands and Islands and in Ireland, where the term 'turf' is more usually employed (though *Irish* whiskeys are almost all unpeated).

In the thirteenth century 'peat' is recorded as *pete*, in Anglo-Latin *peta*, and the word occurs from *c*.1200 in Scots-Latin documents, though its origin is unknown. In the sense of a piece of peat, the first attestation occurs in *c*.1200, 'ad ipsas metas abducendas'.

Peat has an important influence on the flavour and character of whisky, both through the water used, and more directly in the *kiln* during malting, where the amount and type of peat used is a very significant factor in determining the character of the finished whisky. Here the noun takes on a verb sense; Cooper, for instance, writes of the process of 'peating the malt' (*Century Companion*, 20). Much of the water used in Scottish distilleries flows over peat and takes characteristics from it. In plants which continue to produce their own *malt*, water is used to steep the *barley*, and the influence of peat may be introduced during that process. In all distilleries water is used during what Jackson calls 'the infusion that precedes fermentation and distillation'. 'These two elements of peatiness each have their own character, and the interplay between them is a part of the complexity of many single malts. In some instances, the water may impart a smokiness even where only a medium-peated malt has been used' (*Malt Whisky Companion*, 11). Jackson also points out that differences of soil types will affect the peat as well as the water, and that 'The age of peat deposits, and their degree of grass-root or heather character, will have its own influence on the malt' (ibid.). It is generally accepted that island and coastal peat produces a smoke with a considerably more pungent aroma than is found further inland, and this is often apparent in the whiskies from such areas. McDowall observes that 'It is not generally realised that peat is a very variable commodity according to the vegetation of which it is formed and to its depth. It may be three to ten feet deep and is commonly cut by hand. At its best it is, when dried, hard like coal and dark in colour, but it may be very soft and friable' (p.103).

Skipworth notes the existence of two kinds of peat, 'marsh peat made up of decomposed mosses, and forest peat made up of decomposed leaves and branches. It is marsh peat that is usually used to flavour malt whisky' (pp.42-3).

Though now largely irrelevant due to centralised maltings and alternative distillery heat sources such as coal and oil, the local availability of peat was formerly a major locational factor which determined sites for distilling.

Writing of those unfortunate souls who have not been persuaded of the pleasures to be had from Scotch whisky, Jackson (*World Guide*, 16) notes that 'What they usually dislike is what they describe as a medicinal (or to be pedantic, *phenolic*) tang. That is the peat'. (See *Islay*.)

Laphroaig is probably the most distinctively peaty of all whiskies, due to its peaty water being used both for steeping in Laphroaig's own maltings and in the main distilling processes. The distillery owns 250 acres of its own peat 'lots', and Lamond notes that they seem to be 'strongly impregnated with moss and this is said to give rise to Laphroaig's particular flavour'(*Malt File*, 98).

S. Russell Grant addresses the issue of peat resources: 'Conservationists as well as anxious whisky lovers sometimes express concern at the considerable quantities of peat currently being used by the industry. There is, however, more peat in Scotland than meets the eye, and experts estimate that even if whisky distilling continues to increase at its present state of growth, the country's reserves will last for at least another thousand years' (Mackinlay et al, 47). Regarding Islay, where much of the peat bog is at least thirty feet deep, Neil Wilson prophesies that 'So long as barley is malted on Islay, there will be peat enough to dry it' (p.67).

It is interesting to note that Japan has its own peat deposits which have been used in whisky-making, though they are not considered ideal, being of a 'distinctively turfy, less carbonic, character', according to Jackson (*World Guide*, 198). Scottish peat is imported for use in Japanese maltings, along with Scottish-peated malt.

peatreek[1] The peat smoke produced in the *kiln* during malting is often referred to in Scotland as *peatreek*, Moss and Hume writing that 'The "peat reek" gives a flavour to the malt which is carried over to the mature whisky' (*The Making of Scotch Whisky*, 48). The Scots variant of 'reek' for 'smoke' dates from the late fourteenth century and is most famously employed in the affectionate sobriquet 'Auld Reekie', bestowed on the city of Edinburgh. The adjective 'reekie' for smoky, smoke-filled, blackened or begrimed by smoke is first recorded during the sixteenth century, and 'peatreek' as pungent smoke from a peat fire occurs from the late eighteenth century.

peatreek²   A transferred colloquialism for illicitly distilled Scotch whisky, which was formerly produced using peat as a fuel source and was therefore noticeably influenced in flavour by peat smoke. The OED considers *peatreek* to be synonymous with *mountain dew*, and also 'loosely Highland whisky generally'. Unromantically it notes that 'The "peat-reek" flavour is really that of amyl alcohol, due to imperfect rectification'. The phrase is first attested in 1824, 'A male o' sic food, washed down by a few glasses of peatreek'. McHardy uses the expression regularly throughout his book, noting in the introduction that 'As most of the [illicit] whisky . . . was made up in the hills in small bothies [turf huts] over peat fires, the whisky became known as peatreek'.

The lexical compound 'peatreek' can be considered a Scottish equivalent of the Irish *poitín*, and many of the frequently tall tales of its production and distribution have strikingly similar parallels in the social history of illicit distillation across the Irish Sea. The manufacture of peatreek is usually considered to be a purely historical phenomenon today, but Morton is inclined to disagree, writing of a retired Speyside coppersmith who has made small stills for domestic production, and noting that 'There are, however, stills around to this day, from Shetland through Orkney to Skye and definitely Glasgow' (p.111).

peg   A slang term for a drink of spirits, Anglo-Indian in origin, and first attested in 1860 according to Partridge *(Historical Slang)*. Writing of sixteenth and seventeenth century silver drinking-vessels, Marian McNeill points out that among the silver tankards from that period which have survived are 'one or two specimens of the rare peg tankards, which have small silver pegs on the inside to mark the diminishing contents – whence the saying, "to drink a peg"' (p.127). Dunkling notes that the tankards would usually hold two quarts, and would be pegged at half-pint intervals; when 'peg' became a term for a drink of spirits it was 'Popularly explained at that time as deriving from the fact that every drink was a peg or nail in one's coffin' (p.19).

phenols   Flavouring chemicals which whisky acquires from *peat* during *kilning*. It is the *phenols* in Islay whiskies which give them their characteristic flavour. As Jackson writes, 'Their nose has been described as "seaweedy", "iodine" or "medicinal". They are the most phenolic of whiskies by far. A phenolic, peaty nose is found to some extent in most Scotch whiskies, and is one of their defining characteristics, but it is at its boldest in the Islay malts *(World Guide*, 36).

In chemical terms phenols are the hydroxl derivatives of aromatic hydrocarbons, 'phenol' having its origins in the Greek φxινο, shining, φxιο-ειο, to bring to light, to cause to appear, show. It was first used by the French chemist Laurent in 1841, in 'hydrate de phényle' and 'acide phénique', 'names which he applied to the substance subsequently called phenol', according to the OED. Phenol is first attested in English in 1857, 'Phenole . . . is the most abundant acid product of the distillation of pit-coal'.

piece   The term applied to a quantity of germinating *barley* while it is on the malting floor. As Cooper puts it, 'When the barley has been raked out on the malting floor it is known as a piece; there may be half a dozen pieces being treated on the floor at any one time, all in different stages of growth' (*Century Companion*, 20). The barley's development is controlled by turning the *piece* at regular intervals, traditionally using *shiels*. The OED definition of a piece as 'a (small) portion of some specific substance' is closest to the whisky-related sense of the term, but this is a unique usage. It is first attested in 1832, 'The turning of his floors or pieces'.

pissed   Colloquialism for *drunk*. *Piss* as a noun for wine and as a verb for urination dates from 1290, and only came to be considered vulgar around *c*.1760.

The Oxford Dictionary of Modern Slang dates first use of the adjective to 1929, also noting the alternative *pissed-up*, *Piss-artist* – 'a drunkard; an extrovert or loud-mouthed fool, someone who messes about' – is first attested in 1975, with the synonymous term *piss-head* dating from 1961. Perhaps 'piss-artist' has its origins in the literal sense of one who draws with piss on a wall, in the snow etc.

On the piss, (first attested in 1942) on a heavy drinking bout, and *piss up*, a drinking session, dating from 1952, while Partridge (*Historical Slang*) includes the obsolete term *piss-factory* to denote a public house, adding the explanatory note that 'liquor makes rapid urine'. The current use of *pissed* clearly has its origins in that particular aspect of alcohol consumption. Partridge also gives *pissy pal*, 'a public house crony', noting that it was principally confined to Cockney usage. He adds the splendid comment that the expression is 'Ex their simultaneous use of the urinal for one discharge of their heavy cargo'.

The common phrase 'He couldn't organise a piss-up in a brewery' implies uselessness, ineffectuality; 'piss-up' also has the sense of 'A mess-up; a bungle or confusion' (*Oxford Slang*). *Piss* is used in the sense of inferior drink, with weak or poor beer in particular being referred to as 'gnat's piss'. In Ecuador a locally produced whisky – possibly named for its manufacturer by a

Scots expatriate with a mischievous sense of humour – rejoices in the name of Auld Piss.

plastered Very *drunk*. The expression is first attested in 1912, and its origins are obscure, perhaps being connected with the original medical sense of *plaster* as an external curative application, and the subsequent figurative usage to imply a healing or soothing means or measure, first recorded prior to 1310. 'Of penaunce in his plastre al'. The OED notes another, figurative sense of plaster which means to 'load to excess', or to 'mend or restore superficially', which could well form the basis of the later drink-related usage.

Poit dhu An Anglicised spelling of the Gaelic *poit dhubh* also sometimes *poit dubh*, literally meaning 'black pot', used both to describe the vessel in which domestic, illicit distillation took place in the Highlands and Islands, and by association also the produce of that still, illicit whisky itself. The pot would be black due to the effects of the fire over which it was heated. The Gaelic term for a commercial still was *poit ruadh*, red pot, presumably because of the copper colour of the stills.

'Ach, I believe you'll have to distill it yourself, Doctor, in a poit dhubh. Oh, I've had a poit dhubh myself and made the stuff. It was a grand sight on a fine summer's morning to see the way the thin blue smoke of it would be stealing up into the sky so quiet' (Compton Mackenzie, *Whisky Galore*, 123).

Poit Dhu has been taken up as a brand name for a *vatted malt* whisky, produced by the Skye company Praban na Linne. Appropriately it contains the Skye malt Talisker along with a number of Speysides, and is a stablemate to the excellent blend *Té Bheag*.

The term 'black pot' occurs in Irish usage, being recorded in 1783 when, as McGuffin writes 'the Government had imposed a £20 fine on a county or a town where any "still, alembic...or blackpot" was found' (p.22).

poitín Illicitly distilled Irish *spirit*, the Hibernian equivalent of *moonshine* or *peatreek*, also sometimes *potheen* or *potsheen*; anglicised as *poteen*. The first attestation occurs in 1812, 'Potsheen, plase your honour; – because it's the little whiskey that's made in the private still or *pot*; and *sheen*, because it's a fond word for whatsoever we'd like, and for what we have little of, and would make much of'. McGuffin writes, 'The word "poitín" itself merely means "a little pot".' The colloquial Scots equivalent is *sma' still*. *Poitín* is a shortened form of *uisge poitín* – little pot whiskey. According to McGuffin, 'In Ireland, through time poitín has come to mean a strong colourless spirit, not unlike whiskey in taste, which is illegally manufactured and upon which no duty is paid' (p.84). Both McGuffin and Magee favour the spelling *poitín*, usually pronounced pŏtee´n, and McGuffin opens his panegyric to the product with a special note which stresses 'Throughout the book I have spelt the word "poitín". This is the correct Irish spelling, the reason for the emasculated "poteen" on the cover is my publisher's idea'.

Behan, perhaps surprisingly, writes in *Brendan Behan's Island*, 'Potheen is just murder. It's the end, you can take it from me, for I have had a wide enough experience of it'. This experience may have been coloured by sampling 'prison poitín' in the Curragh Internment Camp in 1943. Behan had the habit of relieving himself into empty bottles which he proceeded to throw out of the window to eliminate the tiresome business of getting out of bed. Empty bottles for the poitín which was ingeniously distilled by the internees to celebrate Christmas were obviously at a premium, and Behan was duly presented with his share of poitín in a 'recycled' bottle that had been retrieved from below his window. The ingenuity of Irish prisoners clearly remains where poitín is concerned, as a *Daily Telegraph* news item from July 1992 makes clear: 'An investigation was launched at the Maze prison in Belfast yesterday into how Loyalist inmates managed to make alcohol at the jail'.

Magee shares Behan's lowly opinion of poitín, or as it is sometimes known 'wee still', though earlier commentators clearly had different views regarding its comparability with legal whiskey. Writing in 1839, Caesar Otway noted that 'To every Irishman poitín is superior in sweetness, salubriety and gusto, to all that machinery, science and capital can produce in the legalized way' (*A Tour in Connaught*, quoted in McGuffin, 11), and a government report of 1823 stated that 'In Belfast poitín is expensive but it is consumed principally by the better classes where price is no consequence but quality is everything'. It should also be noted, however, that a story is still told of a West Cork man in the 1920s who ran his motorcycle on poitín and allegedly syphoned off a nightcap when he got home each evening.

Traditionally poitín was made from barley, but nowadays, according to McGuffin, 'Each area has its own recipe involving malt or sugar or treacle or beet or potatoes depending on the market price and availability of whatever substance they prefer' (p.84). He adds 'If care and attention is taken poitín made from just malt or beet or treacle or molasses can be every bit as good as that made from barley'. The manufacture of poitín continues as something of a 'cottage industry' today, notably in remoter areas of the west and south-west, though illegal stills are also in operation in the heart of Belfast city. McGuffin notes that 'County Antrim has always been poitín country' (p.94), and Antrim was home to the most famous of all twentieth century Irish poitín makers, Mickey McIlhattan, known as 'The King of the Glens', a highly respected musician and character, as well as a fabled maker of 'wee still'. The craft continues in Antrim, as viewers of the BBC television series *The Duty Men* saw when Customs and Excise officials caught a farmer from Ballymena with ten barrels of wash and over one hundred litres of finished spirit on his premises.

It is all a far cry from the situation in the early nineteenth century, when it is estimated some 3,800,000 of the total 11,400,000 gallons of spirits produced in Ireland in 1806 were illegally distilled rather than being what was often contemptuously referred to as 'parliament whiskey'. In Ireland the 1823 Excise Act helped legal distillers in that it replaced the previous Distillery Act of 1779, which had insisted that each licensed distillery must produce a minimum number of gallons of spirit per week, often far more than could be sold, and taxed the distiller on that level of production. A higher quality product more able to challenge poitín was the result, but in Ireland illicit distilling took longer to die out than it did in Scotland. The famine years of the 1840s and mass emigration did much to reduce poitín making, along with better road communications and law enforcement. A highly effective temperance campaign by the Catholic church in the middle years of the century also played its part.

The golden rule of drinking poitín is always to know its provenance, as it can vary from the excellent to the nearly toxic, and one way of testing an unknown sample which has been suggested to me is to place a little of the spirit in a saucer and add milk. If the milk curdles, opt for a Jameson or a Paddy instead. One fine advertisement for poitín came to light in March 1992 when a birthday party was held in County Kerry for Bertha, the world's oldest cow, who had reached the age of forty-nine, producing thirty-nine calves along the way. According to a *Daily Telegraph* report, Bertha's owner Jerome O'Leary noted that 'She gets pretty nervous when confronted with the public but I give her a drop of whiskey or poitín to build her up.'

pot ale   Also known as *burnt ale* and spent *wash, pot ale* takes its name from the fact that it is the residue of distillation in a *pot still*, with *ale* here having the sense of what the OED terms 'an intoxicating liquor made from an infusion of malt by fermentation'. 'Ale' is first attested in *c*.940, occurring in Old English as *alu*.

Graham and Sue Edwards list a secondary use of the phrase, suggesting that in Ireland pot ale was 'The religious establishments' barley-based spirit. Earliest recorded spirit in the British Isles'.

pot still   *Pot* as a vessel or container is late Old English or early Middle English, *pott*, first attested prior to 1200, 'Nim readstalede harhuna & ysopo & stemp & do on ænne neowna pott...' The *Scots Concise Dictionary* throws useful light on its origin in the context of distillation, defining a pot still as 'A kind of whisky still in which heat is applied directly to the pot. Originally one made by adding an attachment to a cauldron-type cooking pot'. It dates usage from the second half of the eighteenth to the end of the nineteenth century, though obsolescence by the latter date is clearly not accurate.

The pot still is the copper vessel in which *malt* whisky is distilled in Scotland and a blend of malt and unmalted *barley* is distilled in Ireland. Pot stills are also used to distil spirits such as cognac and rum. Jackson notes that a pot still is 'little more than a heated copper pot', and suggests that compared to *patent* still distillation, pot still distillation is 'a most inefficient procedure. However, its very inefficiency produces spirits of a character and individuality that cannot be matched by more modern methods' (*World Guide*, 10).

Essentially there are two connected pot stills in most Scottish distilleries, with the first distillation taking place in the *wash* still and the second in the *low wines* or *spirit* still, the former being larger as it has to accommodate a larger volume of liquid. McDowall describes the pot still as 'a large onion-shaped vessel with a long, narrow neck which leads to a cooling coil or worm' (p.104), and it is interesting to note that the basic pot-still design in use today was developed during the sixteenth century, when, as Moss explains, 'the technique of passing the outlet pipe through cold water was introduced and the copper worm developed'. The great advantage of the 'familiar pear-shaped still' was that it prevented 'unpleasant flavours and noxious substances tainting the spirit' (*Scottish Drink Book*, 89). Though McDowall's description of the pot still is basically valid, it is important to note that the apparatus varies considerably in design from one distillery to another, and that this is a major factor in the differences to be found between various whiskies which on the basis of ingredients, production technique and location ought, in theory, to be very similar. Milstead writes, 'Some are squat onion-shaped affairs, others are the traditional pear shape; still others look like inverted tulip glasses. And each has its own special way of condensing the compounds in whisky. There are 600-800 compounds in whisky and how they relate to each other and how they affect the flavour has never been established' (p.17).

There are many theories about pot-still design, some of which own more to superstition than fact, distillers through the years not unnaturally having been loth to replace a still with one of a different design when it has been producing good spirit. The whole business of making fine whisky has always been so unquantifiable in many respects that it is eminently reasonable that, having found a winning formula for its consistent creation, nothing should be done to jeopardise its continuity. At its most extreme this led to not-so-apocryphal stories of distillers who refused to move cobwebs in the stillroom and who had existing stills copied right down to hammering matching dents into their replacements. Milstead calls this 'The famous dented still myth'. Less extreme is the case of the *Islay* distillery of Laphroaig, where rather than scale up their existing stills and risk altering the distinctive *make*, the number of stills of the same size was increased to meet greater demand. The same logic was applied at a number of mainland Scottish distilleries such as Glenfiddich and Macallan. At other plants, such as Glencadam near Brechin, it was considered that only the overall shape and the neck design of the pot still was important, and larger stills which retained the same 'profile' were installed.

It is generally accepted that tall stills will produce lighter whiskies than short stills, because 'in a large still, some of the vapours condense before they have left the vessel, fall back and are redistilled' (Jackson, *Malt Whisky Companion*, 10). The *Highland* malt Glenmorangie is produced in stills nearly seventeen feet tall, the tallest in Scotland.

Laphroaig's oily, peaty, fully-flavoured malt is produced in small, squat stills which have comparatively short necks, and the *Lomond* still produces what Moss and Hume call a 'heavy, rich whisky'. Long-necked pot stills such as are found at the Islay distillery of Bruichladdich produce a lighter, 'cleaner' spirit. According to Moss and Hume, 'The presence of a bulge in the still neck, sometimes called a 'Balvenie ball' is usually a sign that a lighter yet more flavoursome whisky is required, and the same goes for a lantern head' (*The Making of Scotch Whisky*, 182).

Another general rule is that the larger the still the lighter the resulting whisky, and it is interesting to note that Irish pot stills have almost always been larger than those used in Scotland, perhaps because when large stills came into use, Ireland's distilleries were catering for cities – Dublin, Cork and Belfast. The largest pot still in the world, with a capacity of 31,648 gallons, is to be found at the Old Midleton distillery in County Cork. By comparison the pot stills of the New Midleton distillery each hold 16,500 gallons.

There is an old distiller's theory that the smaller the pot still, the finer the whisky, in much the same way that in cooking small boilings are usually considered to produce better flavour. It is hardly surprising that Scotland's smallest distillery, Edradour in Perthshire – with stills of five hundred gallons' capacity – should make use of the old theory in its promotional material, and the company notes that 'Our copper stills are the smallest allowed under Excise regulations – any smaller the theory goes and they'd be hidden away in a hillside'.

Copper is universally used in the construction of pot stills as it has the best heat transference of any metal, and John Wilson records that at the *Campbeltown* distillery of Glen Scotia, 'The stills are left unpolished to keep them cooler' (*Scotland's Distilleries*). Originally pot stills were heated by peat or coal, but today stills are heated by coke, gas or steam, steam heating having been pioneered in the 1880s. Some distilleries, such as Glenfiddich on Speyside and Springbank in Campbeltown, have persisted with direct heating, however, believing that it 'seals in' the malt flavours, and in 1984 Glen Grant reverted to the use of coal-fired stills. Internal steam-coil firing makes for more precise control of the distilling process and an even spread of heat, removing the possibilities of particles of malt burning on the bottom of the still and therefore the necessity of *rummagers*. It also reduces the chances of the wash boiling over. Modern stills have sighting windows so that boiling can easily be monitored, but in the past a large wooden ball would often be hung alongside a still and bounced off its side, so that the *stillman* could tell by the note produced what was happening within the vessel.

The term 'pot still whisky' is now rarely encountered, though Daiches uses it, declaring that 'the whisky distilled from malted barley in the manner perfected in the Scottish Highlands in the eighteenth century and still produced in essentially the same manner – what we call Pot Still Highland Malt Scotch Whisky – has proved to be inimitable outside Scotland (*Scotch Whisky*, 4-5). Gunn employs the expression as a synonym for malt whisky which was current during the 1930s, 'some essential principle is retained that gives pot-still whisky its peculiar, desirable, and unmistakable flavour' (p.144).

According to Jackson, 'The product of this distillation [of malt and unmalted barley] is known in Ireland simply as pot still whiskey, and that term is used very specifically in the industry and in labelling (*World Guide*, 103). Magee notes, however, that 'Irish pot still continues to be a highly favoured drink, but there is not so much of it around nowadays. The appellation has gradually disappeared from the labels of both the home and export products over the last few years' (p.94).

potable Fit for drinking, and more specifically liquor suitable for drinking. After the French *potable*, adapted from the Late Latin *pōtābilis*, drinkable, from *pōtāre*, to drink. The first attestation occurs in 1572, 'The water there is altogyther potable', and with the sense of liquor in 1623, 'In a well-knit body, a poor parsnip will play his prize above their strong potabiles'. In *Scotch Whisky: Questions and Answers*, the Scotch Whisky Association notes 'Spirits for human consumption, or potable spirits, are the distillates of alcoholic liquids...'.

poteen A widely used anglicisation of the Irish *poitín*.

Prohibition The action of forbidding by or as by authority; an edict, decree, or order forbidding or debarring; a negative command. The word *prohibition* comes from the French *prohibition*, itself an adaptation of the Latin *prohibitiōn-em*, a noun of action from *prohib-ēre*, to prohibit.

In the specific sense of the forbidding by law of the manufacture and sale of alcoholic drink, which is now most usually employed, Prohibition is recorded in the United States in 1851, 'The state of Vermont has struggled arduously to arrive at the summit level of entire prohibition.' In 1869 the Prohibition Party was formed, with the aim of nominating and supporting only people pledged to vote for the abolition of the liquor trade. The term *prohibitionist* is first recorded in 1846, 'Prohibitionist, an advocate for prohibitory measures'. Colloquially prohibitionists were frequently known as 'drys', just as their opponents were labelled 'wets', and the two appellations are used by Sir Robert Bruce Lockhart 'During the war, too, the teetotallers were well-organised and very active. The "wets" were apathetic' (p.141).

'Prohibition' is now usually taken as being synonymous with that period from 1919 to 1933 when alcoholic drink was, in theory at least, banned in the United States, though it should be noted that prohibition is still in force in some American counties, mainly in the South. According to Lockhart, Prohibition was 'the most puzzling episode in American history', and he observes that 'The biggest blow to the Scottish distillers after the First World War was the introduction of total prohibition by the Government of the United States' (p.143). A number of 'dry' states were already in existence, but complete Prohibition was first introduced as a war measure in 1917, being authorised by the Eighteenth Amendment. After the war the National Prohibition Law became part of the American Constitution, and the Volstead Act laid down the measures for its enforcement. Writing of the national state of mind that accepted the introduction of Prohibition with very little protest, Lockhart notes the 'wave of Spartan idealism' that accompanied American entry into the First World War. 'Alcohol was a menace to the American effort, and to be dry became the patriotic duty of American men and especially of American women who had not yet experienced the delights of cocktail orgies and chain-smoking' (p.140). 'What was extraordinary', he suggests, 'was the fervour with which the American people accepted prohibition *after* the war. For total prohibition did not enter into full force until January, 1920, and at first it swept the country like a best-seller'. This mood was not to last, however, and illicit distillation of frequently very questionable *moonshine* and the illegal importation of *the real McCoy* were soon occurring on a grand scale. In 1921 some 96,000 illicit stills were located by the authorities, and by 1930 that figure had increased to 282,000.

Lockhart spent some time in America during Prohibition, and he comments, 'I have seen much drinking in many countries, but the United States of the "dry" period surpassed all that I had previously experienced or, indeed, that I could have imagined' (p.142). Tales of alcoholic hardship do occur, however, W.C. Fields lamenting that 'once during Prohibition, I was forced to live for days on nothing but food and water'. In 1933 President Roosevelt repealed the Volstead Act, 'rightly interpreting public opinion', as Lockhart puts it. He considers that prohibition was ultimately not particularly damaging to the Scotch whisky industry, as previous markets were recaptured and expansion achieved due to the previously high reputation Scotch had enjoyed in the United States.

Another factor that led to increased sales of Scotch whisky after Prohibition was the inability of the distillers of Irish whiskey to respond to the renewed demand for their product. If, as Morrice concludes, 'On balance, Prohibition was far from being a bad thing for the Scotch whisky industry' (p.71), it was clearly something of a disaster for the Irish distillers. It was also a major contributory factor in the dramatic decline of the old Scottish 'whisky capital' of *Campbeltown*, whose products gained a reputation for poor quality and inconsistency due to excessive demand from the United States during the period of Prohibition.

'Prohibition' inevitably conjures up American-derived images of *bootleg* whisky and Al-Capone-style gangster operations, but 'dryness' was not limited to America; British temperance activities led to a little-known period of Prohibition in the far north of Scotland which lasted for eleven years longer than the 'experiment' in the United States. As the Caithness historian Iain Sutherland records, 'For a quarter of a century, between 28th May 1922 and 28th May 1947, there were no public houses or licenced grocers in Wick open for the sale of alcohol to the public. They had been closed as the result of an election which had been held on 10th December 1920, under the terms of the Temperance (Scotland) Act of 1913...' (p.3). 'Wick is the old herring capital of Scotland', notes Morrice 'and once had an appalling reputation for lawlessness due to the influx of transient workers from the Hebrides, intent on making a killing during the herring season' (p.350). As in the United States 'Prohibition' was regularly used to describe the situation in Wick, appearing in the publicity material of both 'wets' and 'drys', and also as in the States, the fishing port was never actually 'dry', with alcohol still being legally obtainable from a number of premises with wholesale licences. Sutherland comments 'Unfortunately for the prohibitionists the same effect which had been seen in America began to show itself in Wick after a short time. By 1922 doctors in Chicago were prescribing 200,000 gallons of spirit for medicinal purposes a year, and while Wick could not reach that level it was beginning to discover a variety of ailments which required treatment by alcohol' (p.25). Another inevitable outcome was the development of illicit drinking and illicit distillation, with at least two stills in operation. One, at Hill of Newton, was operated by Willag Thomson in conjunction with his uncle and cousin, and the trio even grew their own barley for the whiskey they produced. Sutherland notes:

> The customers were uncritical of quality, although this varied considerably according to the brew and vintage, which was usually measured in days or weeks. Whisky is a naturally clear liquid and acquires its colour from the sherry casks in which it is stored. The organisation at the top of Newton Hill had difficulty in acquiring bottles, not to speak of sherry casks, and they gave the accepted colour to their product by singeing white sugar in a spoon over the fire till it turned a suitable brown and stirred this into their brew. (*Vote No Licence*, 33)

A number of what Sutherland terms *shebeens* sprang up around the town, and he writes 'the most daring of all operated in a restaurant, whose regulars knew that when the fancy silver teapot was in use, that its contents had been brewed some considerable time previously. And not in India or China either' (p.30). My own paternal grandfather, who grew up in Wick, recalled being puzzled at the incongruous sight of large, red-faced countrymen apparently taking tea in the Bridge Street premises.

proof As Daiches explains, 'One of the meanings of the word "proof" at least since the sixteenth century is "of tried strength or quality" and it is this meaning that is involved in the phrase "proof spirit", which simply means spirit of standard and approved strength' (*Scotch Whisky*, 17). In the drink-related sense, *proof* is first attested in 1705: 'For Proof (of the brandy) there was a little Spanish soap clapt into it, and the Scum of the Soap passed on them for the Proof', though with the original meaning to which Daiches alludes a first use is recorded prior to 1225, 'þet hit beo soð, lo her þe preoue'. Proof comes from the Middle English *preove, proeve, preve*, after the Old French *preuve, proeve, preve, proeuve*. In Latin *probāre*, to prove.

The Customs and Excise Act of 1952 defined spirits of proof strength in the following terms: 'Spirits shall be deemed to be at proof if the volume of the ethyl alcohol contained therein made up to the volume of the spirits with distilled water has a weight equal to that of twelve-thirteenths of a volume of distilled water equal to the volume of the spirits, the volume of each liquid being computed at fifty-one degrees Fahrenheit'. *Proof spirit* was, therefore, as the Scotch Whisky Association notes, 'a mixture of spirit and water of a strength of 57.1% of spirit by volume and 42.9% of water' (*Questions and Answers*, 32). 'Proof strength was measured in degrees', writes Morrice, 'starting with proof itself at 100°. Scotch whisky has usually been sold in Britain at 30° under proof, i.e. 70° proof, but it is sometimes found at 75° and 100° proof' (p.140).

Until January 1980 the strength of spirits in Britain was measured by proof strength, using the hydrometer developed by Bartholomew Sikes from models first used in the 1740s. The Sikes apparatus was officially adopted by the 1818 Hydrometer Act, though as Marshall Robb explains, 'In ancient times an idea of the strength of spirits was obtained by several dry rough methods. The spirit was shaken in a bottle and a note taken of the time required for the disappearance of the "bead" or small bubble; the alcohol was ignited and the amount which burnt away was noted. Gunpowder was damped with the spirit and then a light was applied to see if it still ignited' (p.51). As Morrice points out, 'The assessment of duty has for long been based on alcoholic strength, and the accurate measuring of this has always been an obsession of the exciseman' (p.138).

Since 1980 the notion of proof strength has not been officially recognised in Britain, having been replaced by a new method of measurement recommended by the International Organisation of Legal Metrology and adopted throughout the European Community. As the Scotch Whisky Association explains, 'The OIML system measures alcoholic strength as a percentage of alcohol by volume at a temperature of 20°C. It replaced the Sikes system of measuring the proof strength of spirits, which had been used in Britain for over 160 years' (*Questions and Answers*, 29). As a result, the old, familiar British whisky bottle labelling of '70° proof' gave way to the information that the spirit was '40% Vol.'. Neil Wilson notes that 'In the United States a proof system is still operated whereby 100° American Proof equates to 50% alcoholic volume' (p.7).

Jackson points out that 'All spirits are distilled at a higher alcohol content than makes for a pleasant drink. In order that the character of the original material be retained, the law insists that Scotch whisky be distilled at a percentage of alcohol by volume that is clearly under 95 (to ensure this 94.8 is specified). In practice, malts come off the still in the range of 75-60' (*Malt Whisky Companion*, 19). At the opposite end of the strength spectrum there was a vogue for low-priced, low-strength Scotch whisky during the 1980s, but in 1989 EC legislation was introduced prohibiting the sale of whiskies below 40% vol. in order to protect the reputation and integrity of the product.

Most whisky is reduced in strength by the addition of water to 40° or 43° before bottling, but Jackson notes that 'Single malts sold at "cask strength" range in alcohol content from just under 60 to just over 50' (ibid.). The Elgin firm of Gordon & MacPhail, who bottle a range of malts at cask strength, note in their corporate brochure that 'Before the First World War all whisky was bottled straight from the cask – i.e. at about 57% alcohol by volume (100° proof). Then in 1916, as a wartime measure, it was ordained that the strength be reduced to 30%. A bitter fight ensued and a compromise was reached at 40% (70° proof), which has remained the norm ever since.'

punch, whisky   As Daiches explains, 'When Lowlanders drank whisky in the eighteenth century they usually made it into toddy (whisky, hot water and sugar) or punch (whisky, hot water, sugar and lemon') (*A Wee Dram*, 10). The earliest reference to *punch* made with whisky occurs in Captain Edward Burt's *Letters from a Gentleman in the North of Scotland to His Friend in London* (1754), 'When they chuse to qualify it for Punch they sometimes mix it with Water and Honey, or with Milk and Honey.' The first attestation of the term 'whisky punch' is in Burns' poem 'Scotch Drink' (1785). In Glasgow rum punch was popular as a result of the city's trade with the West Indies, but in Edinburgh whisky was almost always the spirit used. Daiches – in a BBC Radio 4 broadcast of January 1981 – commented that whisky punch was 'A terrible waste of good whisky'. He observed that 'The last decadent remnant of the whisky punch habit is whisky and lemonade', noting that the provision of a bottle of lemonade on bar counters is 'A strange aberration found only in Scotland'.

Theodora Fitzgibbon gives recipes for both hot and cold whisky punch (Mackinlay et al, 112). The heated version involves straining hot tea over sugar and lemon and adding a bottle of whisky; the resultant mixture is lit and served in punch glasses. Cold whisky punch consists of pouring boiling water over squeezed lemons and sugar. Once cold this is strained and a bottle of whisky is added. *The Dictionary of Drink* offers a recipe for whisky punch *cocktail*, and specifies two measures of whisky to one of rum, along with lemon juice, sugar, and a dash of Angostura. The mixture is served on ice with a dash of soda water and a slice of orange soaked in Curaçao.

With the sense of a drink usually composed of wine or spirits mixed with hot water, flavoured with sugar, lemon, and spice or cordial, punch is first attested in 1632, 'I hope you will keep a good house together and drincke punch by no allowanc'. It has been suggested that it derives from the Marāthī and Hindī word for five – *pānch* – as it was originally made from five ingredients. However, as Dunkling points out, 'The *Oxford English Dictionary* long ago pointed out that this was unlikely on phonetic grounds. There is also no evidence that punch was originally made from five ingredients. The word is more likely to be an abbreviation of "puncheon", a kind of large cask' (p.203).

puncheon A large *cask*, usually with a specific capacity which differed according to commodities. As a liquid measure it varied from 72 gallons for beer to 120 gallons for whisky. The first attestation occurs in 1479, 'Gevin...to John of Tyre to by a pwncion of wyne'. *Puncheon* has its origins in the thirteenth century Old French word *ponçon*, and according to Russell Sharp the puncheon and the *dump* puncheon, with respective capacities of 558 litres and 463 litres, are two of the five 'main types of cask used in Scotland' (*Scots on Scotch*, 170).

Q **uaich** 'The quaich is of Highland origin, the name being a corruption of the Gaelic *cuach*, a cup', according to McNeill (p.125). In Gaelic *cuaich* is the genitive singular of *cuach*, and in Old Irish *cúach* occurs, probably being an adaptation of the Latin *caucus*. The first attestation of *quaich* occurs prior to 1673, 'A quech weighting 18 unce and 10 drop'. The first recorded usage with the current spelling dates from 1884, and other variants include *queich, quaigh, queff, coif,* and *quaff*.

McNeill describes the quaich as 'wide and shallow, with wedge-shaped horizontal handles which, to the convivially-minded, "seem to invite a hearty grasp", and which certainly facilitate its being passed from hand to hand when circulated as a loving-cup'. Gordon Brown of the Malt Whisky Association, writing in issue 3 of *The Malt Letter*, notes that the double handle of the quaich 'symbolises the social bond of drinking and sharing, the cup having the means of being passed on in friendship and being received by the person beside you'. Dunford records that the quaich was 'Created in wood, in later years craftsmen started to embellish it in silver, and by the end of the seventeenth century when Scottish life was becoming more opulent, it was sometimes made entirely of silver' (n.p.). According to McNeill, 'Long after cups and glasses came into general use, the smaller quaichs continued to be used for brandy or whisky.' Sir Walter Scott made a point of serving whisky to his guests at Abbotsford in quaichs, and as Dunford observes, 'on many a Highland Army mess table for years the most characteristic feature was the silver-bound quaich of whisky, circulated frequently during the evening'.

The role of the quaich as the archetypal historical vessel for whisky-drinking in Scotland has led to its adoption as a kind of emblem by a prestigious organisation founded in 1989 by employees of what is now the Guinness-owned United Distillers. This exclusive company rejoices in the name of 'The Keepers of the Quaich', and its avowed intention is to act as 'custodian of the traditions and prestige of Scotch whisky...to promote the image and prestige of Scotch whisky...to rekindle the magic and mystery of the product'. Alongside a photograph of 'The Keepers' in full Highland regalia, accompanied by a singularly opulent example of hallmarked silver quaich design, the caption writer of *Scots on Scotch* rather tartly observes 'Tradition is reinvented'.

quarter In whisky terms a *quarter* is a *cask* with a capacity of approximately 28 gallons or 127 litres. It is a quarter the size of a *butt*, just as an *octave* is an eighth of a butt. As a cask, quarter is first attested in 1882, 'There is a trifle of oil, a quarter barrel'.

R **at-arsed** An adjective which, according to *The Oxford Dictionary of Modern Slang*, means 'Intoxicated or incapacitated by drink, drunk'. First attestation occurs in 1984, but the synonymous adjective *ratted* pre-dates that by a year. The expression probably evolved from the existing phrase 'drunk as a rat', one of the many rather inappropriate, unfactual similes for intoxication. (See also *drunk*.) The use of *arsed* here arises perhaps from the sense of an arse as a foolish person, and/or of *arse around*, to mess about. The term *arseholed* to mean drunk also occurs, probably from the sense of an arsehole as 'a stupid or obnoxious person' *(Oxford Slang)*. Partridge notes *(Historical Slang)* 'rat' as 'A drunken person taken into custody', dating usage from the late seventeenth century to the early nineteenth. He suggests the possibility that the term 'drowned rat' may be the origin of the expression, but speculates that it is more likely to be from 'drunk as a rat', which is thereby effectively dated to at least the late seventeenth century.

real McCoy See *McCoy*.

receiver The *malt* whisky distillery contains four types of *receiver*, the large collecting vessels which 'receive' *feints*, *low wines*, *spirit* or *worts* once they have been produced. Wilson writes 'When the distillate reaches the required strength it is diverted into the spirit receiver' (p.27).

With the sense of a tank or vessel, receiver is first attested in 1538, 'Much ground therabout is playne and low, and as a Pan or Receyver of most parte of the Water of Wyleshire.' The word was originally adopted from the Anglo-French *receivers* or *receivour*, *receyvour*, which equal the Old French *recevere* and *recevour*. In Modern French *receveur* from *receivre*, *recevoir*, to receive.

rectification With the chemical sense of 'To purify or refine a substance by a renewed or repeated distillation, or by some chemical process; to raise *to* a required strength in this way...' the verb *to rectify* is first attested in c.1450. 'Ffirst departyng of the foure Ellementys, And afftirward...Euerych of hem for to Recteffye'. It is adopted from the fourteenth century French *rectifier*, itself adapted from the third century Late Latin *rectificāre*.

162

Moss & Hume state that in the nineteenth century, 'Most grain whisky was sent to London for rectification (a further distillation process) and compounding into gin' (*The Making of Scotch Whisky*, 26). As well as meaning to purify, to distil spirit close to neutrality, *rectification* can also encompass the flavouring of a liquor with some substance, as in the manufacture of gin, which is flavoured with juniper.

Rectifier – the apparatus for rectifying spirit – is first recorded in 1854, 'The upper part forming a heater for the wash, while the lower compartment acts as a rectifier'. The *Dictionary of Drink* defines the rectifier as 'Part of the Continuous-still (patent or Coffey still) which produces the pure spirit. Condenses a hot vapour (the spirits) to a liquid in distillation'.

road, one for the   A final drink before departure, the English language equivalent to the Gaelic *deoch an doras*, 'a drink at the door'. 'Inside snug MacLellan's/Old Rab, the earth's salt,/Knocks one back *for the road*'. (W.S. Graham, 'The Murdered Drinker'). Brewer's *Twentieth Century Phrase and Fable* notes, 'One last drink before departing, formerly a popular call at the end of a party. However, since the introduction of strict drink-driving codes this is rarely heard'.

The term is not always used with total sincerity; often intentions are good but flesh is weak. Sometimes several ones for the road are consumed prior to leaving a house or bar, and in the case of a drinking acquaintance of my father, the consumption of one for the road was invariably followed by the declaration 'And now let's have one for no reason at all'.

rummager   An apparatus fitted inside a *pot still*, consisting of four rotating arms which carry a copper chain mesh. When stills are direct-fired by either coal or *peat*, there is an ever-present danger that solid particles in the *wash* will scorch the still bottom and the resultant *spirit* will be tainted as a result. As Moss & Hume explain, 'From the late eighteenth century, "rummagers", devices made of chains for scouring the bottom of stills during distillation, were fitted to help prevent scorching. In recent times, most stills have been converted to steam heating, which avoids the problem and gives more accurate heat control' (*The Making of Scotch Whisky*, 20). Milsted describes the rummager as being 'a large, slow-motion whisk', noting that one fine whisky bluff is to carefully sample a *malt* and exclaim, 'This has all the hallmarks of being cut from an imperfectly rummaged run' (p.19).

In its distillation-related context, *rummager* is a term peculiar to Scotland, with most dictionary entries offering nautical uses, relating to the arranging of ships' cargoes, storage capacity, or a search of a vessel, though the sense of miscellaneous goods, lumber or rubbish also occurs.

With the meaning of 'to disarrange or disorder; to knock, stir, or drive about, to force or rout out by searching or making a stir', which is the one applicable to distillation, first attestation occurs in 1591, 'Our Ships being all pestered and romaging euerie thing out of order'. The OED offers an application, obsolete except in Scotland, of rummage to mean 'bustle, commotion, turmoil', first attested in 1575.

run   A term used in Ireland, Scotland and the United States for the flow of spirit from a still during any one period of *distillation*. The first recorded use of *run* with the sense of the amount of liquid produced or allowed to flow at one time occurs in 1710, 'And being seldom tryed when melted, their coins are of different value, as the run happens to be good or bad, Plate, Dollars, and old Copeeks, being all melted together'. The first attestation which makes specific reference to distillation is in 1838, 'The second run of the still . . . is of a strength from 23° to 26°.'

Writing of *poitín*-making in County Donegal, McGuffin quotes from the novelist Seamas MacGrianna's autobiography, *Nuair a bhí mé óg (When I was Young)*: 'Hudai Hugh was helping me with the run' (p.106). The term *doubling run* is used in America to denote a second distillation, 'One by one you'd distill each barrel and you'd get six to eight gallons of singlings from each. Then you'd cook them through the still again. That's your doubling run. That's when you get your real alcohol (McGuffin, 58). *First run* – which produces *low wines* – and *second run* also occur in general usage. McGuffin quotes Long Kesh internee 'Uncle Doc' on the subject of prison poitín: 'The first run would come out and be caught in half of a large plastic fruit juice container. We normally always drank the singlings rather than give it a second run. This meant that although we got drunk we also got shocking hangovers because the fusel oil hadn't been eliminated' (p.44). The *middle cut* of spirit is also sometimes referred to as the *heart of the run*.

rusty nail   The usual recipe is for one and a half measures of Scotch whisky and half a measure of Drambuie *liqueur*. The two ingredients are stirred *on the rocks* and a twist of lemon is added. The drink is served in an *Old-fashioned glass*. Jackson, however, notes that 'Some suggest that the ingredients should be matched 1:1. Even 2:1 produces too sticky a drink'. He is inclined to serve the *rusty nail* without ice, floating the Drambuie on the top. 'Do not stir, not even with a rusty nail', he insists (*Pocket Bar Book*, 134).

The most obvious provenance of the drink's name has to do with its colour, but it is hardly unique in being rust-coloured. Grindal speculates on this, pointing out that 'No one has ever been able to give a satisfactory explanation for the origin of this name. Could it be because the drink might be the one rusty nail in the coffin-lid, enabling an otherwise doomed over-indulger to make a last-minute escape?' (p.198). Quite why a large, strong, spirit-based drink should somehow offer the over-enthusiastic drinker redemption is not explained by Grindal.

rye   Along with *Bourbon*, *rye* whiskey is one of the two distinctive indigenous whiskeys of the United States, possibly dating back to the 1600s. Rye is a food grain obtained from the plant *secale cereale*, and is first recorded in *c*. 725 as *ryʒe* (Old English), Old Norse *rug-r*. According to the OED 'It is probable that the original home of the word was Eastern Europe'. In the United States rye has developed an elliptical, colloquial usage to connote rye whiskey, first attested in 1894, 'I knew better than to put straight rye on top of it [cider]'.

Whereas *Scotch*, *Irish* and Bourbon whiskies are defined by strict geographical parameters, rye whiskey – produced in a *continuous still* – is not, and is distilled in the United States and Canada. In the former it must, by definition, contain a minimum of 51% rye, but as Jackson notes, 'It is difficult to produce a whiskey exclusively from rye, and a small quantity of barley malt is introduced during fermentation' (*World Guide*, 130). Rye whiskey is basically made from three different kinds of grain, as Jackson also makes the point that 'in palate the intensity of the rye is offset by a substantial proportion of corn'. In terms of its character he writes that the rye grains which give a slight bitterness to bread also affect the whisky, 'It is reminiscent of a bittersweet fruit – perhaps a hint of apricot – spicy, a little oily, almost peppermint. The bitterness arouses the appetite, like quinine in a patent aperitif, or hops in beer' (ibid.). There is no legal minimum *maturation* period for rye whiskey, though by law it must be held in new, charred oak *casks*, and it cannot be called *straight* rye whiskey in the United States unless it has been aged for a minimum of two years, and if it is younger than four years old when bottled, then the label must state that fact.

The Canadians are altogether more relaxed about what can pass for rye whiskey, merely stating 'Canadian Whisky (Canadian Rye Whisky, Rye Whisky) shall be whisky distilled in Canada, and shall possess the aroma, taste and character generally attributed to Canadian Whisky'. In practice, all Canadian whiskies are blends of rye, other whiskies like Bourbon, and spirit that has been rectified close to neutrality. The country produces no straight rye whiskies. One interesting difference between American and Canadian ryes is that in Canada malted rye is often used as well as unmalted rye. The American version is definitely 'the original rye', according to Jackson.

One result of EC regulations which banned spirits below 40° alcohol by volume from being marketed as 'whisky' or 'whiskey' has been the arrival on British supermarket and off-licence shelves of many Canadian rye whiskies, many at 30° abv. Labelling carefully avoids mention of whisky in any way, usually just proclaiming 'Finest Canadian Rye' or 'Imported Spirits'. These 'spirits' usually sell for little more than half the price of a bottle of reputable blended Scotch whisky, but sampling experience suggests that this ought to be so.

The development of rye whiskey in the United States owes much to the Irish and Scottish settlers who found rye less difficult to grow than the *barley* which they were accustomed to raising for distilling purposes, though the Irish were already used to using rye in whisky-making. It was particularly associated with Pennsylvania and Maryland, but their importance as distilling centres has declined considerably, and most rye is now distilled in Kentucky.

Jackson observes that 'rye has never quite recovered from being upstaged by Kentucky Bourbon, which came later' (*World Guide*, 138) though there were signs during the early 1980s that rye whiskey was staging something of a minor comeback, with several distilleries increasing rye production and even introducing new rye whiskeys. He suggests that one reason for the general decline in demand for rye whiskey was its rather distinctive flavour; it may well have possessed too much character for an age in which increasingly bland spirits gained most favour amongst drinkers. *Prohibition*, too, may well have played its part, as 'Rye-flavoured blends smugged in from Canada confused the customer as to the true nature of the designation and things have never been the same since' (*World Guide*, 147).

The principal straight rye whiskies currently available include Old Overholt, Pikesville, and Rittenhouse, whilst two high-profile names best known to Bourbon drinkers have also been transferred to rye, Jim Beam making an 80° *proof* straight rye, and Wild Turkey producing one at their characteristic 101° proof.

S **aladin** A *malting* process initially used in brewing, invented in the late nineteenth century, but not popular in Scotch distilleries until after the Second World War. Daiches writes: 'Some distilleries use the long concrete or metal trench known as the "Saladin box", after Charles Saladin, the French engineer who invented it. In the Saladin box revolving metal forks move slowly up and down its length to keep the grain turned and aerated' (*Scotch Whisky*, 9).

Scotch The contraction of *Scottish* into *Scotch* is not recorded before 1570 – when it appears in the compound *Scotchman* – though the OED considers it likely that usage occurred at a considerably earlier date. The first use of *Scotch* with the sense of pertaining to Scotland occurs in 1591, as 'Scotch cap', and specifically relating to whisky in 1855, 'While malt liquors give our Scotch and Irish whiskies'. In current usage, the word Scotch is only considered acceptable in a few instances, such as relating to whisky, broth, eggs and mist. McCallum's 'Perfection' blended whisky is unique in being labelled 'Scots Whisky'.

Clearly Scotch whisky here is just whisky made in Scotland, there is no sense of Scotch implying a *blended* whisky rather than a *malt*, as is generally now the case. The first elliptical use of 'Scotch' with reference to whisky where the substantive is contextually known is recorded between 1886 and 1896 – 'In the early evening watches he had started well on Scotches' – and the date would suggest that the product in question was blended whisky, though we have to wait until 1898 for a quotation which leaves us in no doubt that Scotch means blended whisky. 'Scotch and syphon for you, sir? Here the presence of a soda dispenser is conclusive. Partridge *(Historical Slang)* dates the first use of 'Scotch' for a drink of Scotch whisky to *c*.1885, noting that this colloquialism had become Standard English by *c*.1905. Today the definition of 'Scotch' is not entirely clear cut, though it would seem that when the word is used in isolation the reference is usually to a blended whisky, and when used in conjunction with whisky the implication is whisky – of any kind – distilled in Scotland. Jackson uses the term Scotch when writing of what he calls 'single malt Scotch'. For him 'The term Scotch means that the

167

whisky was distilled and matured in the country whose name it bears' (*Malt Whisky Companion*, 8).

The Scotch Whisky Association poses the question 'When Consumers ask for a Scotch, what exactly do they mean?' and answers 'They usually mean a blended Scotch Whisky...' (*Questions and Answers*, 9). Cooper observes that 'As far as I know the Scots are the only race in the world to have an internationally renowned drink named after them and that is surprising because "Scotch" was only invented in the middle of the nineteenth century' (*Whisky Roads*, 11).

The first legal definition of Scotch whisky was made in 1909, as a result of the 'What is Whisky?' case, and after defining whiskey (as the Royal Commission spelt it) in general, its report stated '"Scotch whiskey" is whiskey, as above defined, distilled in Scotland...'. Current legislation specifies that 'The expression "Scotch Whisky" shall mean whisky which has been distilled and matured in Scotland', and in order to retail within the EC it must also be of a strength of at least 40% alcohol by volume.

Morrice makes the interesting observation that 'To ask for "Scotch" in Scotland is to identify yourself as a stranger. Whisky means different things to different people in different places. Only in Scotland will the request for a "whisky" guarantee that you are served with the native spirit, Scotch...' (p.7). If one wished to be served with a malt whisky in a bar one would need to stress the fact, and not to specify a particular *single malt* would probably be taken as a sign of lamentable ignorance.

self *Self* whisky is the old term for what is usually now referred to as *single malt* whisky, and the expression is almost obsolete. It was regularly employed by whisky writers such as Gunn and Robb during the 1930s and 1940s, Gunn noting, 'I know that pot stills with a very indifferent reputation as single or self-whiskies have had their perfect periods, and famous names out of the Glenlivet country, and elsewhere can definitely on occasion be "not so good"' (p.178). Robb comments that 'in fact a large number of pure malts called self whiskies are not put on the market in bottle in the pure state' (p.47).

The first recorded use of the adjective 'self' with regard to whisky occurs in 1904, 'Of whisky: not blended', and in the same year a specifically Scottish use of the expression occurs in the *Dundee Advertiser*, 'In the market for self-whiskies there has been a pronounced want of activity'. The first use of 'self' with this sense of 'the same throughout, uniform', is in the context of colour, e.g. self-silver, self-black, in 1601, 'In a peece of selfe russet cloth'.

sensation Often preceded by the diminutive 'wee', *sensation* is used in Scotland to imply a drink of whisky (although it is not commonly used now, except in a self-consciously arch manner), and is generally taken to mean spirits of one sort or another. With its basic sense of 'an operation of any of the senses', it is first attested in 1615, and the later drink-related usage perhaps has its origins in the interpretation of sensation as 'a condition of excited feeling, an emotion', such as might be induced by the consumption of strong drink. (See *tired and emotional*.) The first recorded use of 'sensation' relating to alcohol occurs in 1859, 'A sensation (i.e.) Half-a-glass of sherry'. In the same year it was also defined as 'a quartern of gin'. Partridge specifies 'A (very) small quantity, esp. of liquor, occ. of food, rather rarely of other things', dating usage from the mid-nineteenth century. 'Lit., just so much as can be perceived by the senses', he adds, suggesting comparisons with the French *soupçon*.

shebeen A 1903 Act of Parliament stated that 'the word "shebeen" shall mean and include every house, shop, room, premises or place in which exciseable liquors are trafficked in, by retail, without a certificate and excise licence in that behalf.' The term is chiefly Irish in use, though Scottish examples do occur, and the meaning has extended to include any wayside public house, generally one with a poor reputation. The word is first attested in *c*.1787, 'With de stuff to a *shebeen* we hied'.

Writing of *prohibition* in the Scottish town of Wick, Sutherland notes that 'And so the system of illicit drinking places, known as *Shebeens* gradually spread' (p.30). He also uses the term *shebeeners*, for those who operated the illegal premises. 'Shebeen' is Anglo-Irish in origin, but the word's formation remains obscure. The diminutive suffix is clearly Irish – as in *boneen*, 'little pig' – and it has been conjectured that the word is from the Irish *seapa*, an adaptation of the English *shop*. In Irish dictionaries it is usually given as *sibin*. In Maria Edgeworth's *Castle Rackrent* (1800) a note on shebeen – or 'shebean' as it is spelt, with the definition of 'a hedge alehouse' – offers 'Shebean properly means weak small-beer, taplash'.

shiel A term employed in Scotland and Ireland for the wooden shovel used to turn *barley* during *malting*. Moss and Hume write 'The barley remains on the malting floor for between seven and fourteen days and is turned regularly to allow even germination and to prevent a build-up of heat. This is called "turning the piece" and is traditionally done by tossing the malt into the air with wooden shovels called shiels' (*The Making of Malt Whisky*, 13). Modern drum and *Saladin* malting processes have removed the necessity for hand-turning with *shiels*, though the practice survives at distilleries which maintain their own floor maltings, e.g. Laphroaig.

'Shiel' is a Scots variant of shovel, also sometimes *shuil*, and is recorded from the late eighteenth century, with usage chiefly being restricted to the north of Scotland. As well as being a malt shovel, a shiel can also be a long-bladed *peat*-cutter, and this sense is recorded from the early twentieth century, principally being used in the northernmost mainland county of Caithness.

shot A single measure of spirits, usually drunk *neat* or *straight*. Usage is chiefly confined to America, though it does occur in Britain, as in a *hangover* cure suggested by Floyd, 'In a glass jug pour in one shot each of Pernod and dry Vermouth, and add one egg white and the juice of one lemon' (p.23). It also gives its name to the *shot glass*, a small vessel designed to hold a single measure of spirits, the equivalent to a *jigger*. 'Shot' as a supply or amount of drink is first attested in 1676, 'Their vain way of drinking shots'. 'Shot' also has a second application as a synonym for *drunk*, with Partridge *(Historical Slang)* noting this adjectival usage as dating from *c*.1870. He suggests that its origins lie in the parallel with 'being wounded by a shot', presumably in terms of the physical effects of such a wound, including staggering etc., and the use of the existing sense as a measure of drink.

Partridge offers the American expression *shot in the neck* as the immediate origin of shot, and variants such as *shot in the arm* also occur, as in Sinclair Lewis's *Babbitt*: 'All afternoon he snorted and chuckled over his ability to "give the Boys a real shot in the arm" to-night.' The nautical alternative *shot-away* occurs from the late nineteenth century, and *overshot*, for very drunk, is first used by Marston in 1605, 'Death! Colonel, I knew you were overshot'. The sense here developed from the figurative one of to venture too far, to go beyond what is intended or proper. A drugs-related usage of 'shot', 'An injection of narcotics', according to *The New Dictionary of American Slang*, is first attested in the late 1920s.

silent Just as a theatre is said to be 'dark' or to have 'gone dark' when not in use, so a distillery is considered *silent* when it is not currently operational, although retaining its productive capacity. If silent for an indefinite period it is sometimes said to be 'mothballed'. The term 'silent' is in common usage in the Scotch whisky industry; Lamond notes of Tobermory distillery on Mull, 'Established by one John Sinclair. Taken over by DCL in 1916. Silent 1930-72. Now owned by a Yorkshire property company' *(Malt File*, 131). 'Silent' here has the sense first attested in 1745 of 'Inactive, quiescent, not operative'.

Every distillery has what is known as a *silent season*, though this is usually shorter than it used to be, and is no longer necessarily so seasonally-orientated. At one time, as distilling worked 'into the economy of the Highlands', as Gunn puts it (p.155), the process began in the autumn after the *barley* was harvested and while clear water was plentiful. It continued until spring, when the water supply became less certain, grain supplies were exhausted, and there was no longer a ready market for *draff* from farmers whose cattle did not require artificial feeding during the summer months. As Cooper observes, 'there was a "Silent Season" between May and October. Now that most of the barley is malted mechanically the only reason a distillery has for closing is to give the staff their annual holiday. The "Silent Season" has become just a holiday and annual maintenance break' (*Century Companion*, 17). In some cases necessity continues to dictate a silent season, as, for example, at Edradour in Perthshire, where distilling has to be suspended in summer when the Edradour burn dries up or falls to a very low level. At the end of one season the *feints* and *foreshots* from the final run are kept and re-distilled at the start of the next season in order to maintain continuity.

The sense of silent as 'inactive, quiescent, not operative' also occurs in the term *silent palate*, used by Gunn to describe the distressing affliction suffered by those whose palate is not sufficiently educated or discriminating to truly appreciate fine malt whiskies, 'Glenfiddich and Strathisla . . . are both very sound whiskies, the true Speyside flavour requiring perhaps a slight cultivation by what I may call a "silent" palate' (p.181). Gunn also notes that 'a pure spirit in the trade is known as a "silent" spirit', and this sense with the meaning of 'possessing no flavour' is first attested in 1839, 'Well purified or clean spirits, such as the distillers call silent whiskey'.

single A *single* whisky or single *malt* whisky as it is now more usually known, was formerly referred to as a *self* whisky. Hills notes that 'As the 1970s progressed, so did single malt whiskies, as they came to be called . . .' (p.13). Jackson stresses that 'The term SINGLE has a very clear and precise meaning. It indicates that the whisky was made in only one distillery, and has not been blended with any from elsewhere' (*Malt Whisky Companion*, 8). The single whisky may, however, come from between fifty and one hundred different *casks* of varying ages, and as with blended whiskies, any age statement made on a bottle of single malt must refer to the youngest component whisky. The Scotch Whisky Association notes that 'A single Malt Whisky is the product of one Malt Whisky distillery and a single Grain Whisky is the product of one Grain Whisky distillery' (*Questions and Answers*, 9). Jackson declares that 'The Classic whiskies of Scotland are the *straight* – or "single" – malts. In most cases, a single malt simply has the same name as the distillery that produced it' (*World Guide*, 16). Single malts are not entirely the preserve of Scotland, however, with Bushmills marketing an Irish single malt, while in Japan a number of single whiskies were introduced in the 1980s, most notably Suntory's Yamazaki and Sanraku Ocean's Karuizawa.

The sense of 'single' used with regard to whiskies is that of 'separate, distinct from each other or from others, not combined or taken together', and its first attestation occurs between 1432 and 1450, 'Iacob... blessenge his childer with single benedicciones'. It is adapted from the Old French *single, sengle*; in Latin *singulum* – one, individual, separate. It is interesting to note that whilst a large whisky, twice the size of a standard measure, is usually referred to as a 'double', nobody would ever ask a barman for a single whisky when they wanted a small glass of spirits.

The dramatically increased availability of a wide range of single malts has been one happy development in the drinks industry during the past two decades, something which has happened, paradoxically, as the whisky business has become concentrated into ever fewer hands. When Gunn was writing about whisky during the 1930s, single malts had all but disappeared, and even when McDowall's *The Whiskies of Scotland* was published in 1967 the range of single malts generally available was comparatively limited. He writes, 'There are about 110 malt distilleries in operation, but more are under construction. Less than 30 of their whiskies are available to the public in bottle' (p.9). The idea of a *Malt Whisky Almanac* (Milroy) or a *Malt Whisky Companion* (Jackson) that was of anything more than pamphlet proportions would have been inconceivable until quite recently. Milroy remarks that his

> Almanac was first published because malt whiskies were no longer the domain of an exclusive body of academic tasters and connoisseurs, but were to be found in increasing numbers in supermarkets, wine shops and duty free outlets at home and abroad. As distillers continue to budget greater amounts on the marketing of their malts, the public are at last getting access to a national asset as valuable to Scotland as the brandy houses are to France (p.6).

Hills considers the change that led to single malts being relatively common in England by the end of the 1970s to have been 'purely demand-led; the distillers, with a very few, laudable exceptions, were slow indeed to discern a potential market. The demand originated in Scotland, where it grew in the later 1960s' (p.13). Writing in 1987, Skipworth notes that 'Although it only represents a small slice of the market, *single* malt whisky is doing well. The pioneering work was done by Glenfiddich, the world's leading malt whisky' (p.39). The market share of single malts is, indeed, small, and to take a random but not untypical example, just 3 per cent of the *Lowland* malt Bladnoch is sold as a single whisky rather than disappearing into a variety of Guinness-owned blends.

Nonetheless, the days are gone when single malts were largely the preserve of a handful of dedicated specialist companies such as Gordon & MacPhail and Cadenhead catering for an almost equally small number of connoisseurs. Today many more singles are bottled and vigorously promoted by the distillers themselves, the promotion frequently being supported by visitor facilities at the distilleries where the whiskies are produced. Between 1974 and 1990, world sales of bottled-in-Scotland malt whisky rose from just over 2 million lpa to more than 10 million lpa, and in the fifteen years from 1972 to 1987 worldwide sales of single malts rose by nearly 600 per cent. Considering that single malts account for only some 3 per cent of domestic whisky sales it is interesting to note that their promotion accounts for nearly a quarter of all whisky-related advertising. Morton makes the point that the single malt market is attractive to distillers because of the comparatively high profit margins involved. 'Nobody except the taxman can make much money charging £8.00 for a bottle of supermarket blend. But something taxed at the same rate, because it's the same alcoholic strength, which you can charge nearly £30 for is a different story' (p.67).

single cask *Single cask* malt is the ultimate single whisky. Whereas most bottles of single malt contain spirit from between fifty and a hundred *casks*, mixed to give consistency, single cask whisky is just what its name implies, whisky taken from one individual cask, the product of just one distillation, producing a maximum of three hundred bottles. It is usually sold at *cask strength* – around 60% – rather than being diluted to 40% as is standard practice, and the process of *chill-filtering* is frequently omitted.

Cadenhead, Gordon & MacPhail, MacArthur and Signatory all bottle single cask malts, and the Scotch Malt Whisky Society was founded purely to make single cask whiskies available to a wider public. Based in Leith and now boasting some 14,000 members, the society was formed in 1983 by Phillip Hills and a number of like-minded associates, and it now offers whisky from more than thirty casks, all bottled under its own label. Writing of the usual bottled single malt whiskies which have been diluted and chill-filtered, Hills comments, 'The result is by any standard a fine liquor, but it lacks some of the character of malt whisky taken, unfiltered, from a single cask' (p.14).

singlings A synonym for *low wines*, the product of the *first run*. The term is not used in professional Scotch whisky distillation, but occurs in Irish and American *poitín* and *moonshine* manufacturing circles. It is also the standard term used in brandy distillation. *Singlings* here is a verbal substantive, the sense being selection from a number, separation from others. In a specifically distillation-related content – defined in 1884 as 'the first to come over, the crude spirit of distillation' – 'singlings' is first attested in 1830, 'The distillation may proceed as rapidly as (it) can run without coming foul or muddy, until 2400 gallons have been drawn off; these constitute what are called singlings.'

sippin' The Jack Daniel company advertises its famous product as 'Smooth sippin' Tennessee whiskey', the implication being that this is a delicate, subtle spirit to be sipped and savoured, not a fiery *moonshine* drink.

Lynchburg is the home of Jack Daniel's, and it boasts a population of three hundred, a fact which is frequently pointed out in the amazingly successful series of advertisements for Jack Daniel's whiskey, which have lasted for thirty-eight years with a virtually unchanged format. The term *sippin'* is not restricted to American usage; the Scotch Malt Whisky Association describes the *Highland* malt Linkwood as 'A sipping whisky' in its *tasting* notes.

'Sipping' – the action of the verb to sip, drinking by sips – is first attested *c*.1440, 'Cyppynge of drynke', and in 1648 the combination 'sipping drinke' occurs. 'Sip' – first recorded *c*.1386 – is of obscure origin, 'possibly a modification of sup, intended to express a slighter action', suggests the OED.

skalk Anglicisation of the Gaelic *sgailc*, which has the meaning of a smart knock or blow, and also formerly 'a full draught of any liquid', and specifically 'a bumper of spirits taken before breakfast ... a morning dram', according to Edward Dwelly *(Illustrated Gaelic-English Dictionary)*. Although 'skalk' and 'sgailc' are obsolete in terms of general usage in both English and Gaelic, skalk and the variant *scalch* are listed in Chambers' *Scots Dialect Dictionary*. Samuel Johnson *(A Journey to the Western Isles of Scotland*, 1775) records that 'A man of the Hebrides as soon as he appears in the morning swallows a glass of whisky; yet they are not a drunken race, at least I was never present at much intemperance;

but no man is so abstemious as to refuse the morning dram which they call a skalk'. Dwelly mentions the *sgailc-sheide*, an obsolete term for 'a dram taken before rising in the morning', and itemises a fascinating list of early morning drams usually offered to the guest in a house in Gaeldom. First came the *sgailc-nide*, 'a full bumper of whisky while still lying down', followed by the *friochd-uilinn*, 'an elbow nip, when he was first propped up', after which came the *deoch chas-ruisgte*, 'when still barefoot', and finally the *deoch bhléth*, 'while his breakfast porrage oats were being ground'. Quite how the guest was able to do anything other than fall back into bed without eating is not made clear.

slainte A Scots equivalent of the ubiquitous English *cheers*, almost exclusively used as a toast when drinking whisky. '"Another one?" "Aye, ta, Slainte".' (James White, *A Fine White Stoor*, 1992, p.101). Although a Gaelic expression, *slainte* is widely used by non-Gaelic speakers throughout Scotland. In Gaelic it means 'health', and is actually a contraction of the traditional Gaelic toast *slàinte mhath, slàinte mhór*, 'good health, great health': 'as we raise the uisge beatha to our lips with a devout "slàinte mhaht, slàinte mhór", we feel that we are indeed privileged visitors to Tir nan Òg' (*Whisky Galore*, 20). Dunkling considers the second element of the toast to be by way of a response, noting that Compton Mackenzie offered the Anglicised pronunciation slahnje vay, slahnje vor.

slug A draught of strong liquor, a *dram*, with usage principally being confined to the United States since *c.*1880, according to Partridge *(Historical Slang)*. The *Dictionary of Drink* specifies 'a single measure of spirit, usually served in a very small glass and drunk in one mouthful'. Originally *slug* was a British slang term for strong drink, first attested in 1756, 'Gunpowder, slug, wild-fire, knock-me-down', which was obsolete by 1790. The current, drink-related sense of 'slug' is first recorded in 1762, 'That he might cast a slug into his bread-room', and Partridge *(Historical Slang)* also notes the American expression 'fire a slug, to take a drink of potent liquor'. The origins are obscure, though one possible explanation is that 'slug' suggests the lethargy-provoking element of drinking, having the sense of a slow, lazy fellow, anything that moves slowly. It is part of the same aggressive, macho, imagery of American drinking vocabulary as *belt* and *shot*, with which there is perhaps a parallel in that 'slug' can also be slang for a bullet, as well as being a verb, to hit.

Dunkling notes the special Scottish application of the word, quoting from George Douglas's *The House With The Green Shutters*, 'He was what the Scotch call a "slug for drink". A slug for the drink is a man who soaks and never succumbs' (*Guinness Companion*, p.21).

sma' still   A Scottish and Anglo-Irish term, *sma'* being a colloquial form of *small* which has had currency since the late fourteenth century. As the *Concise Scots Dictionary* explains, the expression 'sma' still' was current during much of the nineteenth century and was frequently used 'implying illicit distillation – a type of small still, supposed to produce mellower whisky'. This is another example of the old distillers' maxim that stills of modest capacity generally produce whisky of superior quality. The sma' still was necessarily one that operated outwith the knowledge of the *excise* authorities, as the minimum legal size of still allowed effectively limited distillation to a large-scale, professional basis. The Small Stills Act of 1816 was an attempt by the government to reduce illicit distillation in Scotland, and for the purposes of this piece of legislation a 'small still' was defined as being one of not less than forty gallons in capacity. Previously five hundred gallons had been the minimum legal size. The term 'sma' still' was also applied to the whisky produced in the still, with first attestation occurring in 1822, 'Taste the whisky, Mr Gordon – it is sma' still, and will do no harm to no man.' In Irish *poitín*-making circles the equivalent – and still current – term is 'wee still', and the word *poitín* itself means 'small pot'.

smashed   Drunk. Originally an American adjective, according to *The Oxford Dictionary of Modern Slang*, and in 1859 one definition of a *smash* was a beverage made of *spirit*, ice, water, sugar, and flavoured with mint. The OED notes in the same year 'A smash, ice, brandy, and water'. The sense of *smashed* as *drunk* certainly originates in the early meaning of smash as a hard or heavy blow, first attested in 1779, with *smashed* having the sense of severely or extensively crushed or broken. As with many terms originally associated with intoxication – such as *white lightning*, *snifter* and *snort* – smashed came to be absorbed into the vocabulary of drug-taking, with first usage in this context occurring in 1962, according to *The Oxford Dictionary of Modern Slang*.

snifter   A small drink of spirits, a *dram*. First use is recorded in America in 1844, with Anglicisation occurring in *c*.1880, according to Partridge (*Historical Slang*). Again a drug-related usage developed, with *The Oxford Dictionary of Modern Slang* noting *snifter* as a colloquial synonym for a cocaine addict from 1925, also a small quantity of cocaine inhaled through the nose. 'Snifter' additionally has the sense of 'Any thing or person excellent, or very big or strong' (*Historical Slang*), being synonymous in this respect with *snorter*.

'Snifter' is also the name given to a 'balloon' *nosing* glass, presumably from the sense of sniff as a transitive verb to take up through the nose. Writing in *Wine* magazine (January 1993), Gordon Brown comments that 'the snifter nipped our noses by concentrating alcohol below them so that we lost track of the aromas...'.

snort Also *snorter*. A small drink of spirits, synonymous with a *snifter*, and probably having the same origins in the sense of something exceptional in severity or strength. Dunkling suggests, rather unconvincingly, that *snort* derives 'From the sound made by the drinker' (p.21). Like 'snifter', 'snort' is American in origin, first being attested in 1889, and has also become part of drug-taking vocabulary, being used as a noun for an inhaled amount of cocaine or heroin since 1951, and as a verb to inhale such substances, from 1935.

soak As a verb in relation to drinking, *soak* means to drink immoderately and consistently, to saturate oneself with liquor, the first attestation occurring in 1687, 'You keep soaking in Taverns'. The adjective *soaked* for drunk first occurs in 1737. From 1820 'soak' also developed as a noun, with the sense of a drunkard, one who soaks. 'Exposed by Lord, Barnard comes across not so much as a crusy barfly but as a mean and miserable soak who was often violent when drunk' (Alan Taylor's 'Diary' in *Scotland On Sunday*, 8 November 1992).

soap A substance formed by the combination of certain oils and fats with alkaline bases, first attested in *c.* 1000, 'Meng wiþ sote, sealt, teoro...eald sape'. The word *soap* derives from the Old English *sāpe*, and is widely represented in European languages, though as the OED notes, 'its occurrence in some of the Tartar languages may indicate that it was introduced by early trade from the East'.

The link between distilling and soap may seem tenuous to say the least, none the less soap has played an important part in traditional still-craft. As Neil Wilson writes, 'Why is soap used? Simply because it acts as a surfactant and reduces frothing within the still, particularly when it is directly heated by coal or gas' (p.34). Ian Allan of the Islay distillery of Bruichladdich remarked to the present author that soap was still occasionally used by stillmen, and recalled that 'There was always a soap box on stills when I started. It stopped your still frothing right up. Just a slice of a piece of unscented soap went in. With modern steam heating and sight glasses in the still you can see it bubbling up now, and it's easier to control with the steam than it was with coal or gas.' Writing in an era when most stills were direct-fired by coal and gas, Marshall Robb notes that during distillation, 'There is some production of froth or "head" in the still, and in order to diminish this a small proportion of a special soap (about 8 ounces to 5,000 gallons) is inserted into the wash still by means of a container under excise locks' (p.35). Soap had another role in illicit distilling during the nineteenth century, as Graham Nown explains: 'The first spirit through the worm was distilled a second time to remove impurities, and finally – an unusual touch – they added a small square of soap to make the new whisky clear' (p.19).

sour mash   See *mashing*.

sour, whiskey   Jackson considers the *sour* to be the original of the 'several classic mixed-drink categories which comprise spirit, citrus and sugar' (*Pocket Bar Book*, 136). The drink derives its name from the effect of the lemon, which should indeed be sour. He specifies the use of *Bourbon* or *rye*, hence spelling it 'whiskey', though the Scottish variant also occurs, being used by Theodora Fitzgibbon. She does not specify any type of whisky, and also suggests the option of adding egg white and a dash of soda to the basic *cocktail* of a double measure of whisky or whiskey, the juice of half a lemon, crushed ice and half a teaspoon of sugar (p.115). McNulty recommends using the *liqueur* Southern Comfort instead of Bourbon or rye when making a whiskey sour.

sparge   A noun used in the *mashing* stage of brewing or distilling to denote what Daiches calls 'the product of the later washings'; 'The sparge becomes the first and second extractions of the next batch' (*Scotch Whisky*, 11). The nominal sense of *sparge* developed from an original verb, *sparging* being the process of spraying the *grist* with hot water, first attested in 1830, 'It would keep up an uniform temperature in the goods, without requiring them to be sparged with very hot liquor'. It is thought to be adapted from the Old French *espargier* or the Latin *spargĕre*, to sprinkle, and with its earliest sense of to plaster, to rough-cast, it is recorded in 1560, and in 1786 it occurs with the sense of to bespatter or besprinkle, to dash or splash with water. The variant *spairge* also occurs in specifically Scottish usage, meaning, according to the *Concise Scots Dictionary*, 'a drink, a mouthful, a drop of spirits, as much liquid as will moisten one's lips', and was extant from the nineteenth to the early twentieth century.

spent lees   The residue left in the *spirit still* after distillation. Unlike the leftovers from the *low wines* or *wash still* – *burnt* or *pot ale* – the *spent lees* have no recyclable use and are simply disposed of. Cooper writes, 'When the hydrometer indicates that water is beginning to flow this, known as *spent lees*, is run to waste. In these days of conservation and concern for ecology the *spent lees* are treated and cleaned before being discharged into any open stream or burn' (*Century Companion*, 24). Whilst 'spent lees' is the term used in whisky distilling, 'spent liquor' is also applied in other distillations, and in brewing the term 'spent grains' is applied to the left-over grain after *mashing*, what is known in whisky-making as *draff*.

With the sense of expended, consumed, used up completely, 'spent' is first attested in *c*.1440, 'Spent, expensus, dispensatus', and in specific relation to brewing practice in 1826, 'If the disorder do not subside readily, a gyle of spent hops will generally be advantageous'. It is the past participle of the verb *spend*, from the Old English *spendan*, adapted from the Latin *expendĕre*. 'Lees' as the sediment deposited in the containing vessel from wine or other liquids, the dregs or refuse, is first recorded *c*.1384, 'Boystes Crammed ful of lyes As euer vessel was with lyes'. The plural form is now always employed, and the word is adopted from the French *lie*, Gaulish Latin *lia*, plural *liæ* (in the tenth century).

spirit   Until it has been matured for a minimum of three years in oak in its country of origin, *Scotch* whisky and *Irish* whiskey is not, officially speaking, whisky/whiskey at all, and is always referred to simply as *spirit*. It is produced in the *spirit still*, monitored and separated in the *spirit safe* and collected in the *spirit receiver*. The *stillroom* pipes are colour coded, as Cooper explains: 'all pipes through which wash flows should be painted red; pipes through which low wines, feints or foreshots flow are painted blue, pipes through which clean spirit flows are painted black' (*Century Companion*, 24).

The plural form 'spirits' is more usually used outwith the specific context of *distillation*, and the Scotch Whisky Association defines spirits as 'the produce of distillation, whatever the raw materials, or whether it be in a pure state or contaminated by impurities normally present in any distillate. Generally, the word refers to any volatile inflammable liquid obtained by distillation' (*Questions and Answers*, 12). Spirits intended for human consumption are known as *potable* spirits.

'Spirit' is an adaptation of the Anglo-French *spirit (espirit)*, *spirite*, the equivalent of Old French *esperit*, *-ite*, *esprit*, or an adaptation of the Latin *spīritus*, breathing, breath, air etc. related to *spīrāre*, to breathe. With the sense of a liquid of the nature of an essence or extract from some substance, especially one obtained by distillation, the first attestation of 'spirit' occurs in 1610, 'H'is busie with his spirits, but wee'll vpon him'. With the specific sense of strong alcoholic liquor obtained by distillation from various substances and employed for drinking, the first recorded use is in 1684, 'He gave me also a piece of a Honey-comb, and a little Bottle of Spirits'. The use of spirit or spirits in a drink-related sense derives from the early meaning of spirit – first attested in c.1250 – as what the OED calls 'The animating or vital principle in man (and animals): that which gives life to the physical organism; in contrast to its purely material elements; the breath of life'.

From 'spirit' come the adjectives *spiritous* and *spirity*, the latter being used in a pejorative way to describe the *nose* or taste of whisky which has not benefited from *maturation* as it might have done, a whisky which has failed to become well-rounded. 'Spirity' is also sometimes applied to wines, notably fortified ones such as port. Jackson notes of a 1964 sample of the Inverness whisky Glen Albyn, 'A Signatory 1964 (58 vol) was spirity in the nose, but more perfumy and flowery in the palate' (*Malt Whisky Companion*, 81). The terms *grain spirit, neutral grain spirit, proof spirit* and *silent spirit* also occur.

spirit safe   Also sometimes known as a distiller's or whisky safe and in America as a *try box*; here the crucial process of *cutting* takes place. As a receptacle for the safe storage of articles, especially meat, usually in the form of a ventilated chest or cupboard, 'safe' is first attested c.1440, 'Almery of mete kepynge, or a *saue* for mete'. As a secure, locked, metal receptacle the first recorded use occurs in 1838: 'A penknife...and a letter...were found lying near the safe'. In Middle English it occurs as *sauf, sāf*, after the French *sauf*; in Latin *salvus* – uninjured, entire, healthy.

Moss describes the *spirit safe* as consisting of 'a long brass box, usually highly polished, with a glass door at the front secured by a stout brass bar with padlocks at either end'. He explains that 'Inside the spirit safe are two brandy-shaped glasses with a chute down which the distillate flows. This can be directed by a lever on the outside of the spirit safe to allow the stillman either to discard or retain the distillate without coming into contact with it. There are also hydrometers in the spirit safe, once again operated from outside, so that the specific gravity of the distillate can be tested' (*Scottish Drink Book*, 81). In some modern or modernised distilleries, such as the now *silent* Lowland plant of Bladnoch, the flow of spirit in the safe is controlled by a computer. According to Morton, Bladnoch possesses 'the only automatic spirit-safe I've ever seen. Sensors detect when the middle cut, the purest spirit, is coursing from the spirit-still, and automatically divert it through the steel spirit-safe to the spirit-receiver using compressed air to move the pourer' (p.162).

The spirit safe was invented by Septimus Fox in the early 1820s,

and its use was made compulsory in 1823, though in practice the
first safes were introduced in 1825. Lamond observes when writing of the Islay distillery of Port Ellen that 'The Excise Act of
1824 enforced the introduction of the spirit safe in distilleries.
Tests had to be made to ensure that it had no harmful effects on
the make. The official experiments were carried out in Port Ellen'
(p.116).

spot   A small drink, figuratively a drop of liquor, the first attestation of which is recorded in 1885, 'A little spot of rum, William,
with a squeeze of lemon in it'. Partridge *(Historical Slang)* notes
'In C.20 Anglo-Irish coll, it has a specific sense: a half-glass of
whiskey'. The drink-related use derives from spot as a small quantity or piece, a drop, first recorded in *c*.1400. Writing of the names
given to measures of whisky, Fleming notes that 'The traditional
and colloquial words in Scotland are "tot", "dram", "nip" and
"spot"' (p.39).

squiffy   Chiefly British slang adjective for slightly *drunk*, first
attested in 1874, 'Squiffy, slightly inebriated'. The meaning
gradually changed to mean drunk in any degree. Partridge *(Historical Slang)* suggests the formation is based on *skew-whiff*
('crooked, askew'), perhaps on *swipey*, a colloquialism for slightly
drunk, in use from *c*.1820 and obsolete by 1900. *Swipey* has its
origins in the verb *swipe*, 'To drink hastily and copiously...'
(Historical Slang), probably taken from the sense of 'swipe' as a
heavy blow, interestingly comparable with other drink-related
terms such as *cut*, *shot*, *slug* and *smashed*.

steep   Like the term *sparge*, *steep* may be applied both as a verb
and a noun, the former giving rise to the latter. As a verb, 'steep'
in the whisky-making sense is the process of soaking or steeping
the *barley* to promote germination, a process which takes place
in a vessel known as a 'steep'. Neil Wilson explains that 'the
requirements of a modern distillery normally dictate the use of
large cylindrical vessels, varying in capacity from 8 tonnes at
Laphroaig to the huge 25-tonne steeps at Port Ellen Maltings'
(p.23).

As a verb meaning to soak barley or *malt*, the first attestation
of steep occurs in 1390/91, 'Pro ij fattes... pro stepying in'. It
comes from the Old English *stiepan, stēpan,* equivalents to which
occur in Danish, Norwegian and Swedish; in the Norwegian
støypa – to steep seeds and barley for malting. In Old Norse *staup*
and *stoup* occur as vessels for liquor, leading to the modern *stoup*
– a flagon, beaker or drinking-vessel.

Steep has a third, hyperbolic verb use – to *soak* in liquor, with
reference to constant or excessive drinking, also to deaden or

stupefy one's memory or senses, to drown sorrows etc. in drink. With this sense the first attestation is recorded prior to 1592, 'Our iolly horsekeeper, being well stept in licor, confessed to me the stealing of my maisters writings'.

still 'An apparatus for distillation, consisting essentially of a closed vessel (alembic, retort, boiler) in which the substance to be distilled is subjected to the action of heat, and of arrangements for the condensation of the vapour produced. Also applied to the alembic or retort separately', according to the OED. It derives from the Latin *stillāre*, to drop, and the first attestation occurs in 1562, 'A horned still, Bagpipe still, pelican still'.

The person directly in charge of the *distillation* process is known as a *stillsman* or *stillman*, a term first recorded prior to 1864, and distillation takes place in a *still room* or *still house*, the latter term first being attested around the same time as *still*. Gunn observes that 'The stillman's job is one of great responsibility, for negligence on his part may not only wreck the still, but, what can hardly be detected at the time, ruin the flavour of the final spirit' (p.141). Moss and Hume suggest 'the distillation of alcohol was not developed until the eleventh century AD, as the techniques used in earlier times did not cool the vapour from the still sufficiently to collect the liquid'. They note that 'The earliest stills used air cooling to condense the vapours, and the yield of spirit must have been small'. During the sixteenth century one very significant improvement was the development of water-cooling, and the still head was modified, 'either by elongation to produce the familiar pear-shape of a pot still or by water cooling, which increased the reflux of condensate back into the still, giving better separation of alcohol from water and reducing the carry-over of noxious impurities' (*The Making of Scotch Whisky*, 31). The effect of these improvements was to produce a more palatable whisky, and Moss and Hume date its widespread use in Scotland to the introduction of those developments.

As Morrice observes, 'If the pagoda roof is the most familiar external feature of a malt whisky distillery, the pear-shaped, gleaming copper still, with its Loch Ness monster neck, is easily the most memorable internal feature' (p.27). Whisky-making closely resembles the brewing of beer until production moves into the stillhouse after *fermentation* has taken place. Distillation is 'the process characteristic of whisky making, indeed of all spirit making', notes McDowall. Essentially what happens in a still is that

the liquid wash is heated to a point at which the alcohol becomes vapour. This rises up the still and is passed into the cooling plant where it is condensed into liquid state. The cooling plant may take the form of a coiled copper tube or *worm* that is kept in continuously running cold water, or it may be another type of condenser'. (*Questions and Answers*, 17)

See *Coffey still*, *Lomond still*, *patent still*, *pot still*; also *Irish*.

straight   Unmixed, undiluted *spirits*, an adjective usually applied to whisky, according to *The Dictionary of Drink*. A drink served *straight up* is one to which ice has not been added. Originally colloquial American, it is first attested in 1874, '"Straight", an American phrase peculiar to dram-drinkers; similar to our word neat.' Writing of 'macho' drinking and the mistaken belief that 'real men drink their whisky straight', Hills is apt to lay the blame for this particular misconception on Ernest Hemingway. 'There are two things everyone should know about Hemingway', he writes, 'that the whisky he drank straight was 70° proof, having been diluted substantially by the distillers before he got it; secondly, that the man was an awful fool' (p.184).

The word has its origins in the Middle English *stregt*, *stragt*, originally an adjectival use of the past participle of *strecchen* – to stretch. The now obsolete sense of 'extended at full stretch' existed, as well as 'direct, undeviating, not deflected'. The drinks-related usage as not mixed or 'adulterated' obviously has its origins in the second sense.

A further drink-related use of 'straight' is as a synonym for *single* or *single malt*, i.e. a Scotch whisky which has not been blended in any way.

In the United States the term *straight Bourbon* occurs in popular usage, as in the country song 'Kentucky Straight Bourbon Blues'. Jackson notes that 'the term straight applied to *rye* or Bourbon indicates not only that the whisky has been aged according to the regulations but also that it has not been "stretched" with neutral spirit. A "straight" may contain more than one distillation of its specified type, perhaps even from more than one location, but it conforms strictly to the designation on the label, whether that is rye or Bourbon' (*World Guide*, 140). Jackson also observes that 'In the United States, a distiller who puts together more than one mature Bourbon or Rye may describe the result as a blended straight whiskey. This contradiction in terms distinguishes his product from a blend of bourbon or rye with an inferior whisky or neutral spirit (*Pocket Bar Book*, 84).

'Straight' is another word to have developed a drugs-related usage, though this has evolved from the sense of straight as not deviating, also used for heterosexuality and general conventionality. The *Oxford Dictionary of Modern Slang* defines it as 'Not using or under the influence of drugs', dating this sense from 1959, though somewhat confusingly, it also notes the earlier (1946) meaning of under the influence of drugs, 'drugged, high'.

streah An Anglicisation of the Gaelic *sreath*, a row. John Stanhope in his *Journal of 1806* noted 'Little variation seems to have taken place in the manner of living since the time of Dr Johnson. In the Hebrides they still continue to take their streah, or glass of whisky, before breakfast...Additional streahs are never refused in the daytime'. Twenty-two years later, Samuel Morewood *(Inebriating Liquors)* wrote of the way in which old drinking customs had survived in the Western Islands, noting that 'In former times, large companies assembled, composed principally of the chief respectable men of the islands. This assemblage was called a "sheate", "streah" or "round", from the company always sitting in a circle'. The men tended to drink for at least a day until no liquor remained. Morewood suggests that 'in this practice our "round of glasses" is supposed to have originated'.

switcher A *switcher* or *switch* is a mechanism consisting of rotating arms which is fitted to a *washback* to reduce excessive frothing during *fermentation*. As Michael Moss explains, 'Sometimes the wash can bubble over and small boys used to be employed to beat it down with heather switches. This process was mechanised from the late eighteenth century. Today most washbacks are fitted with electric switches. These are rarely used as fermentation is much less violent than it used to be, as yeasts are more stable and the process more scientifically controlled' (*Scottish Drink Book*, 79). Gunn uses 'switch' as a verb, 'It [the wort] would, of course, come right over the top if the brewer did not switch it back'. He continues, 'Nowadays wooden switchers are rotated by mechanism, but I have seen men in past days, stripped to the waist, with long birch sticks laying into the ebullient yeast-froth for dear life in a battle in which they were not always completely victorious' (p.137).

   With the sense of a whip, something used to strike, flog or beat, 'switch' is first attested in 1592 in *Romeo and Juliet*, 'Swits and spurs'. *The Concise Scots Dictionary* also gives the nineteenth century use of switch as a verb to thresh grain or beat flax. *Switch, swits, switz* is thought to be an adaptation of a Flemish or Low German word, as in the Hanoverian *swutsche*, a variant of the Low German *zwukse*, a long, thin stick; also *swuksen* – to bend up and down, and to make a swishing noise like a lash.

T **ail** See *feints*.

   tasting   The action of the verb *to taste*. With the sense of trying or testing, the first attestation occurs after 1300, 'It is ywrite þat euery þing Hym self sheweþ in þe tastying'. The OED notes a specific sense of tasting as a small portion taken to try the taste, especially of alcoholic liquor, and in this context taste is first recorded in 1530, 'He sent for the tast of wyne...dew to him of every hoggshed'. The word taste has its origins in the Old French *tast* – touching, touch.

   Cooper suggests that the correct procedure when sampling whiskies is first to *nose* the spirit, then taste it *neat*, and finally take it with the addition of some suitable water (*Century Companion*, 64). Writing in his *Malt Whisky Companion* (p.22), Jackson points out that 'A tasting note cannot be definitive, but it can be a useful guide', and he breaks his notes down into colour, nose, *body*, *palate* and *finish*.

   The language employed in relation to whisky tasting can often be self-indulgent. Grindal inveighs against pretentious description:

> From the pages of the many books on *Scotch* that have been published one can compile a litany of curious nouns and adjectives used to describe the flavour of different *single malt* whiskies: marzipan, linseed, bitter chocolate, peppermint, flowering currants, orangey, buttery and the evocative 'wet grass on a rainy day'. They say much for the inventive imagination of the authors, but one doubts whether after reading them the whisky lover is any the wiser (p.212).

McDiarmid was very much of the same opinion, declaring 'I have little patience with the pseudo-poetical attempts to describe the differences in flavour of the various malts' (quoted in Mackinlay et al., 23).

   Within the whisky industry a 'flavour wheel' exists for use by professionals, designed in the late 1970s by a working party from Pentlands Scotch Whisky Research Ltd. The aim of the group was to 'devise a vocabulary which would enable blenders and distillers to communicate flavour descriptions more accurately than had been possible in the past', as Cooper puts it, though he goes on to point out that 'Blenders have tended to use their own

185

repertoire of words; ambiguity has reigned' (*Century Companion*, 66). Russell Sharp explains that 'In the whisky industry, systems for describing the taste and smell of whisky have been developed, which use terms standardised against particular chemical compounds. Staff are trained to use these terms together with scales of intensity to describe whiskies' (*Scots on Scotch*, 175-6).

The problem of finding a useful vocabulary remains. This was something addressed by Phillip Hills and the Scotch Malt Whisky Society, whose aim was to make new converts to the cause of good whisky. Writing of what he calls 'good drink', Hills explains that 'The only problem is that we don't have an adequate vocabulary to talk about it with, much as desert dwellers don't have a lot of words for fish' (p.182). The Society decided to ignore the language of wine tasting and everything else that had gone before: 'We had to create the language we required, or rather to adopt plain English, but in a way that would allow most reasonably sensible people to gain access' (Hills, 183). Hills offers a selection of the Society's tasting notes as examples of what its tasting committee has come up with, including such comments as 'Golden in colour it has an estery, fruity, citrusy aroma and a delicate, smooth flavour – a memorable dram' (Bladnoch), and 'Pale gold, this is slightly peaty, with a cut barley, grassy aroma. Exceptionally smooth and mellow with a slightly winey, raisiny flavour' (Royal Brackla).

United Distillers produce a list of fifty 'Tasting Vocabulary Descriptors' to guide members of the public when they hold 'Classic Malts' tasting sessions, and the list contains such sensible and useful offerings as 'hint of *peat*', 'full bodied', 'good aftertaste', as well as the slightly less taxing 'delightful', 'pleasant' and 'attractive'.

Capitalising on the sometimes esoteric and rather startling similes and metaphors of tasting, the Oddbins chain of off-licences ran a newspaper advertisement in late 1992 to promote a free tasting day in which they offered 'Jetty sheds, oily ropes, rotting bladder-wrack, Dundee marmalade and even dead hedgehogs... All available when you taste Lagavulin, Laphroaig, Talisker, Highland Park, Glenkinchie, Dalwhinnie, Bunnahabhain, The Balvenie, Oban, Bowmore, Aberlour and Cragganmore at your local Oddbins this Saturday.'

te bheag   This 'is used widely in the Hebrides as an affectionate term for a dram', according to Morrice (p.321). Literally, it translates from the Gaelic as 'little lady', and is also a contraction of the brand name *Te Bheag nan Eilean*, 'Little Lady of the Islands'. This is a superior blended whisky with an all-Gaelic label, produced by Iain Noble's Skye-based Praban na Linne Ltd, and a stable-mate to the *vatted malt Poit Dhu*. Writing of time spent on Skye, Morton suggests that 'If any of my new acquaintances had been Gaels, they would perhaps have ordered a "wee one" – *te bheag*. Hence the name given to Sir Iain Noble's Talisker-based blend' (p.16).

Tennessee *The Dictionary of Drink* defines *Tennessee* whiskey as 'A straight Whiskey distilled in Tennessee with no specific grain criteria', but rather than just being defined by geographical boundaries, Tennessee is one of the three distinctive, stylistically-orientated classifications of American whiskey, along with *Bourbon* and *rye*. Jackson notes, 'In practice the famous Tennessee whiskeys are in the bourbon style, using the sour mash process, with charcoal filtration' (*Pocket Bar Book*, 85).

The best-known Tennessee whiskey is Jack Daniel's, and the distillers proclaim 'Jack Daniel's is not a bourbon. While it has some of the characteristics of bourbon, it falls in a distinctive product classification called Tennessee Whiskey. Like bourbon, however, it's strictly a product of the United States... and more specifically, the hills of Tennessee'. (See also 'sour mash' under *mash*.) Jack Daniel's distillers note that if their whiskey was simply casked and matured directly after distillation it would be just another bourbon. 'Our whiskey is trickled very slowly through 10 feet of hard maple charcoal, right after distillation. It's this extra step in the whiskey-making process that makes Jack Daniel's more than a bourbon... and provides the special character known only to Tennessee Whiskey.' They explain that 'the Charcoal Mellowing process removes the unpleasant congenerics and harsh fusel oils which are always present in any grain alcohol. We like to think of this old process as giving our Jack Daniel's Whiskey a "head start".'

Jackson points out that the Tennessee method of filtration is unique in that it is done before barrelling, which means that a 'cleaner' spirit goes into the barrel, and because it is 'such an exhaustive process', lasting for ten days in a ten-feet-deep filter. 'This is not so much a filtration as leaching out of fusel oils', notes Jackson (*World Guide*, 184). Most of these have already been eliminated during distillation, however, and Jackson muses on whether some flavour characteristics and texture are actually lost in the filtration process. He also considers whether the charcoal filtering adds to the taste, noting that 'Some drinkers find in Jack Daniel's a faint but distinctive smokiness'. He notes of Jack Daniel's that it 'has the intensely dry, aromatic lightness that makes Tennessee whiskeys so different' (*World Guide*, 183).

Jack Daniel's became the first registered distillery in America in 1866, when the Federal Government introduced a whiskey tax, but whiskey-making in Tennessee dates back at least until the late eighteenth century, when some of the state was settled from North Carolina, and the settlers brought the secrets of distillation with them. In the nineteenth century there were hundreds of *stills*, but Tennessee became 'dry' in 1910 and distilling remained illegal until 1938, so the existence of just two distilleries in the state today – Jack Daniel's at Lynchburg and George Dickel's at Tullahoma – is hardly surprising.

Jack Daniel is thought to have been born in 1846, and at the age of seven he went to work for a preacher and distiller called Dan Call, who apparently employed charcoal leaching. The Jack Daniel's distillery literature mentions 'an old leaching process that had traditionally been used in Lincoln County to smooth the new-made whiskey after it came from the still'. The charcoal leaching process was actually invented in 1825 by Alfred Eaton of Tullahoma, close to where the Dickel distillery operates today.

The formal adoption of the classification of Tennessee whiskey as a distinctive style of whisky can be dated to 1941, and a United States tax authority letter to Jack Daniel distillers.

tight   Drunk. Partridge *(Historical Slang)* notes the use of *tight* in America in 1843, and its first British attestation occurs a decade later, 'For the one word drunk, besides the authorised synonyms tipsy, inebriated, intoxicated, I find of unauthorised or slang equivalents…thirty-two, viz: in liquor…half-seas-over, far-gone, tight…'. He suggests the origins of 'tight' in relation to drunkenness are to be found in the slang synonym *screwed*, first attested in 1838, '(lit. screwed *tight*, hence) drunk'. 'Screwed' probably developed as a synonym for intoxicated from its sense of twisted round or awry, particularly in relation to the face when contorted and the eyes when contracted. The expression 'tight as a drum' also occurs, first being attested in 1908, according to Partridge *(Historical Slang)*, and clearly deriving from the tension essential to a drum skin.

three sheets to the wind   Also *three sheets in the wind*. Slang synonym for *drunk*, sometimes shortened to 'three sheets', and first recorded in 1857, 'He said "A man will do anything when he is tight, or three sheets" – he had been drinking.' According to *The Dictionary of Drink* (p.957), in the expression the state of intoxication 'Is likened to the sails (sheets) of a ship that are flapping around in a variable wind', though Gyles Brandreth *(Modern Phrase and Fable)* writes that 'The expression is a nautical one, a sheet being a rope attached to a sail. If the sheet is not tied down to secure the sail it flaps freely in the wind'. He considers the phrase to connote a state of extreme drunkenness, noting that '"a sheet in the wind" is applied to someone who is tipsy; one who is three sheets in the wind has had more to drink'.

tipple   As a noun *tipple* is a slang term for a drink. According to *The Dictionary of Drink* it 'Usually denotes a persons *[sic]* favourite drink'. The first attestation occurs in 1581, 'Of pleasant wine their tipple in they take'. The agent noun *tippler* occurs as an established and apparently legal term in 1396, having the sense of a retailer of liquor, an inn-keeper, and from 1580 it took on the additional meaning of one who tipples. The implication of 'tippler' is of a habitual drinker, one who frequently drinks small quantities of alcohol, with an element of excess, though full-blown drunkenness is not usually implied.

As an intransitive verb, to drink intoxicating liquor, 'tipple' is first recorded in 1560, 'In this conflict was hurt Albert Brunswick, the sonne of Duke Philip, going vnaduisadly after he had well tippled'. The original sense in this usage was to drink freely or hard, to *booze*, but the modern implication has shifted slightly to mean to indulge habitually and to some degree of excess in strong drink. Used transitively, the verb tipple first occurs in 1581, 'Tippling the pleasant wine they downe to table sit'.

Partridge *(Historical Slang)* notes the existence in the eighteenth century of *tippling*-ken for a tavern, and *tipply* for unsteady (1906), 'Lit., apt to tip over', though this is not necessarily intoxicant-related. It does, however, suggest a derivation similar to that of *tipsy*.

tipsy   A slang expression for *drunk* or partially intoxicated, though the usual implication is of relatively good natured and perhaps even humorous or comical inebriation. *Tipsy* is 'often euphemistic for intoxicated, inebriated, drunk', according to the OED, which also suggests an element of unsteadiness due to the amount of alcohol consumed. 'Tipsy' was used as a synonym for a less than 'good-natured' state of drunkenness in a *Daily Telegraph* report of a court case (December 1992), where the prosecuting counsel was quoted as saying the defendants were 'tipsy' prior to an alleged assault which led to charges of causing grievous bodily harm with intent to assault. The story was run under the headling 'Man "injured in attack by tipsy PCs"'. The first attestation occurs in 1577, 'About ten of the clock whenas they were somewhat tipsie...', and the adjective has its origins in the sense of *tip* to fall by overbalancing, to tumble or topple over. This use is first recorded prior to 1530, 'His carte typed over...'.

tired and emotional   Euphemism for *drunk*. First attested in 1981

(The Daily Telegraph), 'Sensing that Penrose's efforts might have left him tired and emotional...' The euphemism is based on *Private Eye*'s 1967 use of *tired and overwrought*: 'Mr Brown had been tired and overwrought on many occasions'. In August 1992 in a *Sporting Life* feature on racing at Deauville in Normandy, William Hughes writes 'Chat among the Brits was more down to earth: it concerned the extremely "tired and emotional" behaviour of a Newmarket trainer...' (See *sensation*).

toddy   In Britain *toddy* is traditionally a mixture of whisky, hot water and sugar, commonly known as a *hot toddy*, though the drink has a number of permutations and can be served either hot or cold. Grindal's recipe for toddy specifies 'Scotch, Lemon juice and honey, with perhaps a stick of cinnamon' (p.200). Cooper considers the toddy to consist of three or four lumps of sugar dissolved in boiling water in a tumbler, to which lemon juice and 'a well matured malt' are added, though he notes that 'purists of the old school would regard lemon juice as a blasphemy' (*Little Book*, 56). Marshall Robb is blunt: the toddy is 'A terrible waste of good whisky!' (p.32). Some recipes recommend the use of blended whisky, which may seem a prudent alternative to Cooper's 'well matured malt', but when mixed with hot water blended whiskies do tend to give off rather unpleasant fumes, and the economy is probably not worthwhile.

'The chief use of toddy in modern times is to relieve the symptoms of a cold', writes Daiches (*Scotch Whisky*, 46), and most commentators repeat the hoary old dictum that one should hang a shoe, bowler hat or other object over the end of the bed before retiring to drink toddy until two shoes, hats etc appear. Cooper writes that 'Of all the rituals associated with whisky none is more civilised than the making of toddy' (*Little Book*, 56). Grindal writes of toddy, 'They say it should be drunk out of a silver mug and never a glass' (p.200), whilst Daiches considers that the drink should be stirred with a silver spoon, noting 'There used to be an elaborate ritual in both making and drinking toddy'. Toddy is a close relation to whisky *punch*, with which it shared great popularity amongst Lowland Scots during the second half of the eighteenth century. 'Toddy was drunk by gentlemen', notes Daiches.

The drink can appear quite perverse to those outwith the Caledonian tradition in terms of its ingredients and the way they interact, and Lockhart quotes an old Russian friend, M. Baleiev, to very good effect in this respect, 'First you put in whisky to make it strong; then you add water to make it weak; next you put in lemon to make it sour, then you put in sugar to make it sweet. You put in more whisky to kill the water. Then you say "Here's to you" – and you drink it yourself' (*Scotch*, 14).

The first attestation comes in the Edinburgh poet Allan Ramsay's 'The Morning Interview' (1721), where he writes of 'Kettles full of Todian spring'. In a note to the poem, Ramsay explains that by 'The Todian spring' he means Tod's Well on the slopes of Arthur's Seat, which supplied Edinburgh with much of its fresh water. Ramsay thinks that 'when it is borne in mind that whisky derives its name from water, it is highly probable that toddy in like manner was a facetious term for the pure element'. The first use of the term *whisky toddy* occurs in 1812, 'I sat down with some whisky toddy...'. An alternative explanation for the word's origins lies in the fact that toddy is also the name given to the sap obtained from some palm-trees, especially the *caryota urens*, also wild date, coconut and palmyra, which is used as a drink in some tropical countries. It is also the name given to the intoxicating liquor produced by its *fermentation*, extant in India, Sri Lanka, the East Indies and South-East Asia. The *Dictionary of Drink* notes that in the United States toddy was 'originally the fermented sap of palm trees. Now classed for a tot of spirit' (p.963). With the palm-related sense, 'toddy' is first recorded in 1609/10, being adapted from the Hindi *tārī*, from *tār*, palm-tree.

The term *toddy kettle* occurs, McNeill explaining that the 'special equipage' that went with toddy-making, 'included a toddy-kettle, usually made of copper, a spatula of glass or metal for stirring, and a small deep ladle for serving the brew...On Hogmanay the toddy-kettle was used for the brewing of Het Pint...' (p.130).

Toddy was also the name given to a small measure of drink, a *nip*, from which the term *toddy lifter* developed. The first toddy lifter was manufactured *c.*1800 and the implement is described by the *Dictionary of Drink* as 'a bottle-shaped glass with a hole at the base so that when placed in a *cask* of spirit the thumb is placed over the top to prevent the contents returning to the cask' (p.963). The toddy lifter could also be a metal or glass cup fixed to a long handle, used for extracting a toddy from a cask.

top dressing   A blending term used to denote high quality *malts* which are known to *marry* well and are used to give the blended whisky a depth and a veneer of character, hence the use of the word *dressing*. Cooper quotes Barnard's use of the term in 1887, 'When blending it is always as well to have a proportion, even if it be small, of very old for "top dressing" and giving the appearance of age; while it improves the bouquet it also adds to the average age of the blend' (*Century Companion*, 43). Writing of

The Edradour malt whisky, Lamond notes 'The output of the single malt is 2,000 cases a year, the balance being kept as "top dressing" principally for the "House of Lords" blend' (*Malt File*, 51).

tot A small quantity of alcoholic liquor, invariably *spirits*, of no specific measurement, though a single measure is usually implied in a bar. *Tot* is first recorded in relation to a quantity of alcohol in 1857, and the reference is to whisky, 'We jabbed the stopper down the whiskey-tin and gave you a tot of it'. In contemporary usage, Daiches (in a Radio 4 broadcast of January 1981) talked of 'A tot of whisky followed by a pint or half pint of beer'.

Partridge *(Historical Slang)* dates tot with the sense of 'A very small quantity, esp. of liquor', from before 1828, noting that from the same time it also had the meaning of a child's drinking vessel. He suggests that the drink-related usage emanates from tot as 'a very young or small child', an application first recorded in 1725. *Tottr* occurs in Icelandic as the nickname of a dwarfish person, and *tommel-tot* is Danish for Tom Thumb, but no connection between these forms and the English 'tot' has been established.

trestarig When writing about the Outer Hebridean island of Lewis, Martin Martin (*A Description of the Western Islands of Scotland*, 1703) noted that 'The air is temperately cold and moist, and for the corrective the natives use a dose of trestarig or usquebaugh'. He describes *trestarig* as 'aquavitae, three times distilled, which is strong and hot'. It was apparently made of oats rather than *barley*, and Daiches notes that 'trestarig' comes from two Gaelic words meaning 'triple strength', and in fact it is an anglicisation of *treas-tarruing* (*Scotch Whisky*, 24). Daiches also writes that very little is known of the drink called trestarig or of the even more fearsome **usquebauch-baul** which Martin also describes. In Jamieson's *Dictionary of the Scottish Language*, trestarig is defined as 'A kind of ardent spirits distilled from oats', and its origins are ascribed to the Isle of Lewis. Clearly the term had currency outwith Lewis and the Hebrides, as McHardy comments whilst writing about mainland **peatreek** production during the eighteenth and early nineteenth centuries that 'The double distilled spirit was the Tarraing dubailt, and being distilled again would become *Treasturring*, or triple distilled' (p.160).

tun In the lexicon of brewing and *distillation*, a *tun* is the vessel in which *mashing* takes place, usually known as a *mash tun*. The area in which the mash tuns are situated is known as 'the mash house', though, somewhat perversely, what is usually called the *tun room* is the place where the *washbacks* are situated. 'When things have quietened down a bit, it is a trick of some of the tun-room men to slide back a section of the wooden lid and ask a visitor to sniff the aroma' (Gunn, 138). 'The process [mashing] is carried out in a large cylindrical tank (often 20 feet across) called a mashtun. The more modern covered, or roofed tuns are usually constructed of stainless steel...', (Neil Wilson, 26).

With the sense of a large *cask* or *barrel*, 'tun' is first attested prior to *c.*725, and as a large vessel, a tub or vat, the first record occurs prior to *c.*1205, 'Heo makeden ane tunne of golde al of ʒimme'. As Neil Wilson explains, tun also had the meaning of a cask of specific capacity, 'Duart, MacLeod and Gorm were all restricted to four tuns of wine a year, amounting to the not inconsiderable sum of over 1,000 gallons (4540 litres)' (p.13). According to the *Dictionary of Drink* a tun is 'an old cask of 250 gallons' or 'A wine cask, 9454 litres, 210 Imp. gallons, 252 US gallons' (p.977).

U isge beatha   The Scots Gaelic for 'water of life'. Neil Wilson explains that *aquavitae* is 'The Latin for "water of life" from which the Gaelic *uisge beatha* and *usquebaugh* were derived' (p.6). Paradoxically, 'whisky' is simply an anglicisation of the Gaelic word for water. The Irish equivalent to *uisge beatha*, *uisci* or *uisce beatha*, is first recorded in 1276, 'with a mighty draft of uisce beatha'. *Usquebaugh* is, as Daiches puts it 'an earlier form of the word "whisky", intermediate between the Gaelic uisge beatha and the modern word...' (*Scotch Whisky*, 24) and its first attestation occurs in 1610, though the form *vskebeaghe* is recorded in 1581, 'She filles them then with Vskbeaghe'. The exact modern spelling *whisky* is first recorded in 1746, with *whiskie* occurring from 1715.

Cooper writes: 'The heady concocting of intoxicating water from grape and grain is almost as old as cultivation itself. Semantically it surfaces in French as *eau de vie*, in Danish as *akvavit*, in Erse as usquebaugh and in Gaelic as uisge beatha. Gradually the soft-vowelled sound *ooska* became on Anglo-Saxon tongues ooskie and eventually whisky' (*Century Companion*, 5). Spelling variants both in the Scots and Irish Gaelic and as anglicisation progresses are very numerous, including uisce betha, uisce beathadh, iskiebae, usque, usqueba, usqubae, usquebagh, usquebah, usquabae, usquebey, usquibae, whisky bae and whisquy-beath. Irish Distillers write that 'the word whiskey comes from the Irish words *Uisce Beatha* (phonetically "isk'ke-ba-'ha")', and express the view that the name was absorbed into English as a result of the presence of King Henry II's army in Ireland in 1170. The soldiers 'never learned how to pronounce the word Uisce Beatha and so, during the following centuries, the word was gradually anglicised, first to Uisce, then to Fuisce, and then finally to the word *whiskey* that we know to-day' (*Whisky With an 'E'*, 1).

The Scotch Whisky Association notes that 'One of the earliest references to "uiskie" occurs in the funeral account of a Highland laird about 1618' (*Questions and Answers*, 14), which would suggest that a parallel progress towards a modern spelling of whisky was taking place in Scotland. Moss and Hume write that during the first third of the eighteenth century, 'the term acqua vitae, or in the Gaelic "uisge beatha", began generally to be corrupted, first to usky, then to whisky. The older terms, however, continued in use for some time'. They consider usquebaugh 'the name given to Irish spirit' (*The Making of Scotch Whisky*, 34), and in 1602-3 the dramatist John Marston used this form in relation to Irish whiskey, 'The Irishman for usquebaugh...'.

In Dr Johnson's *Dictionary* (1755) the whisky entry is under usquebaugh, which he defines as 'a compound distilled spirit, being drawn on aromaticks; and the Irish sort is particularly distinguished for its pleasant and mild flavour. The Highland sort is somewhat hotter; and by corruption, in Scottish they call it whisky.' As newly distilled spirit was harsh and unpalatable, spices, berries and herbs were often added, hence perhaps Johnson's reference to 'aromaticks', and Lamond writes 'This concoction was known as Uisgebaugh, from the Irish Gaelic. From the late 18th century, production methods had advanced such that the liquor was gentle enough to be drunk as a spirit in its own right, i.e. neat and unadulterated. This liquid was known as Uisge beatha, from the Scots Gaelic' (*Connoisseur's Book*, 26). Johnson was no connoisseur of whisky, tasting it for the first time in the Argyllshire town of Inverary in 1773, an event faithfully recorded by James Boswell in his *Tour To The Hebrides*. 'We supped well; and after supper, Dr Johnson, whom I had not seen taste any fermented liquor during all our travels, called for a gill of whisky. "Come," said he, "let me know what it is that makes a Scotchman happy!"' By the time of Johnson's *Dictionary* the 'corruption' *whiskey* was clearly also in use in Ireland, as Butler (*Journey through Fermanagh*) wrote in 1760 of 'Aquavitae or Whiskey'. Moss and Hume note that 'By the 1750's...the term aqua vitae seems to have come to mean malt spirit which was drunk as such, whereas usquebaugh was reserved for compounded cordials' (*The Making of Scotch Whisky*, 34).

Martin Martin (*A Description of the Western Highlands*) noted in 1695 the existence in the Hebrides of 'common usquebaugh', *trestarig*, and *usquebaugh-baul*, the last named distilled four times and clearly fearsome stuff. It was made from oats rather than *barley*, and Martin declared that 'at first taste [it] affects all the members of the body; two spoonfuls of this last liquor is a sufficient dose; and if any man exceed this, it would presently stop his breath, and endanger his life'. Daiches records that 'baul' 'is the Gaelic word *ball*, meaning member, part of the body' (*Scotch Whisky*, 24) though Dwelly (*Illustrated Gaelic-English Dictionary*) notes one meaning to be 'bowl', the equivalent of the modern Gaelic *bobhla*. McHardy is faithful to the Gaelic, describing what Martin calls uisgebeatha-baul as 'this extremely potent liquor', and spelling it 'Uisge bea' ba'ol' (p.160).

underback   The collecting *back* or vessel into which *worts* pass from the *mash tun*. The vessel takes its name from its position below the mash tun. 'The mash tun is again filled with hotter water, stirred, and again the fluid is drained off to the worts receiver or underback', (McDowall, 105). 'The wort held in the "underback" is pumped through a refrigerator or a cooler to bring the temperature down to between 22°C and 24°C. It is then pumped to the tun-room and discharged into fermenting vessels called "washbacks"', (Moss, *Scottish Drink Book*, 79). 'Under-back' is also current in the brewing industry and is first attested in 1635, 'Underbacks in the bruehouse'.

V **atting** With regard to whisky, *vatting* is the process of mixing or *blending* components in a vat, though the term also has the wider sense of simply placing liquor in a vat or vats. The first attestation occurs in 1843, 'Vatting of porter', though vat is initially recorded prior to 1225 as *ueat*. 'Vat' is a southern variant of 'fat' – a *cask*, *tun* or other vessel for the preparation of liquor – which is first attested in *c*.950 as *fatto*; it is *fæt* in Old English, which corresponds to the Dutch *vat*.

In Ireland the process of vatting refers to the blending of component parts of each brand of *Irish* whiskey. As Irish Distillers *(Distilling in Ireland)* put it, 'When maturation is complete, precise quantities of the different types of flavouring whiskeys along with requisite quantities of lighter grain whiskeys are assembled in huge vats in the Spirits Store, vatted (mixed) and left to marry for a period of time (2/3 weeks) and subsequently sent for bottling.'

The most regular use of the term 'vatting' in the Scotch whisky industry is in relation to what are known as *vatted malts*, that is the product of blending or vatting two or more *malt* whiskies, usually up to a maximum of six. Moss and Hume note, however, that 'Vatting – the mixing of whiskies from different distillations of various years at the same distillery – was encouraged by the alteration in the laws in 1853, which permitted the process to be carried out under bond'. The Edinburgh spirit merchant Andrew Usher is usually credited with laying the foundations of the blending industry by producing his Ushers Old Vatted *Glenlivet*, but what he actually created was 'the first recorded authentic vatted whisky', as Moss and Hume describe it (*The Making of Scotch Whisky*, 98).

The popular blended whisky Vat 69 acquired its name in 1882 when William Sanderson of Leith decided to produce a new blend and 'made up a hundred vattings and asked his more knowledgeable friends to express their opinion on them. The verdict was unanimous and 69 was the number of the cask' (McDowall, 70).

McDowall disapproves of the whole notion of vatted malts as they are usually defined today, considering that 'For the most part they are gimmicks made to satisfy the demand for more flavoured whiskies and of course at a considerably higher price than most blends'. He suggests they often contain immature whiskies, conceding that 'Some are quite smooth but somehow the mixture of flavours is wrong, as if one took a mixture of different kinds of chocolate into the mouth at the same time' (p.160). It should be said that not all commentators are as critical of vatted malts as McDowall, but a suspicion remains that many of the component whiskies are not of sufficient character and quality to stand as *single* malts in their own right. If they are, then why vat them and hide their individuality? None the less, in a *Wine* magazine whisky-tasting (January 1993), the Japanese vatted malt Suntory Yamazaki came out in second place, ahead of such 'classic' Scottish names as Glenfiddich, The Glenlivet, Glenmorangie and The Macallan.

Gordon & McPhail of Elgin produce four regional vatted malts (*Islay*, Orkney, *Lowland*, Strathspey) in which the intention is to typify the regional style and create a product which is superior to many of the consituent parts. The company notes that 'In many ways it is more difficult to blend malts than it is to blend malt and grain whiskies, since grain whisky is comparatively neutral in flavour and thus provides a sound basis upon which to build the blend' (Corporate Brochure, 3).

In many cases it is far from immediately obvious when examining a bottle of vatted malt whisky that it differs in any way from the single malts alongside which it sits on the off-licence or merchant's shelves. Jackson notes that whiskies labelled as 'pure malt' are often vatted malts, and he also observes that the label frequently only reveals the name of the blender or owner of the brand, failing entirely to mention the distilleries of origin (*Malt Whisky Companion*, 8). Milsted offers the sound advice that 'What you need to look for is the missing word – in this case, "single" or "unblended" – and the missing information: the name and address of the distillery' (p.23).

One vatted malt which is produced for reasons of necessity rather than any form of expediency is the Isle of Mull Tobermory, John Lamond pointing out that 'Because of a shortage of fillings Tobermory is a vatted malt' (*Malt File*, 131). It is labelled as 'Tobermory The Malt Scotch Whisky', and Jackson writes that 'It is a vatted malt, containing some Tobermory whiskies of up to 20-years-old and proportions of newly mature spirit from elsewhere' (*Malt Whisky Companion*, 217). As Tobermory in this form could contain some three-year-old whiskies, it is hardly surprising that the bottle bears no age statement.

No more than a dozen vatted malts are produced by distilling companies as opposed to wine merchants, and of these Buchanan's twelve-year-old Strathconon is one of the best known. Jackson offers an insight into some of the factors borne in mind when vatted malts are produced when he quotes from Buchanan's own literature: the four component malts are chosen 'One for bouquet, another for flavour, a third for *body*, the last for its ability to blend all four in a balanced, *mellow* flavour' (*World Guide*, 18). 'In the acquisition of a taste for malt whiskies, the vatted products offer a useful intermediate step but that is also their limitation, and perhaps that is why there are few major labels in this market' (ibid., p.19).

W**ash** According to the Scotch Whisky Association, 'The wort or mash technically becomes wash as soon as yeast is added to start fermentation. However, the term is usually used to refer to the liquid at the end of fermentation' (*Questions and Answers*, 43). Daiches notes that 'At the end of the [fermentation] process, which takes anything from thirty-six to forty hours, we have a clear liquid, known simply as the wash, which consists of water, yeast and a bit over 5 per cent by volume of alcohol (i.e. about 10° *proof*). Thus the wash, like beer, is a liquid that has been brewed but not distilled' (*Scotch Whisky*, 12).

Among older distillery workers it has something of a reputation as a *hangover* cure.

The product of the first distillation is *low wines*, and as Cooper explains, 'the crude alcohol has been separated from the wash and the residue (pot ale, burnt ale or spent wash) as it is variously known is removed for processing into animal feedstuffs' (*Century Companion*, 24).

Wash is *wæsc* in Old English, and is first attested in its current sense prior to 1700 as 'Wash – After-wort'.

Washback The process of *fermentation* takes place in the *washback*, fermenting vat, or 'liquor back' as it is known in the United States, and as Cooper explains, 'When fermentation has ceased, the fermented wort, known as wash, is pumped to a wash receiver ... The wash is now ready for the first distillation which occurs in pear-shaped wash stills' (*Century Companion*, 23).

The washback (the word being first attested in 1839) – or washback as Daiches styles it – is a vat fixed into the floor of the *tun room*, as the brewer needs to be able to reach the top of the washbacks. They were traditionally made of wood, with pine, oak or larch being the most favoured types of timber, and Oregon pine was considered to be particularly suitable as it grows tall and therefore has few knot holes. A wooden washback has a lifespan of some forty years, but is harder to clean than cast iron or stainless steel, and the latter material has largely replaced wood in recently constructed backs. Easily cleaned steel would presumably have been an asset at Highland Park distillery in the Orkney Islands, where Morton notes a highly unorthodox use for washbacks, 'The huge larch washbacks have recovered from their role in the Second

World War as baths for Canadian troops stationed at Scapa Flow...' (p.37). Another unusual adaptation of washbacks is found at the Findhorn Foundation's centre in Morayshire, where disused backs from Speyside are converted into accommodation.

Wash Act This Act of 1784 was an attempt to 'simplify the administration of distilling duties and regulations', as Moss and Hume explain (*The Making of Scotch Whisky*, 44). The Act acquired its name from the fact that 'Under this new legislation, instead of taxing low wines and spirits separately, the fermented wash was subject to excise in Scotland at 5d per gallon'. (See also *Excise*.)

water In Old English *wæter*, first attested in *c*.897 as *wættre*. Of all the various factors which influence the location of distilleries and the ultimate character of their *make*, *water* is perhaps the most crucial. Lamond and Tuček consider the sources of distillery water to be so important as to merit a line entry for each whisky they discuss in their *Malt File*, though Jackson is of the opinion that 'The importance of water can be over-stressed and romanticised' (*World Guide*, 16).

Writing of locational factors which influenced the siting of illicit distilling operations, Cooper notes that 'what was absolutely essential was a supply of clear water not only for soaking the barley and making the mash but for condensing the spirit. So every distillery is either on the banks of a river or burn or on the site of a well or spring. Some distilleries bring their water by pipe from a high-lying loch but wherever the source it must be cold, unpolluted and as constantly flowing as possible' (*Century Companion*, 15). Water is also needed to reduce the strength of the *spirit* prior to casking, and as well as guaranteed quantity and quality, 'The coolness of the water is also important, for this can affect the ultimate flavour of the whisky', according to Morrice (p.19), a factor in the timing of the traditional *silent season*. Many distillers will insist that there is a noticeable difference between whisky made in summer and that made in winter, and that the difference is directly attributable to the temperature of the water used in production.

Water picks up influences from the peat over which it flows, as is evidenced most clearly in the case of *Islay* whiskies, where not only is the peat itself apparent in the end product, but the tang of the sea in the peat gives Islay malts their characteristic 'medicinal' *nose* and flavour. The Scotch Whisky Association consider that 'a source of good soft water is essential to a distillery' (*Questions and Answers*, 20) but it is worth noting that some of the most highly regarded Scottish malts such as Highland Park from Orkney are made with very hard water. Glenmorangie's Tarlogie Spring produces water which is very hard and mineral-rich, the minerals having leached from the local red sandstone. The delicacy of Glenmorangie which commentators frequently note may well be attributable in part to these minerals. Soft water is usually thought to be most desirable for distilling because it is a better solvent than hard water. McDowall considers that soft and slightly peaty water 'can dissolve substances other than maltose from the malt mash and it is well recognised that it is these substances which are largely responsible for the valuable characteristics of malt whisky' (p.115). He dismisses the relevance of water flowing over granite, since 'granite is a very insoluble substance and certainly the water does not stay long enough on it for this to be of any importance', though to most observers the real relevance of granite is precisely that it *does not* pass undesirable minerals to the water. Moss offers the useful generalisation that 'Soft peat water, like that commonly used on Islay and in the once large *Campbeltown* whisky trade, makes for heavier whiskies, while the harder waters of Speyside make for lighter styles' (*Scottish Drink Book*, 78).

Regarding the preponderance of distilleries in and close to the *golden triangle* of Speyside, Cooper writes that 'It's probably true that the peat-covered hills in the Cairngorm drained by the Findhorn, the Deveron and the Spey rivers provide abundant supplies of the finest water' (*Century Companion*, 19). He is of the opinion that the water of the middle Spey basin which flows over granite 'influences the whisky more favourably' than that in the nearby coastal areas where old Red Sandstone or fluvio-glacial sands are an influence.

In the United States the fact that most whiskey has traditionally been produced in a number of contiguous eastern states is said to owe much to a limestone shelf which runs through the region, containing many springs. They provided a vital water source for distillation, and as Jackson explains, 'American distillers say their limestone springs produce water free from iron or any other mineral that might discolour the whiskey; that it contributes to the classic texture and sweet taste; and that calcium aids the enzyme activity in fermentation' (*World Guide*, 146). The Jack Daniel company notes in its promotional literature that the Cave Spring which serves its distillery is 'almost sterile and iron free, which has been proven to make the best whiskey'.

Japan's water, like that of the Highlands, is particularly clean; it mostly rises in granite, but sometimes flows over peat.

If water is a vital element in the production of whisky, then its influence certainly continues to the actual consumption of the product. Much as shooting foxes is the most heinous crime imaginable to the foxhunter, so the addition of anything other than water to whisky is utterly unacceptable to many whisky connoisseurs. 'The only thing a man of taste adds to whisky is water', declares Neil Gunn unequivocally, and the expression 'whisky and water' is first attested in 1827. Even the most fanatical whisky-lover would probably conceded that it matters little what is added to a run-of-the-mill blend, especially if its fate is to be part of the intriguing 'Jelly Beans' *cocktail* as described by Derek Cooper (*Century Companion*, 60). Apparently consumed by habitués of Stornoway's Crown Hotel, the 'Jelly Beans' consists of whisky, gin, vodka, Pernod, cherry brandy, Babycham and lemonade.

When it comes to malts, however, water really is the only acceptable additive, and any dilution at all is frowned on in some quarters; as the arthritic old Scots adage runs: 'There are only two things a Scotsman likes naked, and one of them is whisky.' When adding water, 'The correct proportion, according to Scottish whisky wags, is "half and half, with lots of water". The implication of that instruction is clearer before you have a few. Less water, but enough to release the aroma, is prescribed by more serious samplers' (Jackson, *World Guide*, 14). One should never lose sight of Mark Twain's opinion that 'Water taken in moderation cannot hurt anybody'. McDowall writes, 'It is well to note that to bring out the flavour of a whisky an equal amount of water is usually necessary, but the optimum depends on the individual whisky and its strength' (p.127).

Inevitably, tastes vary around the world, with Japan being an interesting example of a country where whisky is often diluted to a considerable degree. While it does little for the palate of the whisky, Jackson reminds the reader that extreme dilution 'tames its potency' (*World Guide*, 197), an important factor if whisky is to be drunk throughout an entire evening, even accompanying a meal, as is often the case in Japan, where the *mizuwari* is popular.

If water is to be added to whisky, it should not be any common-or-garden water, unless one's garden happens to contain a natural spring of unimpeachable purity. Cooper stipulates 'as soft and pure a water as you can find' (*Century Companion*, 60). Lamond and Tuček advise the avoidance of tap water because of the additives such as chlorine which it contains, suggesting instead the use of still 'clear, pure spring water which has been bottled at source' (*Malt File*, 11-12), although others consider 'decent tap water' acceptable. The suggestion has been made that distilleries could make a useful subsidiary profit from bottling the same water that they use in production and selling it in branded form alongside their whiskies, something that would surely appeal to many drinkers who take their whisky seriously.

western malts   Daiches observes when writing of *Highland* whiskies, 'I have in fact seen Highland malt whisky classified simply as Eastern Malts and Western Malts, the latter including Islays, Campbeltowns and Talisker' (*Scotch Whisky*, 23). Robb classifies the Islays and Campbeltowns as West Highland whiskies, and *The Dictionary of Drink* notes under the entry West Highland Malt Whisky, 'The old name for Islay Malt Whisky'. Though it is neither a Campbeltown nor an Islay, United Distillers continue to use the geographically permissible term West Highland in respect of their Oban malt.

whisky/whiskey   According to the OED, 'In modern trade usage, *Scotch whisky* and *Irish whiskey* are thus distinguished in spelling', but as the Scotch Whisky Association points out, 'The most that can be said with any certainty is that it is a convention that grew up gradually as spellings, which were for a long time very variable, became stabilised' (*Questions and Answers*, 11).

Current British legislation specifies that

the expression 'whisky' or 'whiskey' shall mean spirits which have been distilled from a mash of cereals which have been – (i) saccharified by the diastase of malt contained therein with or without other natural diastases approved for the purpose by the Commissioners; and (ii) fermented by the action of yeast; and (iii) distilled at an alcoholic strength (computed in accordance with section 2 of the Alcoholic Liquor Duties Act (1979)) less than 94.8% in such a way that the distillate has an aroma and flavour derived from the materials used, and which have been matured in wooden casks in warehouses for a period of at least three years.

The report of the Royal Commission on 'Whisky and other Potable Spirits' of 1908/9 produced the first legal definition of Scotch whisky. Its definition was that '"whiskey" is a spirit obtained by distillation from a mash of cereal grains saccharified [i.e. turned into sugar] by the diastase of malt; that "Scotch whiskey" is whiskey, as above defined, distilled in Scotland; and that "Irish whiskey" is whiskey, as above defined, distilled in Ireland'. The respective definitions of Scotch whisky and Irish whiskey remain as they did in 1909, except that it is now specified that maturation takes place in the country of origin. An additional specification, introduced in 1989, is that 'the strength at which any whisky, whiskey, Scotch whisky or Irish whiskey shall be offered for sale shall not be less than 40% alcohol by volume'.

Daiches writes: 'Note that the Commission consistently spelt "whisky" with an "e" – "whiskey" – a spelling then regular in official Government publications on whisky but now confined to Irish and American whiskey" (*Scotch Whisky*, p.71).

With either current spelling variant, the word derives from the Gaelic *uisge beatha* or *usquebaugh*, with progressive anglicisation occurring from the early seventeenth century, from *uiskie* (*c*.1618) to *whiskie* in 1715, 'Whiskie shall put our brains in rage'. The first attestation with the modern Scots spelling occurs in 1746, 'A double Portion of Oatmeal and Whisky', and seven years later the current Irish spelling, 'that accursed spirit whiskey'. Interestingly, the variants *whiskybae* and *whisquy-beath* are first recorded in 1792, despite being apparently much closer to the Gaelic.

When writing of Irish distilleries in the 1880s Barnard continues to use the Scots spelling with no 'e', but then as Magee points out, the 'e' was first regularly inserted in Ireland by Dublin distillers in order to differentiate their product from what they perceived as inferior provincial spirit (p.7). He also notes that 'Paddy, curiously, is the only Irish whiskey spelt in the Scotch manner, without the "e"' (p.124), though since then Paddy has fallen into line with the other whiskeys in the Irish Distillers' stable. Clearly the inconsistency of spelling was not limited to Paddy, a product of Cork rather than Dublin, as Giles Gordon notes in his commemorative poem for George Macbeth, 'Yet the ancient mottled advertisement for Jameson's/behind the bar spelt the stuff the Scots way' (*The Scotsman Weekend*, 19 September 1992). This is interesting, as Jameson was one of the principal Dublin whiskeys.

Even today the usually quite rigid spelling conventions that dictate Canadians use the Scots variant and Americans the Irish are not always adhered to, with Maker's Mark from Kentucky and George Dickel of Tennessee preferring the Scots spelling.

In the United States there are specific definitions of *Bourbon* and *rye* whiskeys in respect of content, and – in the case of Bourbon – country of origin, while with regard to Canadian ryes the only real stipulation refers to production within Canada.

Dunkling writes of the words whisky and whiskey that 'Pronunciation is the same in either case, and was thought to be familiar enough throughout the world to make "whisky" represent the letter "w" in the International Phonetic Alphabet' (p.175).

white lightning   See *lightning*.

white mule   Writing of unmatured *spirit* produced and sold illegally in America during *Prohibition*, Lockhart notes that 'new "corn" whisky has long been honoured by Americans with the name of "white mule", because of its powerful kick' (*Scotch*, 147). The use of the word 'white' in this context is as in *lightning*.

wood   Grindal writes, 'American oak casks, broken down into staves for shipment and reassembled in Scottish cooperages, now make up a large proportion of the "wood", as it is called in the trade, used by the distillers of Scotland' (p.96). With the sense of *casks* used as receptacles for *liquor*, as distinguished from the bottle, *wood* is first attested in *c*.1826, according to the OED, 'When the speerit's been years in the wudd', though Elizabeth Grant *(Memoirs of a Highland Lady)* recalls that on the occasion of King George IV's visit to Scotland in 1822, her father instructed her to send to Edinburgh 'whisky long in wood'.

worm   In the words of the Scotch Whisky Association's *Questions and Answers*, the *worm* in a distillery is 'a coiled copper tube of decreasing diameter attached by the lyne arm to the head of the Pot Still and kept continuously cold by running water' (p.43). The alcoholic vapours from the still condense as they pass through the worm. Both distillation and non-distillation uses of 'worm' in an inanimate sense refer to objects that spiral or coil. In the relevant distilling context, it is first attested in 1641, 'Put it into a Copper Still with a worme', though a captioned illustration of a worm and worm-tub appears in Lonicer's *Naturalis Historiae Opus Novum*, published in Frankfurt in 1551. Robert Burns offers a splendid poetic use of worm in his poem 'Scotch Drink' (1785) when he writes 'Whether through wimplin' [crooked] worms thou jink/Or, richly brown, ream o'er the brink,/In glorious faem . . .'

The worm is situated in a wooden *worm-tub* of water outside the *stillhouse*, and, 'fed by the still, it in turn feeds the receiving vessel with the condensed distillate' (*Questions and Answers*, 43). This traditional condensing apparatus is now found in only a few Scottish distilleries, having been replaced by what Neil Wilson calls 'the more efficient water-jacket condenser' (p.34) which was introduced in the second half of the nineteenth century. Moss and Hume note the introduction from the 1880s of 'tube and shell heat-exchangers' to replace the worm (*The Making of Scotch Whisky*, 186). The Perthshire distillery of Edradour operates a worm which dates from 1825, almost certainly the oldest in use, and Talisker on Skye also continues to rely on this traditional piece of apparatus, as does the *Lowland* plant of Glenkinchie: 'It spirals two storeys high inside an enormous tank of cooling water just outside the stillhouse, the worm-pipes diminishing steadily in diameter as they wind towards the collection point' (*The Malt Letter*, no. 2). The preserved distillery of Dallas Dhu on Speyside also offers a good chance to see worms *in situ*.

The worm was first developed in the sixteenth century. Condensing of spirit had previously been achieved simply by air cooling, consequently production of liquor was limited. Writing of sixteenth-century advances in distillation techniques, Moss and Hume remark, 'The most important innovation involved passing the delivery tube through a tub of water. At first the tube was carried straight across the tub, later diagonally. From about 1540-50 the tube was coiled into a 'worm' which increased the cooling surface available' (*The Making of Scotch Whisky*, 31).

In illicit as well as legal distilling operations the worm has always played a crucial role, being a comparatively difficult and therefore expensive piece of equipment for the coppersmith to fabricate, a *cask* often serving as a makeshift worm-tub. Cooper writes, 'The key to the whole operation was the worm... Not infrequently when a worm was worn beyond all use its whereabouts could be revealed to the Excisemen and a reward of £5 collected for disclosing evidence of illicit distillation. With the £5 you could buy yourself a new and better worm!' (*Century Companion*, 10). The ingenuity of Irish prison distillers was equal to the complexities of worm fabrication, as McGuffin illustrates when he quotes the still-maker 'Uncle Doc' who was a Long Kesh internee for several years. 'I would strip a ½ inch diameter copper pipe from the toilet, fill it with dry salt, plug the ends, warm it and bend it. (The salt is to stop the pipe crimping.) That would make a reasonable worm' (p.44).

wort 'The liquid containing all the sugars of the malt which is drawn off after the malt has been mashed with warm water', as Cooper explains (*Century Companion*, 157). *Wort* is essentially unfermented beer, and its production is paralleled in beer-making. When taken internally it was formerly recommended as a cure for acne. The word is first attested in *c.*1000. 'Bewylle þone þriddan dæel on hwætene wyrt', and from *c.* 1325 with the current spelling.

Morrice notes that after *mashing*, wort is 'a sweet, sticky, semi-transparent liquid and is still a long way from resembling anything like the end product' (p.25). From the *mashtun* the wort passes through a heat exchanger to be cooled and is then transferred to the *washback*, where it is fermented to produce *wash*. In many ways the pre-distillation process for making *grain* whisky is very similar to that for producing *malt* whisky, but 'In some cases, Grain distillers do not separate off wort, passing the complete mash to the fermentation vessels' (*Questions and Answers*, 39).

Cooper stresses the pronunciation *wurt*, and Daiches writes 'wort (pronounced "wurt") or worts. (I have heard the plural form more often than the singular in distilleries)' (*Scotch Whisky*, 11). In my own experience many Scottish distillery staff employ the singular and the pronunciation *wort*.

References

Anon. (1982) *The Annals of the Glenlivet Distillery*, Glenlivet Distillery. (1st edn 1924).

Ayto, John & Simpson, John (1992) *The Oxford Dictionary of Modern Slang*, Oxford: Oxford University Press.

Barnard, Alfred (1887) *The Whisky Distilleries of the United Kingdom*, London: Harper's Weekly Gazette. Also (1984) *The Whisky Distilleries of Scotland 1887*, Gartocharn: Famedram Publishers Limited (a selective reprint of the above title).

Begg, Donald (1979) *The Bottled Malt Whiskies of Scotland*, Edinburgh: Gyle Press.

Behan, Brendan (1962) *Brendan Behan's Island*, London: Century Hutchinson Publishing Group Ltd.

Bell, Colin (1985) *Famous Drambusters Guide – Scotch Whisky*, Newtongrange: Lang Syne Publishers Ltd.

Bold, Alan (ed.) (1982) *Drink to Me Only*, London: Robin Clark Ltd.

Boswell, James (1786) *Journal of a Tour to the Hebrides With Samuel Johnson LL.D*. Also (1984) London: Penguin Books Ltd.

Bramwell, James (1939) *Highland View*, London: Robert Hale Ltd.

Brander, Michael (1975) *A Guide to Scotch Whisky*, Edinburgh: Johnston & Bacon Publishers.

Brandreth, Gyles (1990) *Everyman's Modern Phrase & Fable*, London: J.M. Dent.

Brewer, Dr. E. Cobham (1870) *Dictionary of Phrase & Fable*, London: Cassell (14th edn, 1989).

Broom, John L. (1977) *The Rhythm of the Glass*, Edinburgh: Paul Harris Publishing.

Burns, Robert (1867) *The Complete Works*, Edinburgh: William P. Nimmo.

Burt, Edward (1754) *Letters from a Gentleman in the North of Scotland to his Friend in London*, London.

Chapman, Robert (1986) *A New Dictionary of American Slang*, Basingstoke: The Macmillan Press Limited.

Cooper, Derek (1978) *The Century Companion to Whiskies*, London: Century Publishing Co. Ltd (1983 edn).

Cooper, Derek (1982) *The Whisky Roads of Scotland*, London: Jill Norman & Hobhouse Ltd.

Cooper, Derek (1989) *A Taste of Scotch*, London: André Deutsch.

Cooper, Derek (1992) *The Little Book of Malt Whiskies*, Belfast: The Appletree Press Ltd.

Daiches, David (1969) *Scotch Whisky*, London: André Deutsch.

Daiches, David (1988) *Let's Collect Scotch Whisky*, Norwich: Jarrold Publishing Ltd.

Daiches, David (1990) *A Wee Dram*, London: André Deutsch.

Dunford, Joyce (n.d.) *Drinking the Water of Life*, Dufftown: William Grant & Sons Ltd.

Dunkling, Leslie (1992) *The Guinness Drinking Companion*, London: Guinness Publishing.

Dwelly, Edward (1901-11) *The Illustrated Gaelic-English Dictionary*, Edinburgh.

Edwards, Graham & Sue (1990) *The Dictionary of Drink*, Stroud: Alan Sutton Publishing.

Fleming, Susan (1988) *The Little Whisky Book*, London: Judy Piatkus Publishers Ltd.

Floyd, Keith (1992) *Floyd on Hangovers*, London: Michael Joseph Ltd.

Forsyth, Robert (1805) *The Beauties of Scotland*.

Geikie, Sir Archibald (1904) *Scottish Reminiscences*, Glasgow: Maclehose.

Gordon & MacPhail (1991) *Corporate Brochure*, Elgin: Speymalt Whisky Distributors Ltd.

Graham, W.S. (1979) *Collected Poems 1942-1977*, London: Faber & Faber Ltd.

Grant, Elizabeth of Rothiemurchus (1950) *Memoirs of a Highland Lady 1797-1827*, London: John Murray Ltd.

Grindal, Richard (1992) *The Spirit of Whisky*, London: Warner Books.

Gunn, Neil (1935) *Whisky and Scotland*, London: Souvenir Press (1977 edn).

Hart, F.R. & Pick, J.B. (1981) *Neil M. Gunn – A Highland Life*, London: John Murray Ltd.

Hills, Phillip (ed.) (1991) *Scots on Scotch*, Edinburgh: Mainstream Publishing Company Ltd.

Hume, John R. (1988) *Dallas Dhu Distillery*, Edinburgh: HMSO.

Irish Distillers Ltd (n.d.) *Irish Whiskey: The Water of Life*, Dublin.

Jack Daniel Distillery (n.d.) *product description* literature, Lynchburg.

Jackson, Michael (1979) *Michael Jackson's Pocket Bar Book*, London: Mitchell Beazley Publishers Ltd.

Jackson, Michael (1987) *The World Guide to Whisky*, London: Dorling Kindersley Ltd.

Jackson, Michael (1989) *Michael Jackson's Malt Whisky Companion*, London: Dorling Kindersley Ltd.

Jamieson, John (1808-09) *Etymological Dictionary of the Scottish Language*.

Johnson, Dr Samuel (1755) *The Dictionary*, London.

Johnston, James (1892) *Place-Names of Scotland*: Douglas. Third edition reprinted (1970), Wakefield: SR Publishers Ltd.

Killen, John (ed.) (1987) *The Pure Drop*, Belfast: The Blackstaff Press Limited.

Lamond, John (1992) *The Whisky Connoisseur's Book of Days*, Edinburgh: The Edinburgh Publishing Company Limited.

Lamond, John and Tuček, Robin (1989) *The Malt File*, Largs: The Malt Whisky Association.

Lockhart, J.G. (1828) *Life of Robert Burns*, Edinburgh.

Lockhart, J.G. (1837-38) *Memoirs of the Life of Sir Walter Scott Bart.* (7 vols), Edinburgh.

Lockhart, Sir Robert Bruce (1951) *Scotch*, London: Putnam.

Lovett, Maurice (1981) *Brewing and Breweries*, Aylesbury, Shire Publications Ltd.

MacDiarmid, Hugh (1926) *A Drunk Man Looks at the Thistle*. Reprinted 1993 in *Complete Poems: Volume I*, Manchester: Carcanet Press Ltd.

MacDiarmid, Hugh (1952) 'The Dour Drinkers of Glasgow'. Reprinted 1992 in *Selected Prose*, Manchester: Carcanet Press Limited.

MacDonald, Aeneas (1930) *Whisky*, Edinburgh: The Porpoise Press.

MacDonald, Ian (1914) *Smuggling in the Highlands*, Stirling: Eneas Mackay.

McDowall, R.J.S. (1967) *The Whiskies of Scotland*, London: John Murray Ltd (1975 edn).

McGuffin, John (1978) *In Praise of Poteen*, Belfast: The Appletree Press Ltd.

McHardy, Stuart (1991) *Tales of Whisky and Smuggling*, Moffat: Lochar Publishing Ltd.

Mackenzie, Sir Compton (1947) *Whisky Galore*, London: Penguin Books Ltd (1957 edn).

Mackenzie, Sir Osgood (1921) *A Hundred Years in the Highlands*, London: Geoffrey Bles (1972 edn).

Mackinlay, Donald et al (1974) *Macmillan Scotch Whisky*, London: Macmillan London Ltd.

Maclean, Calum I. (1959) *The Highlands*, Edinburgh: Mainstream Publishing Company Limited.

McNeill, Marian (1956) *The Scots Cellar*, Moffat: Lochar Publishing Ltd (1992 edn).

McNulty, Henry (1985) *Vogue – Liqueurs and Spirits*, London: Octopus Books Ltd.

McPhee, John (1986) *In The Highlands and Islands*, London: Faber and Faber Ltd.

Magee, Malachy (1980) *1000 Years of Irish Whiskey*, Dublin: The O'Brien Press.

Martin, Martin (1703) *A Description of the Western Highlands*, London: Andrew Bell.

Milroy, Wallace (1987) *Wallace Milroy's Malt Whisky Almanac*, Moffat: Lochar Publishing Ltd. (Now published by Neil Wilson Publishing Ltd, Glasgow).

Milsted, David (1991) *The Bluffer's Guide to Whisky*, London: Ravette Books.

Morrice, Philip (1983) *The Schweppes Guide to Scotch*, Sherborne: Alphabooks.

Morton, Tom (1992) *Spirit of Adventure*, Edinburgh: Mainstream Publishing Company Ltd.

Moss, Michael S. et al (1990) *Chambers Scottish Drink Book*, Edinburgh: W. & R. Chambers Ltd.

Moss, Michael S. (1991) *Scotch Whisky*, Edinburgh: W. & R. Chambers Ltd.

Moss, Michael & Hume, John (1981) *The Making of Scotch Whisky*, London: James and James Ltd.

Newlove, Donald (1981) *Those Drinking Days*, USA: Junction Books.

Newton, Norman S. (1991) *Campbeltown's Distilleries – A Guide for Visitors*, Campbeltown: Mid-Argyll, Kintyre and Islay Tourist Board.

Nown, Graham (1988) *Edradour*, Melksham: GB Publications Ltd.

Partridge, Eric (1948) *A Dictionary of Slang and Unconventional English*, London: Routledge & Kegan Paul (8th edn).

Partridge, Eric (1972) *Dictionary of Historical Slang*, London: Penguin Books Ltd.

Rae, Simon (ed.) (1991) *The Faber Book of Drink, Drinkers and Drinking*, London: Faber and Faber Limited.

Ramsay, Allan (1721) *A Morning Interview (Poems)*, Edinburgh.

Reeve-Jones, Alan (1974) *A Dram Like This*, London: Elm Tree Books Ltd.

Robb, J. Marshall (1950) *Scotch Whisky*, Edinburgh: W. & R. Chambers Ltd.

Robinson, Mairi (1985) *The Concise Scots Dictionary*, Aberdeen: Aberdeen University Press.

Scotch Whisky Association (1990 and 1992) *Scotch Whisky Questions and Answers*, Edinburgh.

Seton, Mike (1980) *Distilleries of Moray*, Elgin: Moray District Libraries.

Sinclair, Sir John (1794) *The Statistical Account of Scotland*.

Sillett, Steve (1990) *The Whisky Smugglers*, Glasgow: Lang Syne Publishers Ltd. (First published as *Illicit Scotch* by Beaver Books in 1965.)

Skipworth, Mark (1987) *The Scotch Whisky Book*, London: The Hamlyn Publishing Group Ltd

Sutherland, Iain (n.d.) *Vote No Licence*, Wick: Iain Sutherland.

Taylor, Iain Cameron (1968) *Highland Whisky*, Inverness: An Comunn Gaidhealach.

Walsh, Maurice (1926) *The Key Above The Door*, Edinburgh: W. & R. Chambers Ltd.

Wilson, John (1980) *Scotland's Distilleries*, Gartocharn: Famedram Publishers Ltd.

Wilson, John (1973) Scotland's Malt Whiskies, Gartocharn: Famedram Publishers Ltd.

Wilson, Neil (1985) *Scotch and Water*, Moffat: Lochar Publishing Ltd. (Now published by Neil Wilson Publishing Ltd, Glasgow).